MERCEDES
190 & 300SL
1954-1963

Compiled by
R.M. Clarke

ISBN 1 870642 260

Distributed by
Brooklands Book Distribution Ltd.
'Holmerise', Seven Hills Road,
Cobham, Surrey, England

BROOKLANDS BOOKS

BROOKLANDS BOOKS SERIES
AC Ace & Aceca 1953-1983
AC Cobra 1962-1969
Alfa Romeo Alfasud 1972-1984
Alfa Romeo Alfetta Coupes GT.GTV.GTV6 1974-1987
Alfa Romeo Giulia Berlinas 1962-1976
Alfa Romeo Giulia Coupés 1963-1976
Alfa Romeo Spider 1966-1987
Aston Martin Gold Portfolio 1972-1985
Austin Seven 1922-1982
Austin A30 & A35 1951-1962
Austin Healey 100 1952-1959
Austin Healey 3000 1959-1967
Austin Healey 100 & 3000 Collection No. 1
Austin Healey 'Frogeye' Sprite Collection No. 1
Austin Healey Sprite 1958-1971
Avanti 1962-1983
BMW Six Cylinder Coupés 1969-1975
BMW 1600 Collection No. 1
BMW 2002 1968-1976
Bristol Cars Gold Portfolio 1946-1985
Buick Riviera 1963-1978
Cadillac Automobiles 1949-1959
Cadillac Automobiles 1960-1969
Cadillac Eldorado 1967-1978
Cadillac in the Sixties No. 1
Camaro 1966-1970
High Performance Camaros 1982-1988
Chevrolet 1955-1957
Chevrolet Camaro Collection No. 1
Chevelle & SS 1964-1972
Chevy II Nova & SS 1962-1973
Chrysler 300 1955-1970
Citroen Traction Avant 1934-1957
Citroen DS & ID 1955-1875
Citroen 2CV 1949-1982
Cobras & Replicas 1962-1983
Cortina 1600E & GT 1967-1970
Corvair 1959-1968
Daimler Dart & V-8 250 1959-1969
Datsun 240z 1970-1973
Datsun 280Z & ZX 1975-1983
De Tomaso Collection No. 1
Dodge Charger 1966-1974
Excalibur Collection No. 1
Ferrari Cars 1946-1956
Ferrari Cars 1962-1966
Ferrari Cars 1969-1973
Ferrari Dino 1965-1974
Ferrari Dino 308 1974-1979
Ferrari 308 & Mondial 1980-1984
Ferrari Collection No. 1
Fiat-Bertone X1/9 1973-1988
Ford Falcon 1960-1970
Ford Mustang 1964-1967
Ford Mustang 1967-1973
High Performance Mustangs 1982-1988
Ford RS Escort 1968-1980
Honda CRX 1983-1987
High Performance Escorts MkI 1968-1974
High Performance Escorts MkII 1975-1980
Hudson & Railton Cars 1936-1940
Jaguar Cars 1957-1961
Jaguar Cars 1961-1964
Jaguar Cars 1964-1968
Jaguar MK2 1959-1969
Jaguar E-Type 1961-1966
Jaguar E-Type 1966-1971
Jaguar E-Type V12 1971-1975
Jaguar XKE Collection No. 1
Jaguar XJ6 1968-1972
Jaguar XJ6 Series II 1973-1979
Jaguar XJ6 & XJ12 Series III 1979-1985
Jaguar XJ12 1972-1980
Jaguar XJS 1975-1980
Jensen Cars 1946-1967
Jensen Cars 1967-1979
Jensen Interceptor Gold Portfolio 1966-1986
Lamborghini Cars 1964-1970
Lamborghini Cars 1970-1975
Lamborghini Countach Collection No. 1
Lamborghini Countach & Urraco 1974-1980
Lamborghini Countach & Jalpa 1980-1985
Lancia Stratos 1972-1985
Land Rover 1948-1973
Land Rover Series II & IIa 1958-1971
Land Rover Series III 1971-1985
Lotus Cortina 1963-1970
Lotus Elan 1962-1973
Lotus Elan Collection No. 1
Lotus Elan Collection No. 2
Lotus Elite 1957-1964
Lotus Elite & Eclat 1974-1981
Lotus Turbo Esprit 1980-1986
Lotus Europa 1966-1975
Lotus Europa Collection No. 1
Lotus Seven 1957-1980
Lotus Seven Collection No. 1
Maserati 1965-1970
Maserati 1970-1975
Mazda RX-7 Collection No. 1
Mercedes 190 & 300SL 1954-1963
Mercedes 230/250/280SL 1963-1971
Mercedes 350/450SL & SLC 1971-1980
Mercedes Benz Cars 1949-1954
Mercedes Benz Cars 1954-1957
Mercedes Benz Cars 1957-1961
Mercedes Benz Competition Cars 1950-1957
Metropolitan 1954-1962
MG Cars 1929-1934
MG TC 1945-1949
MG TD 1949-1953
MG TF 1953-1955
MG Cars 1957-1959
MG Cars 1959-1962
MG Midget 1961-1980
MG MGA 1955-1962
MGA Collection No. 1
MGB Roadsters 1962-1980
MGB GT 1965-1980
Mini Cooper 1961-1971
Morgan Cars 1960-1970
Morgan Cars 1969-1979
Morris Minor Collection No. 1
Old's Cutlass & 4-4-2 1964-1972
Oldsmobile Toronado 1966-1978
Opel GT 1968-1973
Packard Gold Portfolio 1946-1958
Pantera 1970-1973
Pantera & Mangusta 1969-1974
Plymouth Barracuda 1964-1974
Pontiac Fiero 1984-1988
Pontiac GTO 1964-1970
Pontiac Firebird 1967-1973
High Performance Firebirds 1982-1988
Pontiac Tempest & GTO 1961-1965
Porsche Cars 1960-1964
Porsche Cars 1964-1968
Porsche Cars 1968-1972
Porsche Cars in the Sixties
Porsche Cars 1972-1975
Porsche 356 1952-1965
Porsche 911 Collection No. 1
Porsche 911 Collection No. 2
Porsche 911 1965-1969
Porsche 911 1970-1972
Porsche 911 1973-1977
Porsche 911 Carrera 1973-1977
Porsche 911 SC 1978-1983
Porsche 911 Turbo 1975-1984
Porsche 914 1969-1975
Porsche 914 Collection No. 1
Porsche 924 1975-1981
Porsche 928 Collection No. 1
Porsche 944 1981-1985
Porsche Turbo Collection No. 1
Reliant Scimitar 1964-1986
Rolls Royce Silver Cloud 1955-1965
Rolls Royce Silver Shadow 1965-1980
Range Rover 1970-1981
Rover 3 & 3.5 Litre 1958-1973
Rover P4 1949-1959
Rover P4 1955-1964
Rover 2000 + 2200 1963-1977
Rover 3500 1968-1977
Rover 3500 & Vitesse 1976-1986
Saab Sonett Collection No. 1
Saab Turbo 1976-1983
Singer Sports Cars 1933-1934
Studebaker Hawks & Larks 1956-1963
Sunbeam Alpine & Tiger 1959-1967
Thunderbird 1955-1957
Thunderbird 1958-1963
Thunderbird 1964-1976
Toyota MR2 1984-1988
Triumph 2000-2.5-2500 1963-1977
Triumph Spitfire 1962-1980
Triumph Spitfire Collection No. 1
Triumph Stag 1970-1980
Triumph Stag Collection No. 1
Triumph TR2 & TR3 1952-1960
Triumph TR4.TR5.TR250 1961-1968
Triumph TR6 1969-1976
Triumph TR6 Collection No. 1
Triumph TR7 & TR8 1975-1982
Triumph GT6 1966-1974
Triumph Vitesse & Herald 1959-1971
TVR Gold Portfolio 1959-1988
Volkswagen Cars 1936-1956
VW Beetle 1956-1977
VW Beetle Collection No. 1
VW Golf GTi 1976-1986
VW Karmann Ghia 1955-1982
VW Scirocco 1974-1981
VW Bus-Camper-Van 1954-1967
VW Bus-Camper-Van 1968-1979
Volvo 1800 1960-1973
Volvo 120 Series 1956-1970

BROOKLANDS MUSCLE CARS SERIES
American Motors Muscle Cars 1966-1970
Buick Muscle Cars 1965-1970
Camaro Muscle Cars 1966-1972
Capri Muscle Cars 1969-1983
Chevrolet Muscle Cars 1966-1972
Dodge Muscle Cars 1967-1970
Mercury Muscle Cars 1966-1971
Mini Muscle Cars 1961-1979
Mopar Muscle Cars 1964-1967
Mopar Muscle Cars 1968-1971
Mustang Muscle Cars 1967-1971
Shelby Mustang Muscle Cars 1965-1970
Oldsmobile Muscle Cars 1964-1970
Plymouth Muscle Cars 1966-1971
Pontiac Muscle Cars 1966-1972
Muscle Cars Compared 1966-1971
Muscle Cars Compared Book 2 1965-1971

BROOKLANDS ROAD & TRACK SERIES
Road & Track on Alfa Romeo 1949-1963
Road & Track on Alfa Romeo 1964-1970
Road & Track on Alfa Romeo 1971-1976
Road & Track on Alfa Romeo 1977-1984
Road & Track on Aston Martin 1962-1984
Road & Track on Auburn Cord & Duesenberg 1952-1984
Road & Track on Audi 1952-1980
Road & Track on Audi 1980-1986
Road & Track on Austin Healey 1953-1970
Road & Track on BMW Cars 1966-1974
Road & Track on BMW Cars 1975-1978
Road & Track on BMW Cars 1979-1983
Road & Track on Cobra, Shelby &
   Ford GT40 1962-1983
Road & Track on Corvette 1953-1967
Road & Track on Corvette 1968-1982
Road & Track on Corvette 1982-1986
Road & Track on Datsun Z 1970-1983
Road & Track on Ferrari 1950-1968
Road & Track on Ferrari 1968-1974
Road & Track on Ferrari 1975-1981
Road & Track on Ferrari 1981-1984
Road & Track on Fiat Sports Cars 1968-1987
Road & Track on Jaguar 1950-1960
Road & Track on Jaguar 1961-1968
Road & Track on Jaguar 1968-1974
Road & Track on Jaguar 1974-1982
Road & Track on Lamborghini 1964-1985
Road & Track on Lotus 1972-1981
Road & Track on Maserati 1952-1974
Road & Track on Maserati 1975-1983
Road & Track on Mazda RX7 1978-1986
Road & Track on Mercedes 1952-1962
Road & Track on Mercedes 1963-1970
Road & Track on Mercedes 1971-1979
Road & Track on Mercedes 1980-1987
Road & Track on MG Sports Cars 1949-1961
Road & Track on MG Sports Cars 1962-1980
Road & Track on Mustang 1964-1977
Road & Track on Peugeot 1955-1986
Road & Track on Pontiac 1960-1983
Road & Track on Porsche 1951-1967
Road & Track on Porsche 1968-1971
Road & Track on Porsche 1972-1975
Road & Track on Porsche 1975-1978
Road & Track on Porsche 1979-1982
Road & Track on Porsche 1982-1985
Road & Track on Rolls Royce & Bentley 1950-1965
Road & Track on Rolls Royce & Bentley 1966-1984
Road & Track on Saab 1955-1985
Road & Track on Toyota Sports & GT Cars 1966-1986
Road & Track on Triumph Sports Cars 1953-1967
Road & Track on Triumph Sports Cars 1967-1974
Road & Track on Triumph Sports Cars 1974-1982
Road & Track on Volkswagen 1951-1968
Road & Track on Volkswagen 1968-1978
Road & Track on Volkswagen 1978-1985
Road & Track on Volvo 1957-1974
Road & Track on Volvo 1975-1985

BROOKLANDS CAR AND DRIVER SERIES
Car and Driver on BMW 1955-1977
Car and Driver on BMW 1977-1985
Car and Driver on Cobra, Shelby & Ford GT40
   1963-1984
Car and Driver on Datsun Z 1600 & 2000
   1966-1984
Car and Driver on Corvette 1956-1967
Car and Driver on Corvette 1968-1977
Car and Driver on Corvette 1978-1982
Car and Driver on Ferrari 1955-1962
Car and Driver on Ferrari 1963-1975
Car and Driver on Ferrari 1976-1983
Car and Driver on Mopar 1956-1967
Car and Driver on Mopar 1968-1975
Car and Driver on Pontiac 1961-1975
Car and Driver on Porsche 1955-1962
Car and Driver on Porsche 1963-1970
Car and Driver on Porsche 1970-1976
Car and Driver on Porsche 1977-1981
Car and Driver on Porsche 1982-1986
Car and Driver on Saab 1956-1985
Car and Driver on Volvo 1955-1986

BROOKLANDS MOTOR & THOROUGHBRED & CLASSIC CAR SERIES
Motor & T & CC on Ferrari 1966-1976
Motor & T & CC on Ferrari 1976-1984
Motor & T & CC on Lotus 1979-1983
Motor & T & CC on Morris Minor 1948-1983

BROOKLANDS PRACTICAL CLASSICS SERIES
Practical Classics on Austin A 40 Restoration
Practical Classics on Land Rover Restoration
Practical Classics on Metalworking in Restoration
Practical Classics on Midget/Sprite Restoration
Practical Classics on Mini Cooper Restoration
Practical Classics on MGB Restoration
Practical Classics on Morris Minor Restoration
Practical Classics on Triumph Herald/Vitesse
Practical Classics on Triumph Spitfire Restoration
Practical Classics on VW Beetle Restoration
Practical Classics on 1930S Car Restoration

BROOKLANDS MILITARY VEHICLES SERIES
Allied Military Vehicles Collection No. 1
Allied Military Vehicles Collection No. 2
Dodge Military Vehicles Collection No. 1
Military Jeeps 1941-1945
Off Road Jeeps 1944-1971
V W Kubelwagen 1940-1975

CONTENTS

5	The Mercedes SL Series	Road & Track	April	1954
9	Mercedes-Benz for Le Mans and Mille Miglia	Autocar	Mar. 21	1952
10	Mercedes-Benz	Automobile Topics	Mar.	1954
12	Mercedes-Benz	Car Life	May	1954
13	Mercedes-Benz	Speed Age	Aug.	1954
16	The Mercedes-Benz 300SL Road Test	Autosport	Jan. 7	1955
19	Mercedes-Benz 300SL Road Test	Autocar	Mar. 25	1955
23	Road Testing the Mercedes-Benz 300SL	Road & Track	April	1955
26	Sampling the 300SL Mercedes-Benz	Motor Sport	Nov.	1954
27	R.V. at Dawn	Motoring Life	June	1955
28	Mille Miglia	Road & Track	Aug.	1955
32	Some Personal Observations on the 300SL	Autocar	Sept.	1955
34	Mercedes 190SL Road Test	Road & Track	Oct.	1955
36	Mercedes 190SL	Motor Trend	Dec.	1955
38	The Mercedes-Benz 190SL Road Test	Autosport	Nov. 11	1955
41	On British Roads with a Mercedes-Benz 300SL	Motor Sport	April	1956
46	Mercedes 300SL	Motor Trend	July	1956
50	The 300SLR Coupe Road Test	Motor Racing	Jan.	1957
54	Germany's Silver Screamers – 300SLR	Sports Cars Illustrated	April	1956
59	Mercedes 190SL	Sports Car World	April	1957
63	Mercedes-Benz 190SL Road Test	Autocar	Jan. 10	1958
67	Mercedes 190SL Road Test	Motor Life	Feb.	1958
70	300SL Roadster Road Test	Road & Track	Jan.	1958
72	Mercedes-Benz 190SL Road Test	Sports Car Illustrated	Sept.	1958
74	The Mercedes-Benz 300SL Roadster Road Test	Autosport	April 24	1959
76	Mercedes 190SL Road Test	Road & Track	Dec.	1960
80	Mercedes-Benz 190SL Road Test	Sports Car Graphic	Dec.	1961
84	Mercedes 300SL Road Test	Road & Track	June	1961
88	Mercedes 190SL Roadster	World Car Catalogue		1963
89	Buying a Mercedes 190SL for Restoration	Practical Classics	Dec.	1985
93	The Gullwing	Classic and Sportscar	June	1982
94	Winged Flight	Classic and Sportscar	June	1982
96	Mercedes-Benz 300SL	Classic Sports Cars		1986

ACKNOWLEDGEMENTS

For some years we have had books in our list covering the 200 and 300 series SLs, and very popular they are. I have been frequently asked when I intend to return to the subject and cover the famous earlier models, but have always replied evasively.

This does not mean that I have no interest in the cars, in fact just the opposite. The problem is the time involved. The 190 and 300 SLs came out when I was in my early twenties, they were the cars to own, to be seen in and failing that to be photographed by. I read about them avidly during this period, glorifying in Moss and Jenkinsons Mille Miglia victory and lamenting the passing of the gullwing versions.

I was right, this book took an age to finish. Not becasue the stories were hard to find but because I nostalgically read and re-read each article, grieved over the ones that could not be fitted in and read them again for good measure. I am pleased that it is done and look forward to occasionally taking it off the shelf and reaquainting myself with my dreams of the fifties.

Brooklands Books can only exist because publishers, authors and photographers generously allow us to reissue their copyright matter for the benefit of today's enthusiasts. We are especially indebted in this instance to the management of Autocar, Automobile Topics, Autosport, Car Life, Classic and Sportscar, Motor Sport, Motor Racing, Motor Trend, Motoring Life, Practical Classics, Road & Track, Road & Track Specials, Sports Car Graphic, Sports Cars Illustrated (now Car and Driver), Sports Car World and The World Car Catalogue for their continued support.

R.M. Clarke

a new car from an old star

The production Mercedes-Benz 300 SL automobile sets new engineering standards by its unusual combination of ultra-high performance, remarkable roadability, great attention to comfort, extreme flexibility and reasonable price (under $7000).

the MERCEDES SL series

A surprise announcement is the 125 bhp, Mercedes-Benz 190 SL convertible coupe. It has a two litre, 4 cylinder, overhead camshaft engine. Priced at under $4000, it is a genuine dual-purpose sports car with a remarkable specification—and future.

The Mercedes 300 SL. Only the one body style will be built.

Hinged steering wheel facilitates entry through the door.

Engine at an angle, huge exhaust headers of the 300 SL.

Average driver's view of the 240 bhp, 160 mph Mercedes.

Mercedes-Benz, one of the oldest names in motordom, has announced two new sports cars, the two-litre 190 SL, and the three-litre 300 SL.

Following a tradition established between the two World Wars (when the S, SS, and SSK sports cars were introduced), the new SL models are developments of standard production models, an interesting contrast to the practice of certain other companies whose sports cars are detuned racing machines.

The 300 SL

The prototype 300 SL models first appeared in 1952 and were universally rated the top sports of the year, with wins at Bern, LeMans, the Nurburgring and Mexico. Perhaps the most remarkable feature of the 300 SL is that most of its major components are based on the German firm's production touring car, the model 300. Engine, transmission, front suspension, and rear end are all standard or modified production assemblies.

The chassis frame is special, a light tubular-truss (fully described and illustrated in *Road & Track*, April 1953), and is largely responsible for the term SL (super light). The dry weight of the production 300 SL coupe is only 2240 pounds.

The most interesting new mechanical feature is the employment of a genuine fuel injection system, not to be confused with injection type carburetion. The Mercedes system, developed by Bosch, is similar to the injection mechanism of a diesel engine. Nozzles spray metered quantities of fuel directly into the cylinders via holes formerly occupied by the spark plugs (which are in the cylinder block). A new cylinder head incorporates the necessary smaller combustion chamber, larger valves and ports, and conventional 14 mm spark plugs. The result is an engine which has nearly perfect fuel distribution to each cylinder, is less sensitive to extreme valve timing, operates on 80 octane fuel, and develops 240 bhp from only 183 cu in.

The engine, with seven main bearings and a single overhead camshaft, is designed to run continuously, reliably, and quietly at 6000 rpm. Maximum recommended revolutions are 6600, yet the car is capable of running smoothly at 15.5 mph in direct drive.

The transmission system includes a stock all syncromesh four-speed and reverse box with central control. The differential weight is sprung and the suspension system is the latest M-B swinging axle system, similar to that used on the 180. Coil springs with large shock absorbers are used all around.

The brakes are similar to those used on the prototype cars, with Al-Fin drums having radial valves to act as air-pumps. A booster reduces pedal pressure and the shoes are self-adjusting for lining wear. Wheels are steel disc, bolt-on, but knock-off hubs are available if desired and most cars will be so-equipped.

Only a two-passenger coupe body will be available on the 300 SL chassis. The frame design necessitates a rather high entry, but the upward door hinging arrangement makes entrance and exit easier than it might seem, especially from a normal curb.

Special attention has been given to visibility and ventilation. The driver can see both front fenders and the road in front of the car at a distance of only 13 feet. Cowl ducts feed air through a double dash panel, while forward ducts supply air directly to the compartment.

No performance data is available, but the factory gives a top speed of over 160 mph with standard 3.42 axle ratio. Acceleration from zero to 60 mph should be close to 6.0 seconds.

The 190 SL

The announcement of the 300 SL was not unexpected, but the new two-litre SL comes as a complete surprise. This model utilizes chassis components of the 180, but is powered by a new high output four-cylinder overhead camshaft engine.

The 180 type floor pan has been redesigned to act as a frame, since the open body of the 190 SL contributes very little to chassis rigidity. Wheelbase has been shortened to 94.5 inches, the same length as the 300 SL. Front and rear suspension systems appear identical to that used on the 180, including the unique wishbone type front crossmember (fully described and illustrated in *Road & Track*, March, 1954).

The new engine follows the pattern established by the touring 220 and 300 types, and has two normal side draft type carburetors. Cylinder bore is identical to the 300 (3.35") but the stroke is slightly shorter (3.29"), giving 1898 cc. The four-cylinder engine develops 1.08 bhp/cu in. compared to 1.31 bhp/cu in. for the 300 SL. However a fairer way to compare is to also consider rpm, and on this basis the 190 SL gives .197 bhp/cu in./1000 rpm, the 300 SL gives .218.

The transmission of the 190 SL carries syncromesh on all four forward speeds and is the 180 box with central control. The differential is also 180 but uses a 3.70 ratio instead of 3.89 to 1. Bolt-on, steel disc wheels are used, carrying the passenger car size tires—6.40 x 13. Brakes are two leading shoe hydraulic with cast iron drums.

Body of the 190 is quite different from the 300 SL, though the front end treatment shows a marked similarity. The 190 SL is a somewhat unique approach to the American sports car market in that it is a dual purpose vehicle with many luxury items of design and specification, yet is light enough to be definitely competitive. As a touring convertible, it weighs 2320 pounds curbside. This includes wind-up windows, heating system, a one-man jump seat (transverse) and 16 gallons of fuel. For those who are not "watchers," the lighter doors (see illustration) and elimination of various non-essentials can bring the weight down by nearly 300 pounds. In "competition trim" the 190 SL will be a hard car to beat in its class (Class E for engines up to 2000 cc). Top speed, for example, is given by the factory as 118 mph at 6100 rpm. Using the same rev limit, the speeds in the gears are: 1st, 29 mph; 2nd, 50 mph; 3rd, 77 mph.

No data is available on acceleration performance but the power to weight ratio of 18.5 lbs/hp with full touring equipment is remarkably close to similarly priced equipment which is capable of reaching 60 mph from a standing start in around 10 seconds.

Finally, the Mercedes SL cars are unique in that they come from the factory already "hopped up." The average sports car buyer usually starts a search for more urge, but engines which produce well over 1 hp/cu in. leave no scope for further modification. Knowing the engineering integrity of Daimler-Benz AG, the sports car enthusiast can do nothing but enthuse over these new entries in the field. ●

Complete tabulated data and specifications appear on the next page.

The stock 190 SL windshield and door with wind-up windows.

With optional light weight doors and aero screen in place.

Engine room of Mercedes 190 SL, with high opening hood.

Side view of the 190 SL convertible. Either a bench type seat or bucket seats are available. An extra seat can be fitted behind the driver if desired.

The Mercedes 300 SL engine features fuel injection (center, bottom) which feeds metered fuel directly into the cylinders.

Mercedes-Benz Specifications

General—	190 SL	300 SL
Wheelbase	94.5 in.	94.5 in.
Tread, front	55.9 in.	54.6 in.
rear	57.1 in.	56.5 in.
Dry weight	2140 lbs	2240 lbs.
Curb weight	2320 lbs	2490 lbs
Tire size	6.40 x 13	6.70 x 15
Overall length	166 in.	176 in.
Overall width	68.5 in.	70.5 in.
Overall height	52.0 in.	50.0 in.
Engine—		
No. of cylinders	4	6
Valves	sohc	sohc
Cylinder bore	3.35 in.	3.35 in.
stroke	3.29 in.	3.47 in.
Displacement	116 cu in.	183 cu in.
	(1897 cc)	(2996 cc)
Compression ratio	8.0	8.6
Max. bhp	125	240
Peaking speed, rpm	5500	6000
equivalent mph (std. axle)	106	145
Rev limit, rpm	6100	6600
Max. torque, ft/lbs	114	202
Carburetion	2 sd.	injection
Camshaft drive	chain	chain
No. main bearings	3	7
Lubrication	wet	dry sump
Transmission—		
No. of forward speeds	4	4
No. speeds syncromesh	4	4
Oil pump	No	Yes
Ratios, 4th	1.00	1.00
3rd	1.53	1.33
2nd	2.38	1.85
1st	4.05	3.19
Clutch	sdp	sdp
Differential—		
Type gears	hypoid	hypoid
Standard ratio	3.70	3.42
Optional ratio	3.89	3.25

	190 SL	300 SL
Overall ratios (std.)		
4th	3.70	3.42
3rd	5.66	4.53
2nd	8.81	6.32
1st	15.0	10.9
Chassis—		
Frame	steel platform	multi-tube
Front suspension	independent	independent
type	SLA	SLA
springs	coil	coil
sub-frame	yes	no
Rear suspension	independent	independent
type	half-swing	half-swing
springs	coil	coil
trailing links	yes	yes
Steering ratio	N.A.	11.05
turns l. to l.	N.A.	1¾
steering damper	hydraulic	hydraulic
Brake type	hydraulic	hydraulic
front shoes	2 ls.	2 ls.
rear shoes	non-servo	non-servo
shoe material	aluminum	aluminum
drum material	cast iron	Al-Fin
cooling vanes	yes	yes
booster type	none	vacuum
Fuel tank, gals.	16	34
Body—		
Type	convertible	coupe
Seats	3	2
Panels	steel	aluminum
Heater	yes	yes
Performance—		
Speeds in gears		
top speed	118	165
3rd	80	120
2nd	50	86
1st	29	50
Approx. fuel mpg.	N.A.	9/15
R & T perf. factor	45.0	60.0

The long-expected return of Mercedes-Benz to international motor racing will be with this streamlined 3-litre coupé, the 300SL. Three of them will run in the Mille Miglia and at Le Mans.

Mercedes-Benz for Le Mans and Mille Miglia

TYPE 300SL COUPÉ FOR SPORTS CAR RACING

AS forecast in the description of the Type 300S Mercedes-Benz in *The Autocar* of February 22, a team of special lightweight racing coupés has now been produced and will be known as the Type 300SL (*Super Leicht*). They are on a new chassis of 7ft 10½in wheelbase, which is over 19in shorter than that of the 300S. Overall length of the streamlined coupé is 13ft 10½in. The compression ratio has been increased from 7.5 to 8 to 1 and this, with other modifications, has increased the power output from 147 to 172 b.h.p. at 5,200 r.p.m. Maximum torque is 187.5 lb ft at 4,000 r.p.m.

The new chassis frame follows the Mercedes tradition, being made from steel tubes, but is much lighter than the standard frame. The normal suspension layout is used, with double wishbones and coil springs at the front pivoted to allow slight fore and aft movement. At the rear there is independent suspension by swing axles with coil springs. Extra large hydraulic brakes are fitted, with two-leading shoes at the front. Transmission is through a four-speed close-ratio all-synchromesh gear box to a hypoid final drive.

Most startling feature of the beautifully

SPECIFICATION

Engine.—6 cyl, 85 × 88 mm, 2,996 c.c., single overhead camshaft. Compression ratio 8 to 1. 172 b.h.p. at 5,200 r.p.m. Max torque 187.5 lb ft at 4,000 r.p.m.
Transmission.—Single-plate clutch. Four-speed, all-synchromesh gear box, hypoid final drive. Gear box ratios 1, 1.45, 2.12, 3.33 to 1. Axle ratios vary according to circuit.
Suspension.—Double wishbones and coil springs with flexible kingpost mounting. Swing axle rear with coil springs.
Dimensions.—Wheelbase 7ft 10½in. Overall length 13ft 10½in, width 5ft 10⅝in, height 4ft 1⅞in.

streamlined light alloy coupé coachwork is the absence of doors. Annexe C of the International Sporting Code stipulates that there must be one door of a size sufficient to bear a rectangle 40 cm by 20 cm, but on some of the open cars which have run at Le Mans a flap of the right size, hinged at the bottom and opening downwards, has been accepted as giving genuine and direct access to seats within the meaning of the regulations. On the Mercedes, the side windows and part of the roof can be hinged upwards to allow access to the seats, and this would appear to meet requirements. The unorthodox method of entry is facilitated by the low build of the car, which is only 4ft 1½in high overall, and the lack of a conventional door opening in the side of the car enables the designer to save considerable weight in the body structure.

The fuel tank holds 37½ Imperial gallons, of which 2½ gallons are in reserve, and the engine is fed by twin pumps. There is a defroster unit designed to keep clear both screen and side windows, and a heater-ventilator system drawing air from an intake behind the radiator grille generates a slight pressure in the interior of the car. Bolt-on steel disc wheels of 15in diameter are used at present, but it seems probable that centre-lock wire wheels will be used for some events. The track of the new chassis and the weight of the complete car have not yet been revealed.

The first competition appearance of the new cars will be in the Mille Miglia Race in Italy on May 3 and 4, when they will be driven by Caracciola, Lang and Kling. Caracciola is no stranger to this race, as he won it in 1931 driving a Mercedes-Benz SSKL.

Although it has a beautifully smooth form the 300SL Mercedes departs from the fully swept tail, usually considered the optimum for streamlined cars, in order to introduce a big rear window giving the driver adequate rearward vision. Access to the interior is by hinging up the side window and part of the roof.

Two New High Cars for U.S

Mercedes

NOW AVAILABLE for U. S. purchase is the revamped Mercedes-Benz 300 SL. Expected price: under $7000.

Mercedes-Benz has introduced two very interesting new sports cars to the American market. Both models—the 300 SL (SL for super light) and the 190 SL—are high performance sports cars, but it is the 300 SL which should be able to challenge the very best other manufacturers can offer.

The first 300 SL models were shown in 1952 but only for the factory racing team, not for sale to the public. During that year they scored an amazing string of victories including the Le Mans 24-Hour Race and the Mexican Road Race—two of the world's toughest events. And the new version now offered for sale to the public has its horsepower boosted to 240 principally by replacing the carburetors with a fuel injection system.

This new car is bound to be in the competition news during the coming year but according to the factory is not restricted to competitive events. It was developed from the Mercedes-Benz model 300 passenger car and is not a pure competition machine, but is designed to serve as a comfortable sports car that can be used equally well in city traffic and on the open road. The car is said to have a range of from 15.5 m.p.h. up to the neighborhood of 165 m.p.h. in top gear, along with exceptional acceleration and roadholding usually found only on pure competition cars. Many parts are interchangeable directly with the 300 and 300 S models.

The OHV 6-cylinder engine has a compression ratio of 8.55 to 1 with a bore and stroke of 3.34 x 3.45 inches and a displacement of 183 cubic inches. Its seven-bearing crankshaft and chain-driven overhead camshaft and valve gear are designed to stand continuous operation at 6000 r.p.m.

The fuel injection system has a thermostat and an altitude compensator at the injection pump that automatically corrects for air temperature and density, doing away with the carburetor adjustments required by many finely-tuned sports cars. Mercedes-Benz has 20 years experience developing and building fuel injection systems for aircraft and diesel engines.

The transmission has syncromesh on all four forward speeds. Engine lubrication is by full-pressure system.

The tubular frame is said to be extremely rigid, partly because there is no door opening to weaken the structure. Independent coil spring suspension is used both front and rear with the Mercedes-Benz swing axle at the rear.

Aluminum brake drums have radial vanes that create a strong air flow to throw off heat. A vacuum booster reduces pedal pressure. Brake shoe adjustment is automatic.

Among the unusual features on the 300 SL are unorthodox doors which are hinged in the roof and open upward, making entrance to this low car easy. Seats are of the bucket type and the driver's seat is adjustable. The hood is low and both fenders can be seen by the driver.

A double partition insulates the passenger compartment from engine heat. Cooling air is forced into the enclosed space through a grid ahead of the windshield and flows out

ENGINE for 300 SL has been equipped with special fuel injectors. The 6-cyl. O.H.C. unit is mounted at 45-degree angle, for low hood.

SPARE TIRE occupies most of trunk area. Note slots in rear of roof to exit cooling air. Wheels are real knock-off type—chrome plated.

Performance Export from Mercedes-Benz

BRAND NEW sports model now offered U. S. buyers is Mercedes 190 SL, with same basic chassis as the 300 SL. Four-cyl., O.H.C. engine supplies power.

at the sides through grille-openings, thus carrying away the heat. Ducts alongside the radiator carry fresh air to the passenger compartment and used air leaves through an air vent in the roof. The side windows have revolving-type panes for additional ventilation.

Steering is very fast with the wheel needing only 1¾ turns from lock to lock. Tires are 6.70 by 15 on disc wheels. Unladen weight is approximately 2250 lbs. Wheelbase is 94 inches, same as the 190 SL.

The new model 190 SL has a frontal appearance similar to the 300 SL, but has a folding top. Standard seating equipment is two bucket seats but a third seat behind the two front ones or a bench seat instead of the bucket type is optional.

The top can be removed for competition events and the windshield can be replaced by a small plexiglas windscreen. Bumpers can also be removed and lighter side doors with cut-out arm rests are available.

The 190 SL is made also for comfort and has a heating system, steering column gear shift and luggage space.

Its 4-cylinder engine is rated at 125 h.p. and gives a top speed of 118 m.p.h. Bore and stroke is 3.34 x 3.36 in. with a 116 cu. in. (1897 c.c.) displacement. Other features include two horizontal carburetors and what the company terms a "small starting carburetor"; overhead camshaft; and a heat exchanger for cooling the lubricating oil.

The four-speed transmission permits up to 80 m.p.h. in 3rd gear and up to 50 m.p.h. in second.

The frame and floor unit makes a very rigid chassis. Independent coil spring suspension is used all around with the Mercedes-Benz swing axle on the rear.

In front the unique "support bridge" has been adopted from the 180 model. This bridge is a U-shaped hollow unit carrying the wishbone arms for the independently suspended front wheels, the coil springs, telescopic shock absorbers, steering housing and intermediary steering lever. Combining all these elements in the support bridge is said to give exceptional steering and roadholding as well as minimizing front tire wear and noise.

Sale of Mercedes-Benz automobiles in the United States was resumed only at the end of 1952. Importing and distribution is handled by the following firms: Mercedes-Benz Distributors, Inc., 443 Park Ave., New York City—Eastern and Mississippi states; Inter-Continental Motors, 2000 Milam Bldg., San Antonio, Texas,—Texas, Rocky Mountain and Western states; Riviera Motors, Inc., 1455 Bush St., San Francisco—Northern Calif., Washington, Oregon and Nevada; International Motors, Inc., 5670 Sunset Boulevard, Hollywood, Southern Calif., Arizona and New Mexico.

Announced retail price of the 300 L is less than $7000 and of the 190 SL, about $3900. ★

SPECIFICATIONS
1954 Mercedes-Benz

ENGINE	300 SL	190 SL
Type	6-cyl. O.H.C.	4-cyl. O.H.C.
Bore and stroke	85 x 88 mm (3.34 x 3.45 in.)	85 x 83.6 mm (3.34 x 3.36 in.)
Piston displ.	2,996 c.c. (183 cu. in.)	1,897 c.c. (116 cu. in.)
Compression ratio	8.55:1	8:1
Brake horsepower	240 h.p.	125 @ 5,500 r.p.m.
Carburetors	Fuel injection	2 side-draft

GENERAL
Transmission .... 4 speed conventional
Front suspension .. Coil spring independent
Rear suspension .... Coil spring independent with swing axle.
Brakes .... hydraulic with vacuum booster, turbo-cooled brake drums.
Frame .... welded tubular steel
Weight, unladen .. 2250 lbs. approx.   2140 lbs. approx.

DIMENSIONS

	300 SL	190 SL
Wheelbase	94 in.	94 in.
Tread, front	54.5 in.	56.5 in.
Tread, rear	56.5 in.	58.5 in.
Overall length	176 in.	166 in.
Overall width	70.3 in.	68.5 in.
Overall height	48.5 in. (loaded)	52 in. (unladen)
Turning circle dia.	39.4 ft. approx.	36 ft. approx.
Gas tank capacity	34 gal.	15 gal.
Tire size	6.70 x 15 racing	6.40 x 13

ULTRA-LIGHT aluminum body can be converted for competition use by removing windshield and installing low-cut doors.

Mercedes-Benz puts in a strong bid for prominence in the American sport-car field with the new 190 SL. Its rather conservative styling gives the appearance of conventional town-car trends, yet it can be adapted quickly for racing.

MERCEDES-BENZ

MERCEDES-BENZ, an almost magic name in European car circles, soon will be better known in this country. The 190 SL model, a combination touring and sport car with two seats, has the passenger and luggage space required for long trips and the powerful speed and ease of handling vital to the racing-type auto.

On special order a small emergency-passenger seat can be installed behind the front seats, which are adjustable. A low engine hood gives the driver an easy survey of fenders and of the road just ahead. Corner posts are narrow, and the one-piece windshield is equipped with an electric windshield wiper. All instruments are arranged for easy observation and are well within the driver's angle of vision.

The Daimler-Benz ventilation and heating system is standard equipment and permits independent regulation of air quantity and temperature on each side of the car's interior. Engine vibration and road noises have been reduced to near-perfect proportions through rubber cushioning.

Speed? The 190 SL has been clocked at approximately 120 mph. ★★

In converting the 190 SL for racing, the doors can be removed and replaced by lighter panels with cut-out arm pits. The top comes off and a smaller, plexiglass screen is substituted for the windshield.

MERCEDES-BENZ

The Mercedes-Benz 300 SL is a greatly improved sport car. In their second appearance at the Berne Grand Prix, the coupes took the first three places. Styling has been emphasized in the new model in competition for the American sport car dollar.

By W. ROBERT NITSKE

WITH THE first public showing of their new Mercedes-Benz 300 SL model competition coupe at the recent Third Annual Motor Sports Show in New York, the German firm began in earnest to compete for a share of the American dollar spent for sport cars.

The announcement of their 190 SL sport roadster, which followed immediately, seems to support that viewpoint.

Both sport cars are of more than cursory interest. And it is the first time since the glorious days of the fabulous S models that a Mercedes-Benz competition model can be purchased by an individual sport car enthusiast.

The new 300 SL is greatly improved over the sensationally successful model of the 1952 racing season. That year three Mercedes-Benz coupes were entered in the tortuous Mille Miglia, against tough international competition. Kling placed second in the difficult 970-mile race through the Italian country. Carraciola placed fourth. Lang slid on the wet cobblestones against a kilometer stone marker when pulling out of a fast turn and damaged the front end of his car. He did not finish the race.

In their second appearance, at the **Grand Prix of Berne**, the 300 SL coupes took the first three places with Kling, Lang and Riess driving.

The gruelling 24-hour trial at Le Mans again saw Mercedes-Benz victorious against strong competition. One of the cars was stopped by light trouble when darkness overtook them. The remaining two took first and second places to astonish all but ardent Mercedes-Benz enthusiasts.

At a Nuerburg Ring event, the four 300 SLs placed one, two, three and four, after a record-breaking spectacular race.

When the Mercedes-Benz cars won the first two places in the sport car category of the Mexican Road Race that year, the superiority of the 300 SL seemed well established. Daimler-Benz did not participate in racing events the following year.

The new 300 SL is a masterpiece of elegance and a greatly improved sport car. It is an example of the progressive engineering to be expected from the Untertuerkheim factory. For instance, it is the first production car to employ the revolutionary fuel injection system.

The six cylinders have an 85 mm. bore and 88 mm. stroke, a displacement of 2,996 cc. The three-liter engine develops an amazing 240 horsepower.

The crankshaft with seven solid four-metal bearings, the dry sump lubrication, the large oil cooler, and the strength of the crankshaft result in a driving system which can easily withstand a continuous engine speed of 6,000 rpm.

Driven by a duplex roller chain, the camshaft is located in the cylinder head, insuring, despite large valves, a relatively light valve mechanism. The entire valve operating mechanism works quietly and reliably up to a speed of 6,000 rpm. The large valves and steep cam ensure perfect filling up to the highest engine speed.

Proper saturation with air is also furthered by large suction line cross sections which, in the case of the fuel injection system, can be most favorably dimensioned without impairing the elasticity of the engine.

At full acceleration the engine draws the air in almost completely unthrottled. Carburetor engines, on the other hand, cannot offer such a perfect fuel-and-air mixture on account of the inevitable throttling in carburetors and suction lines at high engine speeds. Consequently, their performance is lower.

Over the entire engine speed range, from idling to running at high speed, the fuel injection system supplies each cylinder automatically with the exact quantity of fuel required. The engine of the 300 SL can be operated in direct drive, without jerks or faulty shifting, from a speed of 15 mph. to top speed, which is around 165 mph.

Because of the perfectly uniform supply of fuel to the cylinders, the fuel injection system permits higher compression than a corresponding carburetor engine, and thus again increases performance. A thermostat and an altitude compensator at the injection pump correct automatically for air temperature and air density, eliminating the frequent carburetor adjustments required by many sport cars.

A decade of development of the fuel injection system for aircraft and vehicle engines at the Daimler-Benz plants guarantees the absolute operational safety of this method.

Fuel quality and lubrication requirements do not differ from the usual passenger car engines. In fact, many components are from the regular 300 series production models. Normal service station super gasoline with an 80 octane rating and 20 SAE oil are sufficient.

The transmission, and especially the gear wheels, are so sturdily dimensioned as to permit racing operation without any difficulty or premature wear. All four forward speeds are of the controlled syncromesh type, permitting unusually fast shifting. An oil pump supplies all lubrication points with pressure oil. The gear ratios of the 300 SL are: 1st gear, 1:3.16; 2d gear, 1:1.85; 3d gear, 1:1.325; 4th gear, 1:1.0.

A rigid frame is an absolute prerequisite for perfect road holding and high speeds on bad roads. A new type of light three-dimensional tubular frame, of which the individual members have to absorb pulling and pushing stresses but no flexural stresses whatsoever, is used. This sturdy frame prevents twisting and distortion and, consequently, body damage on rough roads.

All wheels have independent suspension. The front axle has wishbone arms and the rear axle consists of a jointed cross shaft. Front and rear axles have friction-free coil springs and large shock absorbers. This axle arrangement provides at the same time pleasant springing on all kinds of roads and excellent road holding. On arched roads, a perfectly straight run at the highest speed is possible.

The turbo brake drums of the 300 SL are of aluminum. Its high conductivity quickly transfers the heat from the cast iron drum to the outside of the brake drum. The radial vanes at the outer periphery cause a strong air stream which conducts the heat away from the drum. A booster reduces the required pressure on the brake pedal. Thus even the most forceful braking can be effected without physical effort. The brake remains sensitive and prevents unintentional blocking of the wheels. Through this system of taking the heat off, the full braking effort is preserved for long periods in racing.

The three-liter engine develops 240 hp. With seven solid four-metal bearings and dry sump lubrication, the crankshaft can take care of a speed of 6,000 rpm.

When the brake linings begin to wear out, the brake shoes adjust themselves automatically.

The body of the 300 SL accommodates two persons comfortably. The seats are of the bucket type and offer a good hold on the sides when curves are negotiated at high speeds. The driver's seat can be adjusted back and forth. The airplane-type doors open upward and permit getting into the very low car without bowing the head. The steering wheel can be removed from the steering column by one movement of the hand, further facilitating getting into the car.

The engine hood is low and the front fenders can be seen easily from the driver's seat. The road can be observed as close as 13 feet in front of the car. The corner posts at the sides of the wide windshield are narrow, making for excellent visibility. A strong windshield wiper motor with two speeds, a pane washing system, and effective window defrosting ensure clear vision even during unfavorable weather. A large glare-free driving mirror permits observation of the road behind the vehicle.

To keep the body cool when the engine is under heavy stress in hot weather, a double partition between engine and passenger compartment has been built. The velocity forces a strong air stream through a grid in front of the windshield. The air moves through the space between the partition walls and leaves through grilles on the sides. Thus, the heat generated in the engine does not come in contact with the partition on the passenger's side. Fresh air is caught at the side of the radiator and directed through air ducts into the body where it is distributed. A water heating element, which can be regulated, is installed inside the duct and guarantees sufficient heating of fresh air during cold weather. The side windows have revolving panes for additional ventilation. The used air leaves through an air scoop in the roof.

The instrument panel is at convenient level for the driver and has a rich array of instruments which are so arranged that they prevent any reflection. The spare wheel, tools, and tank filler cap are accessible when the rear deck lid is opened.

The curb weight of the completely equipped 300 SL, with fuel, is 2,490 pounds.

The new Mercedes-Benz 190 SL is a two-seated combination touring and sport car. It is as much a touring and every day car as it is a racing vehicle for the smaller events. The roadster is equipped with a folding top, and has two bucket-type seats. An emergency seat can be installed behind the front seats. Bench-type seats can be provided in front.

To reduce weight and air resistance in sporting events, the roadster top and windshield can be removed. A small plexiglass windshield provides protection to the driver. Lighter side doors, with cut out arm pits, can be installed and bumpers can be removed.

The 190 SL has all the requirements of a comfortable touring car. It has the Daimler-Benz ventilation and heating system which permits independent regulation of air quantity and temperature on each side. A steering column gearshift and a ring operated horn combined with direction indicating lights are provided. There is plenty of room for luggage.

The streamlined vehicle's front and side appearance is similar to that of the 300 SL model. The engine performance of 125 hp. provides fine acceleration and a clocked maximum speed of 118 mph. The transmission has four syncromesh type forward speeds. Designed on the principles of the larger 220 and 300 models, the 190 SL cruises along in city traffic comfortably and quietly. Springing is designed to combine enjoyable touring over long distances and the perfect skid-proof and road-holding qualities expected in a sport car.

The Mercedes-Benz 190 SL is a car suited for all purposes, the perfect synthesis of touring and sport characteristics.

The four cylinders have a bore of 85 mm. and stroke of 83.6 mm. Displacement is 1,897 cc. Compression ratio is 8 to 1. Engine output is 125 hp. at 5,500 rpm., and maximum engine speed is 6,000 rpm. The overhead camshaft is driven by a roller chain with automatic adjustment. Heat exchanger for cooling of the lubrication oil is installed. The engine design provides excellent torque at even low engine speeds.

The engine is equipped with two horizontal carburetors which insure correct filling of the cylinders and perfect distribution. Automatic warming of the suction lines makes it possible to drive the vehicle like any standard touring car. The engine is started without difficulty, even at the lowest temperatures, by means of a small starting carburetor attached to the operational carburetors.

The controlled syncromesh type forward gears permit quick shifting. Gear ratios are: 1st gear, 1:4.05; 2d gear, 1:2.38; 3d gear, 1:1.53; and 4th gear, 1:1. Speeds of up to 50 mph. are permissible in second gear and up to 80 mph. in third gear.

The general chassis arrangement and many details are the same as the new 180 model. A combined frame-and-floor unit endows the vehicle with extraordinary stiffness against distortion, flexure and vibrations, and with unusual safety in case of collision. The famous support bridge from the 180 model has been taken over. This front bridge is a U-shaped unit carrying the wishbone arms for the independently suspended front wheels, the coil springs, telescopic shock absorbers, steering housing and intermediary steering lever.

Combining all of these elements in the support bridge results in perfect kinematics of wheel guiding and steering. As a consequence the front wheels offer outstanding road holding and a minimum of wear and tire noise. Three large elastic rubber connections join the support bridge and the body's frame and floor combination, thus affording additional isolation against driving noises and vibrations.

The 190 SL shouldn't be overlooked as an elegant model. With a 125 hp. engine the power plant provides excellent torque. Maximum engine speed is 6,000 rpm.

The front part of the engine drive unit also is supported on soft rubber pads by the bridge, providing still another excellent isolation between engine and body interior.

The rear axle is of the jointed cross shaft type. For decades Daimler-Benz has been using independent suspension of front and rear wheels with the springing effected by friction proof coil springs in order to obtain optimum road holding. While the car is sprung very softly, there are no secondary vibrations. Its springs quickly neutralize vibrational movements, eliminating the short vertical vibrations, characteristic of the rigid type axle, against which even the softest cushion seats are of no avail.

The steering mechanism of the 190 SL is of the Daimler-Benz type with recirculating balls and automatic adjustment. This system combines ease of operation and smoothness with good road contact and immediate response.

The brakes are of large dimensions. As in the 300 SL, the turbo brake drums transfer the heat quickly to the outside. They guarantee top effectiveness.

The driver also has the same excellent visibility as in the larger model. Ventilation and heating systems correspond with that of the 180 sedan.

The 190 SL roadster is built on a wheelbase of 95 inches and has an overall length of 165 inches. Its height, including the folding top, is 52 inches. Curb weight, including spare tire and tools, is 2,310 pounds.

While the 300 SL and the 190 SL models are available to the individual sport car enthusiast, Daimler-Benz company has developed a special 300 SL model of its own for the Mille Miglia, the Le Mans and the Mexican Road Race this year. It carries the additional designation R for 'racing'.

The 300 SLRs are outwardly identical with the regular type. However, the factory version has two camshafts and especially designed swing axles. The brakes are located on the inside, similar to the design on the aerodynamic, rear-engined, 1922 Benz racer. The wheels have wire spokes for easier brake cooling. The gearbox and differential housing are in one piece. Five gears are provided, which would suggest that the top speed of the 300 SLR is nearly 190 mph.

With their sturdy, reliable 170 and the new 180 model four-door sedans, available with either gasoline or diesel engines, the stylish 220, and the elegant 300 models, Mercedes-Benz will be well represented on the highways of the world.

Airplane type doors on the 300 SL enable driver and passenger to have easy access despite the extremely low floor level. In the convertible, the regular doors are removable to permit installation of lighter panels for sport car racing events.

JOHN BOLSTER TESTS

THE MERCEDES-B

Germany's 140 m.p.h. 3-litre Coupe a Car of Bea

There is little need to mention the triumphant return to racing of Mercedes-Benz with the 300SL. The team, it will be remembered, had an incredibly successful season in 1952, which included the victory at Le Mans. After that, the cars were withdrawn from competition while their makers prepared to enter the Grand Prix sphere, and we thought we had seen the last of the silver coupés.

How exciting it was, therefore, when it was announced that the engine power had been greatly augmented by the adoption of direct fuel injection, and that the model was to be placed on the market at a not unreasonable price. Obviously, this must be one of the most potent production road cars ever sold, and so I was delighted when the manufacturers offered to lend me one for a week's hard motoring.

The basis of the 300SL is an immensely rigid tubular frame. This consists of a very large number of steel tubes, and extends into the scuttle and also embraces the engine, which is considerably inclined towards the near side to reduce its effective height. In front, there are forged wishbones of unequal length with helical springs, and an anti-roll torsion bar. The Z.F. steering gear operates through a three-piece track rod, which has a hydraulic damper to avoid road shocks and shimmy.

Behind, there are swing axles, also with helical springs, and the final drive is a hypoid bevel. The half shafts are enclosed in tubular housings, which pivot on the differential casing, and there is one universal joint for each side. The brakes are hydraulic, with a vacuum servo, and operate in bimetal drums with turbo fins. A shoe width of no less than 3¼ ins. has been chosen.

The engine is a six-cylinder with a single chain-driven overhead camshaft. The six separate inlet ports each have their own ramming pipe, all of which are fed from a large gallery with a single throttle at its forward end. The exhaust system is on the same side, but the welded-up manifold sweeps downwards, away from the high mounted air intake system, and a shield avoids heat transference.

On the near, or lower, side of the engine is the fuel injection pump, which is driven by a shaft and gears from the front of the crankshaft. The injectors are in the block, and the sparking plugs are in the head, directly above them. The tank for the dry sump lubrication is also on this side, and there is another tank for water on the offside. The radiator block is mounted low down in front, and has an oil radiator alongside it. The wide bonnet is literally full right up of machinery, and two slight bulges are, in fact, necessary to clear the valve cover and the induction manifold.

The body is, perhaps, the most typical feature of the car. To reduce the difficulty of entering the seats, which are low down between the tubes of a space-type triangulated frame, the doors of the coupé body include most of the roof. This is an extremely effective solution, and the frame is covered in and padded. There is quite a useful luggage space behind the seats, for which a fitted suitcase can be supplied. The tail locker contains the spare wheel, and there is room for odds and ends here.

Before entering the car I paused to gaze at its really lovely lines. I then operated the ingenious retractable door handle, and the gull door rose on its counterpoise springs. Folding the special steering wheel out of the way, I slipped easily into my seat. (For a lady to enter the 300SL, a delightful display of nylon is called for, which I do not regard as a disadvantage!) Anyway, once I was installed, I marvelled that at last a car had been made with *every* control in the right place.

The cloth upholstered seats are completely comfortable, and positively locate the driver and passenger. The central remote-control gear lever falls under the right hand (L.H. steering), and the wheel is well away from one's legs, so that a heavy coat can be worn if desired. All-round visibility is first class, and although my head was close to the roof, I was never conscious of this.

On moving off, one applauds the clutch, which succeeds in being very

INCLINED SIX: The 2,996 c.c. single considerable angle to reduce bonnet heig six injectors can be

NZ 300SL
nd Superb Performance

most cars, the acceleration falls off when top gear goes in, but this one continues to leap forward. To take three times at random, imagine a comfortable closed car that can accelerate from 0 to 60 m.p.h. in 7 secs., 0 to 100 m.p.h. in 16.2 secs., or 0 to 120 m.p.h. in 25.8 secs.! I agree; it's fantastic!

As regards the timed-both-ways maximum speed, my car had the lowest of the three alternative gear ratios. In recording a mean of over 140 m.p.h., I had to take the engine up to 6,250 r.p.m. in top. This is obviously well past its peak, and I am confident that one could exceed 150 m.p.h. with a higher ratio. For British roads the one fitted is certainly the best, but I would like to try the "high cog" to record a genuine century and a half, at some future date.

The performance figures could not be achieved unless the traction was exceptionally good. The independent rear suspension helps greatly in this, and two exactly equal black lines are left by both wheels when getting off the mark. I did not treat the clutch and gear lever brutally, so a ruthless driver could possibly better my times.

Fuel injection pays dividends in giving instant response to the throttle, and, at the other end of the scale, it allows the car to accelerate in top gear from little more than walking pace. No luxury limousine has a more flexible power unit. The engine is quiet and smooth when cruising, but takes on the "hard" feel of a racing unit when really extended. The exhaust is at all times virtually inaudible, which is astonishing to say the least.

In spite of its short wheelbase of only 7 ft. 10 ins., the Mercedes-Benz is very comfortable indeed. The springing is definitely soft, but there is no pitching. Even when driving at 140 m.p.h. over bumpy roads, one's head never touches the roof.

To drive this car as a fast road vehicle requires only the skill that very high speeds will always demand. To drive it as a racing car, on the other hand, exacts a somewhat special technique. Very few drivers, I think, would be at home in it without a good deal of practice, and I admit that this applied to me. Once acquired, the knack is difficult to put into words, but I think it goes something like this.

Most of us enter our corners too fast, because we are accustomed to driving positive without being fierce. The gearbox is light in action and has effective synchromesh on all four speeds. Too many sports cars lack synchronization on bottom gear, which is really the ratio for which one needs it most. The indirect gears are not completely silent, but their slight whine is not really obtrusive.

The acceleration is so tremendous that it is almost beyond belief. It is not so much that one has 240 b.h.p. to play with, but that the torque curve is exceptionally flat. The gear ratios are ideally chosen with this in mind, and anywhere between 3,500 and 5,500 r.p.m. the surge of power seems virtually constant. With

OFFSIDE of the engine, showing the ramming pipes to the six separate inlet ports. The exhaust system, set beneath, is shielded off to avoid heat transference.

ine of the 300SL is canted to a Bosch fuel pump which feeds the e near side.

"IF IT LOOKS RIGHT—it is right," is a maxim which can justly be applied to the Mercedes-Benz 300SL, the appearance of which matches its electrifying performance.

cars that lack engine power, and so we need the speed to initiate a drift. The 300SL has high cornering power, but excessive speed causes sudden rear end breakaway. The exceptionally high geared and hydraulically damped steering is heavy when used violently, and so one tends to over-correct, which causes a series of untidy skids.

The right method, it seems, is to begin the corner a little slower and achieve a drift by using a great deal of power. Handled thus, the machine fairly rockets out of the bends, which is, after all, the object of the exercise. More than almost any car, the Mercedes-Benz responds to a good driver, but in the hands of an indifferent one it could be dangerous, and should never be sold to a beginner. A man should gain experience in 100-120 m.p.h. cars before being let loose in this projectile.

The brakes are immensely powerful and do not fade, but once again practice is necessary before one is at home with them. This is due to the vacuum servo, which gives an unusual feeling to the pedal. As soon as I had become accustomed to them, I realized that these brakes have no vices and can be used hard and continuously without diminution of their power. It is, however, possible to lock the wheels easily at 140 m.p.h., with all the drama which that entails. The brakes, in fact, are on a par with the 240 b.h.p. engine, and should be used with similar discretion.

The whole car is really beautifully constructed and finished. One hears no rattle or drumming, and a remarkable lack of wind noise is apparent. There is an elaborate system of heating, ventilation and demisting, and the front window panels also turn. The main door windows do not open in the ordinary way, but may be instantly detached and carried in an envelope in hot weather. The aerodynamics are such that this does not cause a draught. Three small criticisms concern—the instrument lighting, which is too bright; the headlamp high beam indicator, to which the same applies; and the speedometer, which is regrettably optimistic. Surely no car needs a fast speedometer less than this one!

The Mercedes-Benz 300SL is a car of beautiful appearance and almost incredible performance. Its construction and finish are of the very highest class, and its whole design represents a technical *tour de force*. It has perfect traffic manners, and the sheer joy of handling it on the open road has to be experienced to be believed. There are other cars which are kinder to the less experienced driver, but for the man who is competent to exploit its full performance, this is one of the world's greatest cars.

ACCELERATION GRAPH

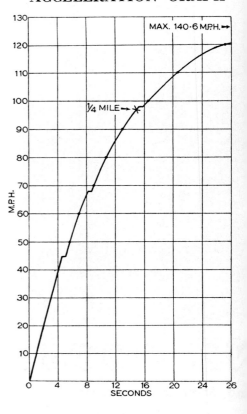

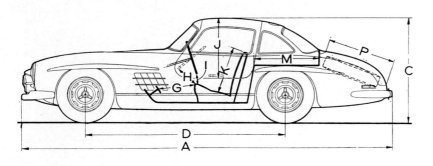

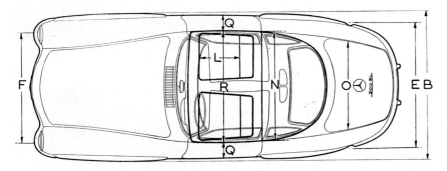

DIMENSIONS OF THE MERCEDES-BENZ 300SL

A Overall length, 14 ft. 7 ins.
B Overall width, 5 ft. 10 ins.
C Overall height, 4 ft. 3 ins.
D Wheelbase, 7 ft. 10 ins.
E Rear track, 4 ft. 8½ ins.
F Front track, 4 ft. 6½ ins.
G Clutch pedal to seat cushion, 1 ft. 6 ins.
H Steering wheel to seat cushion (unlocked position), 7 ins.
I Steering wheel to seat cushion (locked position), 5½ ins.
J Height from step to roof, 2 ft. 4½ ins.
K Length of seat back, 1 ft. 8 ins.
L Length of seat cushion, 1 ft. 6 ins.
M Length of boot, 2 ft. 6 ins.
N Width of boot, 3 ft. 10½ ins.
O Width of spare wheel door, 3 ft. 3 ins.
P Length of spare wheel door, 3 ft. 6 ins.
Q Width of step, 10 ins.
R Width at elbows, 4 ft. 0 in.

SPECIFICATION AND PERFORMANCE DATA

Car Tested: Mercedes-Benz 300SL sports 2-seater coupé, price £3,100 (£4,329 15s. 10d. with P.T.).

Engine: Six cylinders, 85 mm. x 88 mm. (2,996 c.c.). Single overhead camshaft. 8.4 to 1 compression ratio. 240 b.h.p. at 6,100 r.p.m. Direct fuel injection. Bosch coil and distributor.

Transmission: Single dry-plate clutch with steel reinforced linings. Four-speed gearbox with synchromesh on all gears and central remote control, ratios 3.64, 4.73, 7.16, and 12.15 to 1. Hypoid final drive.

Chassis: Welded multi-tubular triangulated frame. Independent front suspension by unequal length wishbones with anti-roll torsion bar. Independent rear suspension by swing axles. Helical springs all round with hydraulic dampers. Z.F. steering box and three-piece track rod. Bolt-on pierced disc wheels, fitted 6.50-15 ins. racing tyres. Hydraulic brakes, 2L.S. in front, with bimetal turbo-finned drums and vacuum servo.

Equipment: 12-volt lighting and starting. Speedometer, rev. counter, ammeter, oil pressure, oil temperature, water temperature and fuel gauges. Clock, two-speed windscreen wiper and washer, flashing indicators, cigar lighter. Heating and demisting.

Dimensions: Wheelbase, 7 ft. 10 ins.; track, front 4 ft. 6½ ins., rear 4 ft. 8½ ins. Overall length, 14 ft. 7 ins., overall width, 5 ft. 10 ins., overall height, 4 ft. 3 ins. Turning circle, 38 ft. Weight, 1 ton (dry).

Performance: Maximum speed, 140.6 m.p.h. Speeds in gears, 3rd 98 m.p.h., 2nd 68 m.p.h., 1st 45 m.p.h. Standing quarter-mile 15.4 secs. Acceleration, 0-50 m.p.h. 5.4 secs., 0-60 m.p.h. 7 secs., 0-70 m.p.h. 8.8 secs., 0-80 m.p.h. 10.6 secs., 0-90 m.p.h. 13 secs., 0-100 m.p.h. 16.2 secs., 0-110 m.p.h. 20.6 secs., 0-120 m.p.h. 25.8 secs.

Fuel Consumption: 15 m.p.g.

The Mercedes-Benz emblem constitutes a focal point in the impressive frontal appearance

The Autocar ROAD TESTS

No. 1560:

MERCEDES-BENZ 300SL

IN 1952 Mercedes-Benz had a successful competition season with their then new sports-racing coupé, the 300SL. Since then, other models have been produced for racing, and the coupé is in full production for sale to those fortunates who have the ability to handle and the means to purchase such a car. As is well known, the two essentials do not often go together.

But the 300SL, in addition to being very fast, is also very safe, and a brief description of the mechanical layout will point some of the reasons why. The chassis frame is built up of a number of steel tubes of small diameter with two main engine cross-members. Suspension at the front is by coil springs and double wishbones, and the usual Mercedes independent rear suspension of coil springs and swinging half-axles is employed. The 3-litre six-cylinder overhead camshaft engine lies at an angle in the frame to assist in keeping the overall height down, and one of its most interesting features is the use of fuel injection. The light alloy body structure is fabricated separately from the chassis, and the two combine to make what is without doubt a most astonishing car.

Provided for test by Mercedes-Benz (Great Britain), Ltd., Mercedes-Benz House, 58, Camberwell New Road, London, S.E.5, the car was fitted with the standard axle ratio of 3.64 to 1. Alternative ratios of 3.42 and 3.25 to 1 are offered. The first thing noticed on sitting in the car is the extremely good view from the driving seat. The forward and downward slope of the long, wide bonnet top with its twin bulges

The small flare over each wheel arch helps to keep the car clean. Air from the engine compartment is vented through the rectangular ports in each side. The twin body vents are seen above the rear window

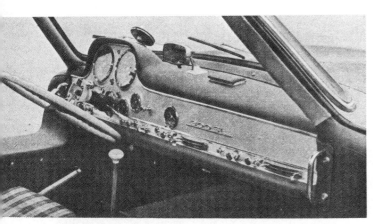

Large diameter rev counter and speedometer are prominent in the facia. Individual ventilation is controlled by the horizontally moving levers on the panel, and an ashtray is provided, placed adjacent to the driving mirror

ROAD TEST . . . . continued

allows the driver to see the road close up to the car, and the thin screen pillars cause less of an obstruction than has been noticed on other cars. The fact that the car tested had left-hand drive did not constitute a handicap.

The 300SL is docile and tractable in dense city traffic, with its innumerable hold-ups, but there is no doubt whatsoever that its true place is outside built-up areas, where it can be allowed to come into its own. After it has trickled along in third and top gears, the time eventually arrives when the driver is able to see opportunity in front of him, and second gear can be selected, so that the car really comes to life.

For a passenger who has not travelled in the 300SL before the effect is electrifying. The driver, of course, knows the precise moment when the car is going to accelerate, but the other occupant of the compartment receives at first a mild pressing back into the seat, and then, as the power comes in between 3,500 and 4,000 r.p.m., he feels as though he is being rocketed through space. Up to 70 m.p.h. is available in second gear, and then can come a quick movement into third. The rev counter needle drops back for a second or two, and again at 4,000 r.p.m. the effect of being urged forward by some irresistible force is felt. There is a somewhat harsh note from the engine, but little exhaust and wind noise; in fact, with the rev counter needle on the red mark at 6,000 r.p.m. it is possible to converse in normal tones.

In the indirect gears, then, and indeed in top, the acceleration of this unusual car is truly remarkable. The effect up to 60 m.p.h. is not so noticeable as higher up when, with over eighty showing on the speedometer, the rev counter needle swinging round rapidly towards the limit mark, and third gear still engaged, the car fairly rockets forward. Gradients, of course, have no meaning except to add to the exhilaration of driving the car, and hump-back bridge signs have to be treated with real respect, as it is only by keeping a wary eye on the instruments that the driver is really sure at what speed he is travelling. It is accurate to say that 60 m.p.h. in the 300SL seems like half that speed, and therefore more than a nodding acquaintance with the car is required before full use of the performance can or should be made.

Although it will accelerate extremely quickly in top gear—for example, it reaches 100 m.p.h. from 16 in top in 35.2sec—it is more amusing to get the full effect and go up to ninety or over on third gear before changing up. It does all this so quickly that opportunities for such performance occur on English roads more frequently than would be the case with a slower car. A satisfying movement of the gear lever and one is into top, when the engine gives the impression of being able to propel the car all day at over 100 m.p.h. Press the accelerator well down even at this speed in top gear, and again there is the feeling of being on the end of a rope which is being pulled hard from in front of the car. The way the 300SL does it all with so little fuss is almost uncanny.

Normally with road tests it is customary to quote cruising speeds, but the 300SL's cruising speed is limited, not by mechanical factors, but by the road and traffic conditions. It is one of the least tiring cars to drive, in the manner of all high-performance cars except those which are very noisy. As does the cruising speed, average speeds or miles in the hour on a long journey depend a great deal on traffic conditions, but the acceleration capabilities of the car enable the driver more frequently to overtake slower moving traffic in safety, and so cut the time for a known route by a very considerable margin and with no feeling of having misbehaved by upsetting other road users. Admittedly, they may have wondered what it was that passed them, but by that time the Mercedes 300SL is over the hills and far away!

Although the door sill is very wide, entry to the seats is not difficult. The doors have spring loaded struts to hold them open. Upholstery and trimming are well carried out. A rail is provided round the luggage compartment to protect the rear window and to act as a cleat when straps are used to secure luggage

Suspension, steering and brakes to match the acceleration and maximum speeds in the gears are part of the character of the car, and considerable experience of other Mercedes-Benz models with similar suspension was found to be most useful. The ride is by no means harsh; in fact, on one four-hundred-mile journey a small child was able to sleep curled up on what is essentially the luggage space behind the seats. When cornering at the speed of other traffic the 300SL goes round firmly on the proverbial rails, taken close to the chosen line and with hardly a movement of the steering wheel. There are but two turns from lock to lock, and the driver is never conscious of actually turning the wheel to direct the car. There is, when cornering fast on open bends, a slight movement of the hands and the car is round. It is reminiscent of a fast motor cycle, which is steered more by leaning the body than by actual movement of the handlebars. There is some slight kick back which gives a useful indication of what the front wheels are doing.

Oversteer is apparent, and unless one is travelling comparatively slowly it is essential to drive the car round a corner. Any inclination to ease the throttle and the rear of the car will tend to swing round. The downhill left- and uphill right-hand bends on a daily route were taken very fast and with complete confidence in the car by adopting these tactics, and there was no trace of misbehaviour.

When taking open, very fast swerves the driver can start to guide—this is the operative word rather than steer—the car round just before he enters the corner and then, using the throttle, make the 300SL come out on the straight in a beautiful movement. There is the typical Mercedes-Benz feeling of the swing axles working. On wet roads the car slides slightly under these conditions, but with judicious handling there is no tail breakaway. It is a car that teaches its lessons sharply, and thus demands respect. Only in

MERCEDES-BENZ 300SL

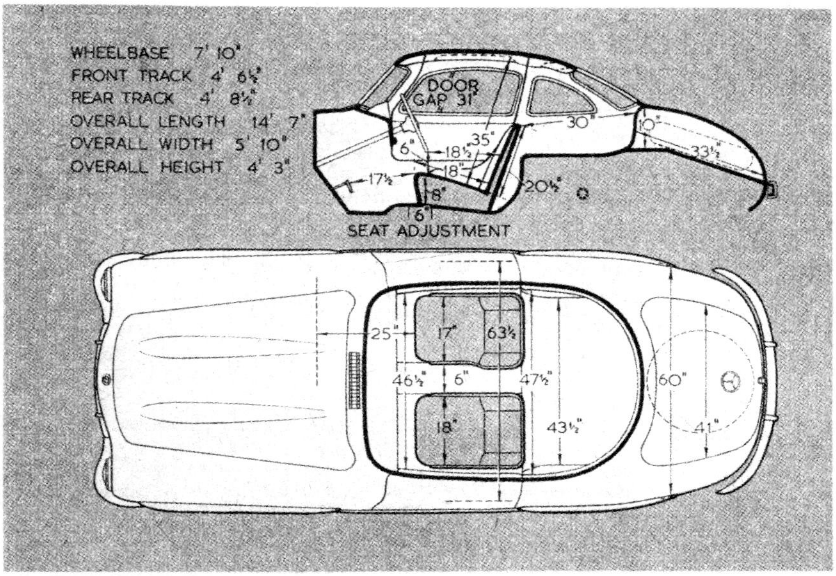

Measurements in these ¼in to 1ft scale body diagrams are taken with the driving seat in the central position of fore and aft adjustment and with the seat cushions uncompressed

PERFORMANCE

ACCELERATION: from constant speeds.
Speed Range, Gear Ratios and Time in sec.

M.P.H.	3.64 to 1	5.04 to 1	7.17 to 1	12.3 to 1
10—30	—	—	4.1	2.6
20—40	7.8	5.5	3.7	—
30—50	7.9	5.4	3.4	—
40—60	7.8	5.0	4.1	—
50—70	7.5	5.0	4.0	—
60—80	8.0	5.1	—	—
80—100	8.2	—	—	—
100—120	9.0	—	—	—

From rest through gears to:

M.P.H.	sec	M.P.H.	sec.
30	3.5	90	16.1
50	7.0	100	21.0
60	8.8	110	30.9
70	11.0	120	56.4
80	13.8		

Standing quarter mile, 16.1 sec.

SPEEDS ON GEARS:

Gear		M.P.H. (normal and max.)	K.P.H. (normal and max.)
Top	(mean)	128.5	206.8
	(best)	135.0	217.3
3rd		84—98	135—157
2nd		58—70	93—112
1st		30—44	48—71

TRACTIVE RESISTANCE: 6.7 lb per ton at 10 M.P.H.

TRACTIVE EFFORT:

	Pull (lb per ton)	Equivalent Gradient
Top	291	1 in 7.6
Third	440	1 in 5.0
Second	660	1 in 3.2

BRAKES:

Efficiency	Pedal Pressure (lb)
87 per cent	90
77 per cent	75
64 per cent	50

FUEL CONSUMPTION:
18.4 m.p.g. overall for 746 miles (15.32 litres per 100 km).
Approximate normal range 15–23 m.p.g. (19–12 litres per 100 km)
Fuel, First grade.

WEATHER: Dry surface, fresh breeze.
Air temperature 30 deg F.
Acceleration figures are the means of several runs in opposite directions.
Tractive effort and resistance obtained by Tapley meter.
Model described in *The Autocar* of 12 February 1954.

SPEEDOMETER CORRECTION: M.P.H.

Car speedometer:	10	20	30	40	50	60	70	80	90	100	110	120	130
True speed:	11	20	29	37	45	54	62	71	80	88	100	110	120

DATA

PRICE (basic), with sports coupé body, £3,100.
British purchase tax, £1,292 15s 10d.
Total (in Great Britain), £4,392 15s 10d.

ENGINE: Capacity: 2,996 c.c. (182.75 cu in).
Number of cylinders: 6.
Bore and stroke: 85 × 88 mm ($3\frac{11}{32} \times 3\frac{15}{32}$in).
Valve gear: single overhead camshaft.
Compression ratio: 8.5 to 1.
B.H.P.: 240 at 6,100 r.p.m. (B.H.P. per ton laden 168).
Torque: 217lb ft at 4,800 r.p.m.
M.P.H. per 1,000 r.p.m. on top gear, 22.2.

WEIGHT: (with 5 gals fuel), 24¼ cwt (2,758lb).
Weight distribution (per cent): F, 52; R, 48.
Laden as tested: 28½ cwt (3,200lb).
Lb per c.c. (laden): 1.06.

BRAKES: Type: F, Two-leading shoe; R, leading and trailing.
Method of operation: F, Hydraulic; R, Hydraulic.
Drum dimensions: F, 10.23in diameter; 3.54in wide. R, 10.23in diameter; 3.54in wide.
Lining area: F, 129 sq in. R, 129 sq in. (180.6 sq in per ton laden).

TYRES: 6.50—15in.
Pressures (lb per sq in): F, 31; R, 40 (normal). F, 43; R, 50 (for fast driving).

TANK CAPACITY: 28 Imperial gallons.
Oil sump, 26.5 pints.
Cooling system, 27 pints.

TURNING CIRCLE: 38ft (L and R).
Steering wheel turns (lock to lock): 2.

DIMENSIONS: Wheelbase: 7ft 10in.
Track: F, 4ft 6½in; R, 4ft 8½in.
Length (overall): 14ft 7in.
Height: 4ft 3in.
Width: 5ft 10in.
Ground clearance: 5⅛in.
Frontal area: 18½ sq ft (approximately).

ELECTRICAL SYSTEM: 12-volt; 56 ampère-hour battery.
Head lights: Double dip; 35-35 watt bulbs.

SUSPENSION: Front, independent, coil springs and wishbones. Rear, independent, coil springs and swinging half axles. Anti-roll bar position front.

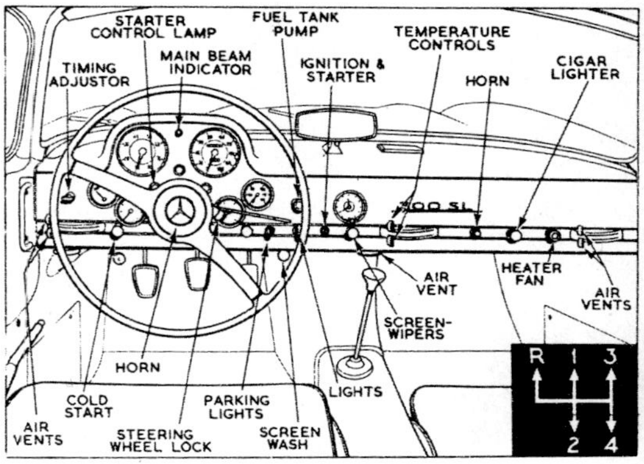

ROAD TEST . . . . continued

traffic or when parking does the steering feel at all heavy.

The driving position and location of the seat enable drivers of varying heights to sit some distance from the wheel, and adopt the almost arms stretched attitude which gives the maximum control. The steering wheel, which can be hinged on its boss to allow ease of entry, is placed at an ideal angle. There is no means of adjusting column length or height.

The brakes are vacuum-servo assisted, and the pedal is completely dead when the engine is switched off. The aluminium drums have cast iron liners and radial vanes to help heat dissipation. There is automatic adjustment to take up wear on the liners. One can only say that the brakes are fully capable of dealing with the high performance of the car. Used repeatedly on a rapid descent of Shap, and when taking the performance figures, there was not the slightest sign of fade or unevenness. The pressure required for all normal stopping and traffic work is comparatively light. On one or two occasions the left front wheel tended to lock, but strangely and fortunately this occurred only at speeds below 40 m.p.h. The brake pedal is just too far away from the accelerator for the driver to indulge in "heel and toe" gear changes. The hand brake lever fits snugly on the outside edge of the driving seat, and is a little far forward when the seat is adjusted for a tall driver.

There is synchromesh on all forward ratios of the gear box, and the movement of the short, stiff central lever can be made very quickly. Part of the pleasure in driving the car is contributed by the gear change. In operation, none of the gears was particularly silent, and even in top there was a slight hum. A car of this nature is all the better for a very small amount of mechanical noise providing that the driver knows what causes the noise and what it indicates.

The clutch is fitted with strong springs to enable the power to be transmitted without slip, and, although by normal touring car standards the pedal pressure is heavy, operation does not become tiring during a long journey. The drive is taken up smoothly, and the clutch stands up well to full throttle gear changes. When accelerating from a standing start the drive passes immediately to the rear wheels, and wheelspin can occur for some distance even on a dry surface. Once the clutch is fully engaged, wheelspin is governed by the amount of throttle used, and with practice it was found that the 300SL could be taken off the mark very quickly indeed, without clutch slip and without overmuch wheelspin. The fact that the electric test speedometer was on the 90 m.p.h. mark at the end of the standing quarter mile is a fair tribute.

The big fuel filler is inside the spare wheel locker. Jack and wheel nut spanner are held in clips on the right-hand side. Flashing direction indicators and stop lights are in the rear lamp assembly

One has been led to expect sports-racing cars, for that is what this Mercedes-Benz basically is, to be noisy and to some degree uncomfortable. In this car the most noise came from the tyres, which were racing pattern, and their sound rose to a not unpleasant crescendo as the speed went up. The window in each door is either closed or can be removed completely; there is no winding mechanism because of the shape of the doors. It is possible to drive at high speeds with the windows removed and without any draught. What wind does come in in these conditions is not felt by the occupants, and it finds its way out through the vents in the coachwork above the rear window. It is perhaps because of the degree of silence of its progress that the car can be driven quickly without attracting unwanted attention. Watching it accelerate away from a standstill is impressive, as there is only a throaty hiss from the big tail pipe as it disappears quickly down the road.

Speed at night is limited by the head lamp beam. One can only assume that when this type of car ran in the Le Mans 24-hour race it was fitted with more powerful lamps than is the present production model. They have a useful spread of light, and the range of beam is adequate for speeds up to 100 m.p.h. on a known road. Most drivers did not find it possible to have the instrument panel lighting switched on at night except for a quick glance now and again, as there is no rheostat incorporated in the switch, and the lighting is very bright; it produces most disturbing reflections in the windscreen. The horn has a good, powerful note and winking indicators are fitted.

Heating and demisting equipment is comprehensive, and driver and passenger have individual controls for supply of hot or cold fresh air. All air taken in from the forward ducts is let out through the rear vents, and it is possible to have both windows closed and fresh air constantly circulating through the car without a draught.

Luggage space is adequate for the type of coachwork, and in addition to the room on the flat floor of the compartment behind the seats there is room for coats and small items in the spare wheel locker. Small tools, the lifting jack and wheel brace are kept here; there is no starting handle.

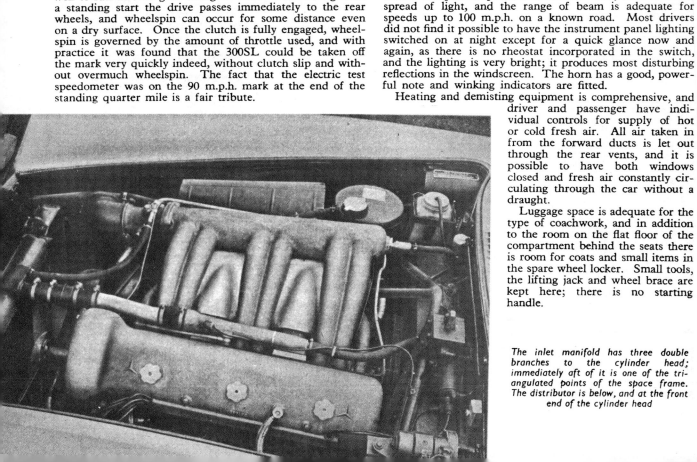

The inlet manifold has three double branches to the cylinder head; immediately aft of it is one of the triangulated points of the space frame. The distributor is below, and at the front end of the cylinder head

Road testing the Mercedes-Benz

photographs by Rolofson

Few cars have been so long anticipated or so long awaited as the first genuine sports car from Mercedes-Benz in over 20 years. Oftentimes a long wait also serves as a cooling-off period and the initial trial turns out to be anti-climactic if not completely disillusioning.

In this case, just when we were beginning to suspect that the 300 SL coupe would prove to be a mediocre performer, we got one for a full scale road test. The new car turned out to be far beyond our boldest expectations. In fact, we can state unequivocally that in our opinion the 300 SL coupe is the ultimate in an all-round sports car. It combines more desirable features in one streamlined package than we ever imagined or hoped would be possible.

Performance? It accelerates from a dead stop to 100 mph in just over 17 seconds.

Top Speed? With standard axle ratio it

Huge intake manifold fills under-hood space.

Trunk is occupied by 35 gal. tank and spare.

The latest style shift lever is shown here.

can approach 140 honest mph in under 2 miles, from a standing start.

Dual Purpose? A production model 300 SL can make a very acceptable showing in any type of sports car competition. Yet the car is extremely tractable and easy to drive in traffic.

Comfort? The fully enclosed 300 SL is the most comfortable (and safe) high-speed "cross-country" car built today.

First Cost? After careful, detailed examination of this car and its performance data, the only question is—"How do they do it for less than $8000?"

Depreciation? Mercedes-Benz reputation for quality and durability, plus the law of supply and demand, lead us to predict that it may be 3 years before you can "pick one up (used) for less than five grand."

One of the joys of publishing an enthusiasts' magazine is—the enthusiasts. M-B dealers have no 300 SL demonstrators, yet on January 11, we met enthusiast supreme, Mr. Vivian A. Corradini, at Santa Anita and proceeded to road test his new 300 SL coupe. (On a lonely desert road—not on the horse track). Mr. Corradini has owned, or owns just about anything interesting ever built to run rapidly on four wheels. His enthusiasm for this car can be shown by his confidence in its ability to stand-up under the fairly rigorous test program undertaken.

With the odometer reading 1732 miles we set off for the desert area. The car is easy and comfortable to handle in traffic. The clutch is just a little heavier than an average car and off-idle throttle response has a slight lag, apparently a characteristic of the unusual fuel injection system employed on the 300 SL. One soon becomes used to this, and other matters receive attention. The seating position is high enough to be comfortable but the knees of a 5 foot 10 driver tend to hit the underside of the steering wheel. Visibility all-around is excellent and the feeling of driving a very wide car is soon lost. (Overall width is only 70.5"). The long cranked gear control lever leaves something to be desired and the action seems a trifle stiff (later models have a typical sports car remote control type shift lever). There is, however, a surprising amount of gear noise from an otherwise very quiet automobile.

The steering is also unusual. It feels light and positive (only 2 turns, lock to lock), but takes extra pressure to make any appreciable change in steering angle. The feeling might be described as exactly the opposite of power steering. After a 100 miles or so, one no longer notices this, and at very high speeds the steering effort is quite light yet remarkably enough does not feel overly sensitive or too quick for a sports car owner. However, an ex-Cadillac owner would be well advised to drive and steer this car with considerable caution for the first few days.

Tramping on the accelerator pedal produces instantaneous acceleration in any gear at any speed. Two aspects of this warrant comment. With first or second gear engaged, full throttle at, say, 1000 rpm literally forces you back in the seat. As the tach needle sweeps toward 4000 rpm, you think—"man, what acceleration!" Then all hell breaks loose, for at 4000 rpm things really begin to happen. The Tapley meter swings way

ROAD AND TRACK ROAD TEST NO. F-3-55

MERCEDES-BENZ 300 SL COUPE

SPECIFICATIONS

List price	$7463
Wheelbase	94.5 in.
Tread, front	54.5 in.
rear	56.5 in.
Tire size	6.70 - 15
Curb weight (no fuel)	2710 lbs.
distribution	49/51
Test weight	3060 lbs.
Engine	6 cyl.
Valves	sohc
Bore & stroke	3.35 x 3.47 in.
Displacement	183 cu in. (2996 cc)
Compression ratio	8.55
Horsepower	240
peaking speed	5800
equivalent mph	127
Torque, ft/lbs.	202
peaking speed (est.)	4000
equivalent mph	88.0
Mph/1000 rpm	22.0
Mph at 2500 fpm	95.1
Gear ratios (overall)	
4th	3.64
3rd	5.04
2nd	7.18
1st	12.2
R & T performance factor	61.0

PERFORMANCE

Top speed	140 mph
2 way avg.	134.2 mph
Max. speeds in gears—	
3rd (6500)	103
2nd (6500)	72.5
1st (6500)	52
Shift points from—	
3rd (6000)	95
2nd (6000)	67
1st (6000)	48
Mileage	18/23.5 mpg

ACCELERATION

0-30 mph	2.7 secs
0-40 mph	4.0 secs
0-50 mph	5.7 secs
0-60 mph	7.4 secs
0-70 mph	9.2 secs
0-80 mph	11.6 secs
0-90 mph	14.2 secs
0-100 mph	17.2 secs
Standing ¼ mile	15.2 secs
best	15.1 secs

TAPLEY READINGS

Gear	Lbs/ton	Mph	Grade
2nd	580	47	30%
3rd	420	62	21%
4th	295	80	15%

Total drag at 60 mph, 130 lbs.

SPEEDO ERROR

Indicated	Actual
10	9.9
20	19.2
30	28.0
40	37.1
50	46.1
60	55.2
70	64.3
80	72.6
90	81.6
100	91.0
110	101.5

Mercedes-Benz 300 SL Coupe
acceleration through the gears

The Mercedes 300 SL gave a fuel consumption of 23.5 mpg at a cruising speed of 65 mph.

off-scale in first, nearly so in second. (600 lbs/ton is top graduation). The engine takes on a hard note and begins to scream. In third gear you are up to an indicated 100 mph almost before you have time to think. Such is the acceleration of the Mercedes.

Then you try the brakes, carefully at first for these are power-boosted. A pressure of only 25 lbs will suffice for a normal, comfortable rate of deceleration. There is a good "feel" here, with perfect control. Applied hard at 120 mph the car's nose goes down slightly and the passenger has trouble with his own rear-end adhesion to the seat. Applied repeatedly, there is absolutely no sign of brake-fade, or loss of control. In our opinion these are the best brakes ever employed on a production automobile.

The comfortable cruising speed of this car can be anything you like. Once we held 120 mph for a few miles. Aside from the dangers of traffic there is no reason for worry at this velocity (and no one can catch you). The engine feels smooth and wind noise is almost non-existent. As a matter of fact, during the first attempt at a timed speed run, with the speedometer reading over 140 mph, Mr. Corradini shut-off as we entered the measured strip when he heard the two stop-watches start, not being familiar with our procedure.

Conditions were not favorable for the high speed tests, and accordingly we credit this car with a genuine top speed of 140 mph, though the two-way average was actually 134.2 mph. The tachometer read 6100 rpm on both runs, and the proper spark plugs for this run should have added 200 rpm. As it was, we changed plugs after the high speed runs in order to be able to proceed. (Bosch No. 280 were used, No. 310 are recommended for competition.) There is no reason to disbelieve the factory claim of 160 mph top speed for this car, when the engine is in good tune and when the optional high speed axle ratio of 3.25 to 1 is used. Our test car, like all the early deliveries, was supplied with a 3.64 axle ratio—a compromise which is an excellent one for the average American enthusiast.

It might also be mentioned that the acceleration data were all obtained without wheelspin and using brisk but not brutal up-shifts. Especially notable was the solid "bite" of the clutch as each gear change was completed. Yet despite the terrific surge forward, the car is easy to control and displays no tendency to yaw under the fiercest acceleration. Here, again, the standard axle ratio contributes to the tremendous acceleration abilities and at the same time gives flexible and tractable low speed driving qualities which appeal to the average owner. Undoubtedly the use of fuel injection in place of normal carburetion has also improved the low speed flexibility of this car. In short, the modest size Mercedes engine has a dual personality—developing over one horsepower per cu in. at high rpm, yet performing at low speed in a manner nearly comparable to the pre-war American powerplant of the era when the time to accelerate from 5 to 25 mph in high gear was all-important.

As recommended in the owners handbook, we used a tire pressure of 43 psi front, 50 psi rear (for competition work). Even so the car proved to be extremely comfortable with a soft suspension that soaks-up the bumps without recourse to low tire pressures.

Comfort has not been sacrificed in any way in this car. In fact, this was the most luxurious sports car road test ever. However much one may appreciate the pleasures of open-air motoring, there is no denying that a fully enclosed coupe has its advantages. Even the fact that the door windows do not crank down proved no drawback, thanks to the efficiency of the very elaborate ventilating and heating system designed as an integral part of the car.

When enclosed comfort is combined with a remarkable ride, uncanny wheel adhesion, quick steering and performance equal to or better than almost any car you can name, the conclusion is inevitable. The sports car of the future is here today!

Knock-off disc wheels on the 300 SL (not included in the list price) underline the gradual demise of the wire-spoked wheel.

SAMPLING THE 300 SL MERCEDES-BENZ

THE 300SL Mercédès-Benz, which created such a sensation in sports-car racing two years ago, until the manufacturers withdrew it from competitions because "they had learnt all they needed to know," was brought to Silverstone on October 14th for the delectation of a few favoured motoring journalists.

Rudolf Uhlenhaut, head of the Mercédès-Benz experimental and racing department, drove each journalist for two or three fast laps of the full Silverstone circuit. This was a wonderful experience, for Uhlenhaut is well known to be nearly as fast as Fangio when it comes to poking a Mercédès round the circuits, and while he may have kept just a little in hand during these demonstration runs, the 300SL was driven very fast indeed, using all the available space on the corners. Uhlenhaut used only top and third gears, bringing the car out of the corners by skilful opening of the throttle, the speed rising to something like 112 m.p.h. along the straights.

Later came the opportunity of trying the 300SL for oneself and while fast "lappery" masks rather than clarifies impressions of a strange car, especially one of this power and speed, we were impressed by the manner in which 6,000 r.p.m. came up in the indirect gears, equal to nearly 100 m.p.h. in third, the comfort and support of the cloth-upholstered bucket driving seat, the high-geared, taut, somewhat heavy steering, the very fine road-holding, swing-axle rear i.s. notwithstanding, and particularly by the great power of the light-to-apply, completely fade-free brakes, with their turbo-finned drums. Naturally, the extreme power and urge of the 300SL impressed. It also created favourable comment for the manner in which it stood up to this continual high-speed without falter, the exhaust showing neither blue haze nor black smoke, the engine starting promptly, and no trouble of any sort remotely thought of, except for a big nail which punctured one of the Dunlops, although this car, with the first production fuel-injection engine, was used as a road-hack and probably did nearly 200 miles of fast work at Silverstone. The accelerator has a short travel and when it is depressed the result is interesting! The car snaked somewhat when taking an adverse camber and it is possible that a de Dion back-end would hold it down better, although it is certainly an outstandingly stable and safe car.

It is a truly delectable motor-car and not surprisingly costs £4,392 15s. 10d. in this country, in spite of the fact that Mercédès have studied cost-reduction and hence use bolt-on wheels, drum brakes and a sheet steel body, etc. Although the price is high, there is, they appreciate, a limit, even for sales to the U.S.A.

The instrument panel is in the modern, even ornate style, with quite modest speedometer and rev.-counter dials before the driver who, in this l.h.d. example, had a hand-brake lever on the left of his seat and a central remote gear-lever, nicely placed and controlling a gearbox with admirable synchromesh. Entry and egress to the two-seater cockpit with its luggage shelf behind the seats entails cocking the legs to negotiate the deep chassis sill, as the spring-loaded lift-up "Le Mans" doors are used, but head-room as you enter or emerge is unrestricted, as the doors form part of the roof. This construction is essential if a properly-stiff chassis frame is to be employed without a heavy weight-penalty; the frame is, indeed, formed of 25 mm. by 1 mm. "bicycle" tubes. The sliding windows seem rather small but visibility is excellent and head-room ample, whilst the luggage boot is capacious.

Mercédès-Benz are building 25 of these 300SL cars a month at present, selling mainly to America, and will soon increase production to 50 a month. They aim to build 500 in all, so that the car qualifies to race in the *Gran Turismo* class.

The engine is a development of the 300 and 300S six-cylinder overhead camshaft 85 by 88 mm., 2,996 c.c. unit. With direct fuel injection, which, from our remarks above, it must be obvious that Stuttgart has got absolutely "taped," the power output is 212 b.h.p. at the clutch, using a compression-ratio of 8.55 to 1. We write "at the clutch" advisedly, for American enthusiasts get 240 b.h.p. by removing cooling fan, exhaust mufflers and such like impediments. The b.m.e.p. is 158.5 lb./sq. in.

The engine peaks at 5,800 r.p.m., but is safe up to 6,000 r.p.m. and will tolerate 6,400 r.p.m. in top gear if the low-ratio back axle is fitted.

Uhlenhaut explained that Mercédès-Benz have adopted fuel-injection because it provides the same strength mixture in each cylinder, so that a higher compression-ratio can be employed than is possible with normal carburation, when the limiting factor is that of the leanest cylinder. The car we tried was using pump National Benzole and S.A.E. 20 Mobiloil. It shows not the slightest tendency to "pink." Besides this advantage of fuel injection, this system provides excellent low-speed torque, from 400 r.p.m. upwards, and makes the engine easier to operate under cosmopolitan conditions, inasmuch as jets do not require changing at high altitudes, as the fuel pump is provided with bellows for automatic altitude adjustment and also has automatic temperature and cold-start adjustments.

Dirt is the enemy of the fuel-pump, as it is of a diesel-injection pump, but a double filter obviates most of the trouble. The only shortcomings of fuel-injection have been difficult hot-starting, cured by using an electric auxiliary pump to prime the system with cool fuel, and a tendency to "hunt," which however is confined to idling speeds and will be cured. A long induction pipe, feeding air to the inlet valves, damps out induction pulsations.

The cost of fuel-injection is approximately £60 greater than that of normal carburation, but later on Mercédès-Benz will probably adopt it for their lower-priced cars.

The 300SL will be available in open as well as coupé form next spring, but not as a four-seater, as Stuttgart consider such addition of weight quite out of keeping with their conception of a *Gran Turismo* motor car.

Three different back axle ratios are available, 3.68 to 1 for normal touring, giving a maximum speed of 150 m.p.h., as used on the car we drove, 3.42 to 1, which provides a maximum of 155 m.p.h. and 3.25 to 1, which gives an all-out speed of 160 m.p.h.—quite a sports car! Using the "town" gear-ratios 40 m.p.h. is possible in first gear, 67 m.p.h. in second gear and 95 m.p.h. in third gear of the four-speed gearbox, but the higher axle ratio gives 75 m.p.h. in second gear and 107 m.p.h. in third. The weight of the coupé, ready to drive and full of fuel, is given as 25.5 cwt., suggesting a dry weight of about 23 cwt. Were a light-alloy body used some 80 kilo. could be saved, but the price would increase.

Fuel consumption is quoted by Uhlenhaut as 44 m.p.g. at 30 m.p.h., 38 m.p.g. at 40 m.p.h., 35 m.p.g. at 60 m.p.h. constant speeds, the average range being between 14.8 and 24 m.p.g. for fast driving, including Alpine work. Uhlenhaut said that motoring "as fast as you can travel on British roads," including town-driving, the 300SL returns 18 to 20 m.p.g., a very conservative consumption for a 3-litre car of this kind, proving that low weight and a good aerodynamic form pay dividends here.

For sports-car racing Mercédès-Benz have the new straight-eight 3-litre fuel-injection 300 SLR (picture on page 622) which MOTOR SPORT described last month.

Uhlenhaut said that next year this car will run in the important sports-car races and they hope to vanquish Ferrari, and Lancia if the latter *marque* runs. Open and closed versions of the 300SLR will be produced, but it is expected that the drivers will prefer the open cars for races like the Mille Miglia, because of the problem of keeping clean the windscreen of a coupé.

Disc brakes are being investigated at Stuttgart, but will not necessarily be used. Already tests of a German-supplied Chrysler disc brake have been completed and Uhlenhaut now places high hopes in the Dunlop disc brake.

He welcomes the increasing competition in Grand Prix racing and looks forward to 1955, when the sports/racing 300SLR will make its debut and the Mercédès-Benz G.P. cars are expected to be faster than they were this year.—W. B.

SEEN AT MONZA.—One of the first production 300SL Mercédès-Benz, used by R. Uhlenhaut for personal transport.

R.V. AT DAWN

A 300 S.L., a clear road, an obliging owner, what more could you want? Asks The Technical Editor.

What the 300 S.L. Can Do

Accelerations	0 — 30 m.p.h.	in	3.5 secs.
	0 — 50 ,,	,,	6 ,,
	0 — 80 ,,	,,	13.8 ,,
	0 — 100 ,,	,,	21 ,,
	0 — 125 ,,	,,	39 ,,
Max. Speed	Top Gear :	165 m.p.h.	
	Third ,, :	100 ,,	
	Second ,, :	75 ,,	
	First ,, :	50 ,,	
Average Fuel Consumption :		20 m.p.g.	

IN 1952, and only a few short days after the Mercedes victory in the 24 Hours Endurance Race at Le Mans we straddled the low sides of a 4-litre 300 S.L. and huddled beside the driver in anticipation of a short sprint down the open highway. The invitation came from none other than Herr Uhlenhaut, engineer-in-chief of the company who also did the driving. The ensuing experience was a memorable one—though much too brief to permit recapitulation into an article at the time.

In those days such a jaunt was a privilege, and we didn't get too nosey about the specification which was then mostly a matter of conjecture. But in 1955 any possessor of an idle three thousand pounds, combined with a yearning to stable the fastest motor car in the world can have himself a 3.0 S.L., as the model is now in series production at Unterturkheim at the rate of five per day. One of these affluential people happens to be a friend of ours and he was glad to give us the chance of an early morning free-for-all in his pride and joy.

When this car was delivered it carried a dossier of literature including a letter from the Mercedes-Benz directorate giving details of various factory tests they had applied to it. These officially certified that the engine had been checked at nearly 240 b.h.p. at 6,000 r.p.m. and that the best fuel to use was a 75% pure petrol, 15% alcohol and 10% benzol mixture. The professional conscience behind such attention explains in part the enthusiam of the connoisseurs for the marque, and justifies the high prices which the 300 S.L. commands.

After somewhat unusually elaborate preliminaries on this occasion—including a few words with our insurance consultant—we took up position behind the steering wheel, swung it back and locked it into the driving position (it swivels up to let you in), and closed over the famous articulated doors.

A quarter turn on the switch key, followed by a further eighth turn automatically threw the starter, and the engine growled into life. This took place on a dual carriage-way "somewhere in England" at 5 a.m. and we waited for a few minutes as the oil temperature needle crept up to the correct operating heat before moving off.

It's the acceleration which hits you first. In a matter of seconds we had to change up through second and third gears. We coasted back and forth along our two mile straight at a modest fifty for a few trips before feeling competent to ease into top gear and open up the throttle. Immediately, or so it seemed, we surged on up past 90 m.p.h., and long after the 100 mark had been passed the car was still rushing forward irresistibly. At this stage one asks oneself if the limit of the thing will ever be reached. On and on (only thirty seconds ago we were standing still) and now, a thousand yards away, we are encompassed in a silvery crouch of machinery moving at the fearsome speed of 150 m.p.h.! And yet the acceleration keeps coming in, until we hit the second mile with the realisation that we have a little wife and family confidently expecting our customary arrival for the evening meal at 6.30. We raise our foot ....150, 140, 135 130 m.p.h., down and down, until we are doing a mere 125 m.p.h. We breathe again.

That was as fast as we dared to go. It wasn't a case of the car not being able to exceed 150 m.p.h., for it is practically guaranteed to make 165 m.p.h. but the limit was quite unashamedly conditioned by a feeling of caution on our part. Needless to say it is practically impossible to get a piece of highway which is straight enough, long enough and clear enough to let the right foot go to the boards and stay there until the 300 .L. won't go any faster.

The acceleration does queer things. It tries to push one's head back off the shoulders and it continues to rush you forward literally at even 100 m.p.h.! It also creates a feeling of fatalism that tends to slow down the inclination to apply the brakes. We have heard of a similar feeling on the part of fighter pilots and our minds turned with sympathy to those brave men who make it their business to give a 300 S.L. its head for twenty-four stretches at a time at Le Mans.

One of the most over-awing characteristics of the 300 S.L. is its silence. The greatest intrusion on a nice quiet conversation at nearly two miles a minute comes from the roar of the tyres as they master the road, and an outside spectator would hardly look twice—he only saw something (that was) and heard an unearthly hiss from the enormous exhaust tail pipe as the car disappeared down the highway.

We felt a bit cheated by our experience. Here was a car which could travel at 165 m.p.h., and yet we had not given it the chance to do so. Perhaps it was as well, for the 300 S.L. is an instrument of fulfillment which is reserved for the skilled racing driver only. Anyone CAN drive it, but not as it should be driven.

Still the Mercedes is not a dangerous car. It is so well designed, and balanced, that it makes speed in itself quite safe. But this is not enough; the human element enters into the scene too dominantly. The car can make sixty miles per hour pass for thirty, but the mind can forget.

The actual acceleration times are shown in the table. Suffice to say that they are easily the fastest we have seen.

The frantic amount of wheelspin which the petrol-injection engine produces at take-off is lethal for the treads. We stopped to feel them once and they were burning hot Racing tyres only, of coures, may be used on the Mercedes-Benz 300 S.L. for moving at 150 m.p.h. in a straight line is in itself dangerous on anything but perfect shoes.

We only tried the brakes once—because of a regard for the owner's rubber bill. They are servo-assisted and deliciously designed so that they will not lock the wheels. They give an impression of not applying themselves nearly hard enough—when you are doing over 120 m.p.h.; but on measurement of stopping distances one finds that their efficiency is excellent.

We continued back to the rendezvous for the last time and thanked our connection for a brief but priceless hour and then got into a car which felt as if it were going backwards for most of a 30-mile journey back to London Airport.

MILLE MIGLIA

by Bernard Cahier

WHETHER OR NOT the ancient gods of Rome looked with special favor on the pair that bore the initials of the race is doubtful, but it is very certain that the accomplishment of Stirling Moss with the new Mercedes 300 SLR sports car in the 22nd Mille Miglia will stand as one of the finest of this or any racing season. Not only did the young Englishman increase the record average speed by almost 10 mph, but he became the second non-Italian and first British driver to win, placed a non-Italian car 1st for only the second time in the race's history (Caracciola with a Mercedes won in 1931), and managed to make a myth of the "who-leads-at-Rome-loses-at-Brescia" jinx. His achievement was all the more remarkable because, according to the Mercedes team strategy as conceived by Manager Neubauer, Moss was not really supposed to win; his task was to set a blistering opening pace to draw out and burn up the Ferraris at the possible sacrifice of his own car, so that teammates Fangio,

Grimy driver Moss and bearded co-pilot Jenkinson shortly after their sensational victory.

Brescia before the start; numbers painted on cars indicate time of departure.

Kling and Herrmann would have a clear field. Moss set the pace well enough, but car and driver held up all the way, and, except for a few dents from a straw-bale encounter, reached the finish in fine condition.

At Brescia before the race, all the elements indicated a great event. Instead of the usual spring rains the weather was hot and clear. With the notable exception of Farina, Ascari, Villoresi, and Behra, most of Europe's top drivers were on hand, and the turn-out of cars—some of them making their racing debut—was the most impressive ever. Out of 648 entries, 533 appeared at the starting line, running in 13 classes ranging from the new category for Diesel cars to the Unlimited Sports class. In the latter, the biggest battle was obviously to be between Mercedes-Benz and Ferrari. The German team was opposed by Ferrari drivers Taruffi, Maglioli, Marzotto, and Siginolfi in the 3.75-litre, 6-cylinder cars, and Castellotti in the new, unraced 4.4-litre 6. No works Lancias appeared, but a 3-litre, 6-cyl. Maserati was on hand driven by Perdisa and also a 3-litre Gordini. The strongest British entry was Collins' Aston-Martin DB3S, but also running in the big-car class were four Austin-Healey 100S models piloted by Donald Healey, Macklin, Abecassis and Flockhart. Gran

An Englishman wins the Mille Miglia in a German car!

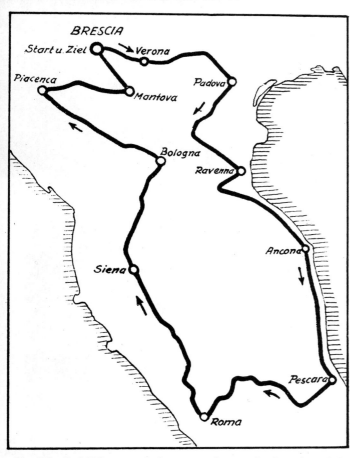

The 992-mile M.M. course makes a sweeping circuit of northern Italy.

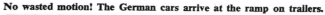

Moss's Mercedes 300SLR awaits the "go" signal on starting ramp.

No wasted motion! The German cars arrive at the ramp on trailers.

Maglioli, in a 3.75 Ferrari, rounds a crowd-thronged corner; he placed a distant 3rd overall.

Turismo competition was provided by three Mercedes 300 SL's (one of them driven by John Fitch), Aston-Martin DB2-4's, Jaguars and a host of smaller cars.

Around the starting ramp Saturday evening, excitement was at a fever pitch. At 9:00 pm the first car, a Diesel-engined Fiat, made its start, to be followed off the mark at one-minute intervals for over ten hours by a steady procession of cars with ever-increasing engine displacement. Not until 7:28 AM Sunday did the last of the big cars rumble off and by then some of the small ones were already past Rome, nearly 600 miles away.

The 992-mile circuit of the Mille Miglia is shaped like a fat bunny with a prominent Adam's apple (at Ravenna), and encounters in its course just about every kind of driving condition. Leaving Brescia, the road leads eastward across the Lombardy plain to Verona and Padua, then turns south across the Po River Valley to Ferrara and Ravena. Along the Adriatic coast are long open straights leading to Ancona and, far to the south, Pescara; swinging west from the sea, the course winds through the Abruzzi mountains to Rome, then starts the long return northward over the plains to Sienna, up through the tortuous hairpins of the Apennines and the Futa Pass, down through Piacenza and Cremona, crossing the Po again to pass through Mantua (Nuvolari's home), and so over the flatlands to Brescia once more. Unlike the PanAmerican race, which, though twice as long, is made

The Austin-Healey 100S of Abecassis ran well, finished 11th overall.

Seidel and Glockler's class-winning Porsche Spyder on the Raticosa.

up of relatively short hops, the Mille Miglia is continuous driving, with stops only for gas and rally-like "book-stampings" at control points. The road is closed until the last of the big cars are past, but the way is dotted with towns and villages and virtually impossible to police effectively, so the Italian fauna, animal and human, is an ever-present danger.

With ideal driving weather, cars of all classes turned in astounding times to Verona, 42 miles away. The Ferraris were the fastest with Marzotto's car averaging an unbelievable 122.7 mph. First control was at Ravenna, 188 miles, and Castellotti in the 4.4 Ferrari 6 arrived with the best average, a stunning 119 mph; Moss was almost two minutes slower, followed (in elapsed time, that is) by Taruffi, Herrmann, Kling, Maglioli, Perdisa, and Fangio whose engine was running roughly. Marzotto was out with a thrown tread and damaged shocks. Heading south, trouble beset the Aston Martins: Collins' DB3S also threw a tread and soon went out with engine failure, while two DB2-4's suffered clutch trouble and retired.

At Ancona, Moss moved into the lead by a scant half minute, but on the coast road to Pescara, Taruffi edged ahead by 15 secs. The "Silver Fox" had a psychological advantage because, starting last, he could learn at each control where he stood in relation to his adversaries; but now he was holding off the German cars almost single-handed. The pace finally took its toll on Castellotti's big Ferrari, forcing it out with engine failure. Just short of Rome, Kling, who had driven thousands of miles on the course in practice, nudged an embankment and crashed, escaping with broken ribs.

At Rome, the crucial half-way point, Moss was again ahead by almost two minutes, and the superstitious shook their heads knowingly. Behind the Englishman in time were Taruffi, Herrmann, Fangio, Perdisa, Maglioli, Siginolfi, Giardini (2-litre Maserati), Musso (2-litre Maserati), and Adianonzo (2-litre Ferrari). In the 750 cc Sports class, Bayol led (long hours before the big cars arrived) in his D.B., while in the unlimited Gran Turismo class Fitch had lost the lead he held at Pescara to Gendebien (300 SL). Two of the A-H 100S's were going strong (Abecassis and Macklin) although Macklin had throttle trouble and was driving on the ignition.

Race favorite Taruffi started last, led Moss, but **failed to finish**.

Beyond Sienna and into Florence, the three Mercedes of Moss, Herrmann, and Fangio dominated the field, but the latter's engine was still having injector trouble. After one of the most gallant efforts of the race, Taruffi's oil pump failed and he was forced to retire, taking with him Ferrari's last hope of winning. Climbing the dizzying Futa Pass, Herrmann's Mercedes became a casualty with a punctured gas tank, but Moss, passing Bologna with nearly a half-hour ad-

Suffering from intermittent injector trouble, Fangio's Mercedes was never able to gain the lead but still took 2nd place.

vantage over Fangio, never eased his pace for a moment. At this point in the route, the D.B. of Storez had overcome Bayol's tired car, Porsches led their classes, and Fitch had regained his class lead. Heading back into Brescia, Maglioli battled to overtake Fangio but missed by 13 minutes, and his lonely teammate, Siginolfi, finished 6th, 40 minutes after Maglioli. John Fitch drove his 300 SL as no one this side of the Atlantic has ever driven one, and came in 5th overall with a Gran Turismo car! Abescassis placed his A-H 100S 11th overall, and the Triumph TR-2 team, having lost two cars, finished one, driven by Brooke, at the creditable average of 70 mph.

The hum of the silver car as Moss crossed the finish line was lost in a roar of applause. His winning time was 10:07:48, for an average speed of 97.93 mph, a new record and one likely to remain unbroken—for a year or so!

All in all, it could be said that the Germans "had a good race": they placed 1-2 in General Category (Mercedes), 1-2-3 in G.T. over 1300 (Mercedes), 1-2-3 in Diesel (Mercedes), 1st in 1500 cc Sports (Porsche), 1-2 in G.T. 1300 (Porsche). The French won two of the small classes with Renault and D.B., and the Italians took the remaining classes with OSCA, Maserati, Fiat, and Alfa Romeo. The Ferraris were the disappointment of the day, and some say that lack of preparation played a larger part in their downfall than did bad luck. Le Mans in next up, however, and there is still time for a comeback—Moss and Fangio will have the car to beat! ●

This battered Alfa Giulietta completed the race but was beaten in class by two Porsches.

1955 Mille Miglia Results

o.a.	Car	Lit.	Driver	Time
1.	Mercedes	3.0	Moss	10:07:48
2.	Mercedes	3.0	Fangio	10:39:33
3.	Ferrari	3.8	Maglioli	10:42:47
4.	Maserati	2.0	Giardini	11:15:32
5.	Mercedes	3.0	Fitch	11:29:21
6.	Ferrari	3.8	Siginolfi	11:33:27
7.	Mercedes	3.0	Gendebien	11:36:00
8.	Porsche	1.5	Seidel	12:08:17
9.	Maserati	2.0	Bellucci	12:09:10
10.	Mercedes	3.0	Casella	12:11:15

Class Winners

Sports Cars over 2-litres
1. Mercedes 300 SLR, Stirling Moss

Sports Cars up to 2 litres:
4. Maserati A6GSC, Giardini

Sports cars up to 1.5 litres:
8. Porsche 550 Spyder, Seidel

Sports cars up to 1.1 litres:
25. OSCA 1100, Bourillot (13:01:21)

Sports cars under 750 cc:
36. D.B.—Panhard, Storez (13:21:03)

Gran Turismo over 1.3 litres:
5. Mercedes 300 SL, John Fitch

Gran Turismo up to 1.3 litres:
21. Porsche 1300, Frankenberg (12:58:39)

Gran Turismo up to 1.1 litres:
83. Fiat TV, Viola (14:32:50)

Special Touring over 1.3 litres:
28. Alfa-Romeo 1900, Cestelli (13:14:05)

Special Touring up to 1.3 litres:
55. Fiat TV, Mandrini (13:48:12)

Special Touring up to 750 cc:
92. Renault 4 CV, Galtier (14:44:58)

Special Diesel Class
202. Mercedes 180D, Retter (16:52:25)

Above: U.S. driver John Fitch placed his 300SL 5th overall, 1st in unlimited Gran Turismo class. Right: the new OSCA 1500 led its class for awhile but lost out to a Porsche. Below: Storez' sleek DB-Panhard 750 cc class winner.

ALL FOR £4,392 15s 10d STERLING

Some Personal Observations on the 300 SL

HOW can any ordinary driver fail to be impressed by the 300 SL? It appeals to the base instincts in the nicest possible way. In its exclusive manner it does almost as much of everything as any other car and rather more than most. Of course it goes faster, accelerates more quickly, stops better and rides more solidly than the average sports car. It also costs more and carries little. That graceful tail houses only a 30-gallon tank and a spare wheel.

Its 130 m.p.h. and over is relatively effortless, yet in traffic it potters on top gear like a town chariot and with revs so low that they do not register on the dial. It can gulp high-octane fuel at speed, but "idling" along at 50 m.p.h. it injects less than a gallon in 30 miles. There is nothing souped up about this Mercedes; rather is it souped down in its production form. It brings the track car's performance to the road in a tractable form and, from all accounts, with reliability as well. A next-generation road vehicle, it exemplifies the direct relationship, in terms of performance with safety, between racing today and touring tomorrow.

Printed sheets should be provided, giving instructions on how to approach this waist-high monster, mentioning perhaps that previous flying experience may be an advantage. To raise the door it is necessary to fan a horizontal trigger which in turn folds out the handle. The first few inches of movement call for some lifting force; after that the spring loading takes over. These doors do not swing as far outside the car's girth as might be expected and so they can be opened freely when the car is tightly parked. There would be a good deal to be said in favour of this door design, even if it were not an essential on the 300 SL.

Quick entry is a matter of knack, practice and physique, and the hinged steering wheel is there to help. Passengers may find it tricky to swing their legs over the side decking outboard of the bucket seats, but once in there is plenty of room and the seat adjustment sensibly provides for height increase with forward movement and vice versa.

The driver sees well from his left-hand position and soon learns that the car is not really ten feet wide, as it appears at first. He sees around him the normal knobs and dials plus seven ventilation controls, a parking light selector switch, a fuel booster pump, hand ignition and a passenger's horn button—none of them labelled. The central gear lever calls for a right-hand change but this does not feel unusual. The four forward gears have synchromesh.

A glance under the engine cover reveals little that is familiar; it might as well be an atomic unit. On closer examination around the shrouded manifolding and piping, a vast cylinder block is seen reclining on its port side. From the forward placed air filter a surprisingly large duct leads to the manifold and thence directly into the cylinders. Equally large holes elsewhere allow the exhaust to depart

The driving position is roomy and comfortable and the knack of sliding in across the side decking is soon mastered. The steering wheel will hinge flat to make entry easier. In the heading picture the 300 SL is seen beside a familiar stretch of the Thames not far from Runnymede

Gentlemen (see also below) as well as ladies of Cheltenham admired the unfamiliar low curves of this visiting vehicle

All for £4,392 15s 10d Sterling . . .

and petrol to be poured directly into the tank. The radiator reservoir is mounted well back on the British offside and the hefty oil tank (it is a dry sump engine) in a corresponding position opposite. The oil radiator is beside the main coolant radiator over on the other side again. Hidden away under the six-cylinder block is the fuel injector.

Except from cold with the choke out, the 300 SL was not always a first push starter, idling was inclined to be "lumpy" nor could you, or should you, blip the engine. This I attributed to the fuel injection system. The starter switch is tied in with the ignition switch—an extra small twist against a light spring bringing life to the engine. You need to remember not to twist back too positively or the ignition key cuts the engine again.

To make full use of the performance of the Merc would, as yet, often be inconsiderate; it alarms the populace by its rapid acceleration or equally rapid stopping power. The noise is distinctive but very moderate. On the open road the driver has to think more than usual for the other man as well as for himself because few motorists have learned to judge the rate of closing with an approaching fast car. They see it 500 yards away, decide that there is time to swing out to pass a vehicle ahead and are then dismayed to find themselves nose to snout with a squealing sports wagon, on their wrong side of the road and technically at fault.

The car I drove was fitted with Dunlop racing tyres which are designed for adhesion and strength before wear or quietness. On smooth road surfaces they set up a merry whine which effectively drowns the other high-speed noises of engine, transmission and exhaust. Of wind noise I could detect nothing, even with the side windows removed. (They cannot slide or wind because of the interrogatory shape of the doors. They are either in the hole or in a bag behind the seat.)

I believe real appreciation of the 300 SL would come after about a month of varied driving, but a short acquaintance with this dramatic vehicle, taken as a main course between an Aston Martin *entrée* and dessert, naturally produced some definite impressions. There is the big push in the back in all gears and from 20 to 120 m.p.h. in top. With a touch of moisture on the roads the wheels spin in the gears and if you drop a ratio or two to pass another vehicle be careful lest the combination of power and camber whips your tail round. Hurrying away on a dry surface it is easy to burn the tyres and tarmac for 30 yards or more, but the sustained forward surge is thoroughly exhilarating.

It is not easy to design steering and suspension to suit such a wide road-speed range and one finds that the Merc has slightly heavy and abrupt steering for town work, while at high speeds it is light and soberingly effective. The suspension is short and hard in the suburbs but comfortingly substantial on the open-country curves.

Racing drivers no doubt take swing-axle and power effects on the turn for granted, but even as a one-time motor cyclist I am not entirely used to steering with the throttle. In the air, I do know how to adjust bank and rudder in a turn to avoid slip or skid, and this is vaguely relevant. The technique for fast cornering with the 300 SL seems to be to introduce the car to the turn at the minimum speed to be used and then to accelerate round and out—a mild version of the Moss technique. Whether right or wrong, for the 300 SL the car felt happy to me when turning under power, less happy if you had to lift your foot in the middle. I would not feel prepared to say without qualification that it understeers or oversteers. On a smooth, flat road it is probably accurate to the break-away point. Camber and bumps may cause a small unbalance towards the over or under. More power leads to over-steer.

The full servo brakes are a joy to use. Smooth and powerful and requiring very little push indeed they are almost up to Derby-cum-Crewe standard and I would definitely exchange them for those on my own car or on other sports cars I have driven. I would not say the same about the gear change on this particular car which, though by no means unpleasant, was to me a little laborious. Perhaps it will loosen up more later; the mileage was only 1,700. The clutch pedal load is a good deal heavier than I have been accustomed to; it also transmits more power.

I finished a fast ride to Cheltenham and back unfatigued but a mite tense. The car gives a contradictory impression; achievement of its performance is relatively effortless, yet it also seems to be working hard. Perhaps there is an animal explanation. Nature approves of straining muscles and makes them lithe and beautiful in their exertions.

It is polite either to love or hate your friends: indifference is an insult. So with a motor car. If it provokes strong feelings all is well, and any criticisms of the thoroughbred Merc are recorded in this spirit. I was sorry to say goodbye to it.

M. A. S.

If you loiter with intent—even to snap a photograph—you must expect the law to take notice. This officer was full of admiration.

road test:

MERCEDES - BENZ
190-SL

Despite a pair of enormous dual Solex carburetors, the 190 SL recorded 31 mpg at 70 mph.

Three special suitcases are available for the trunk, two for behind the seats.

Traditional Mercedes horn-ring also acts as a direction signal control.

Very few new sports cars have been so eagerly awaited or so long in coming as the moderately priced SL version of the Mercedes-Benz. A first description of the 190 SL appeared in R & T as far back as April, 1954, but many modifications have been incorporated since that time. Changes made in the production cars just now arriving in quantity include a redesigned frontal aspect (similar to the 300 SL), and numerous changes in mechanical details brought about as a result of very intensive testing and development work by the Stuttgart engineers.

The net result is a car which is slightly more expensive and a little heavier than was originally planned, but certainly it should be durable, dependable and without "bugs". Furthermore, this machine shows genuine quality in every detail, from the external finish to the smallest bolt and nut.

The car tested was handed over to us with 973 miles on the odometer by Mr. Harold F. Coole, General Manager for Mercedes-Benz in Los Angeles. We were also accompanied by Mr. Victor R. Gross, the factory export service engineer who proved to be a most enjoyable companion, making no complaint as to our driving methods—so long as we did not exceed 6000 rpm.

The outstanding achievement of the 190 SL is without a doubt its quality in design and workmanship. But a close second is the general feeling of solidity which it immediately conveys. It weighs exactly 2500 lbs with a full tank, and it feels like a 4000 lb car on the road. The ride is very difficult to describe; at times there is a slow easy motion, especially on long, rolling undulations. At other times, particularly on choppy surfaces, there is a feeling of firmness which indicates that the shock absorbers really "snub" the car.

Like all Mercedes cars, the steering is a little heavy, even at high speeds. The car understeers slightly, but the force required to round a fast bend tends to cause one to oversteer a bit until more experienced. The car is at its best at high speeds, one of the easiest cars to cruise at 80 plus mph we have ever encountered. Fast bends cause absolutely no anxiety but sharp, right-angle corners taken vigorously in 2nd gear are not this car's *forte*. True, it adheres firmly to the road and the low-pivot swing axles at the rear "stick" very well over bumpy corners, but the tire squeal in this type of test is appalling, and there is considerable roll. Most sports car people would prefer something a little less noisy in tire choice.

Mr. Gross, the factory engineer was frankly disappointed over the results of the performance tests. Possibly the acceleration figures could be improved upon slightly, and certainly the top speed should be better, with more miles on the engine. The odometer read only 1175 miles at the start of the tests and only two high speed runs were made, in deference to the low mileage. The factory states that "the top speed, with sports car windscreen, is about 180 km/hr (111.8 mph)" but we, of course, test in full touring trim. Wind noise is moderate up to 80 mph, above that, noticeable, and at over 90 mph there is a shrill whistle, with windows closed tightly.

During the acceleration tests we used a rev limit of 6000 rpm in each gear, with one exception. Strictly as a "not recomended" procedure we hit an actual 60 mph (63 mph indicated) in 2nd gear, during one standing start test. The time recorded was 12.1 seconds, but this required 6500 rpm and though the engine did not object, Mr. Gross did.

Obviously the 190 SL is not a "bomb" in acceleration; nor is it "Super-Leicht," but the acceleration times are very good for a 2-litre car of this weight. It is easy to overlook the fact that this engine is very small, by U.S. standards, for 1897 cc is only 115.7 cu. in. Yet at no time is there any impression of being underpowered, and despite the fact that over one horsepower per cu. in. is developed, their is no temperament. With engine idling there is a little "cam-clatter" but inside the car there is no noticeable engine noise. In fact this is one of the smoothest and quietest four-cylinder cars on the market, and it is absolutely impossible to tell the number of cylinders from driving the car. The only criticism which might be made by the non-enthusiast is that the car feels "high-geared" in 4th, and 3rd is necessary for rapid ascents of long steep grades. About 20 mph is the minimum speed in 4th gear, and we used 3rd gear at all times below 35 mph. The transmission is, incidentally, one of the best. It is nearly dead silent in all ratios and the synchronizers (on all four forward speeds) work perfectly—at no time is there a "crunch" when shifting, even during the most energetic use.

Seated at the wheel the driving position is ideal, the controls are well placed and visibility is excellent. The seat cushions are quite firm and far less tiring after several hours of driving than the super-soft types which "sell" cars in the showroom. Two semi-bucket seats are standard equipment but a bench seat is optional. In addition a third seat can be ordered which sits transversely behind the two front ones.

A built-in heater is standard equipment and has adjustments for fresh air on each side of the dash panel in lieu of vent panes in the side windows. This is of course a true convertible coupe rather than a roadster. Mercedes describe the 190 SL as a "touring-sports" model but a racing screen and lighter, cut-away doors can be supplied, which the factory states "make it possible to participate with success in sporting events on a modest scale."

As far as Class E competition is concerned, "modest" is probably the right word, but for a rally type event, we could hardly think of a more suitable car than the 190 SL.

ROAD & TRACK TEST NO. F-12-55

MERCEDES-BENZ 190SL

SPECIFICATIONS

List price (N.Y.C.)	$3998
Wheelbase	94.5 in.
Tread, front	56.3 in.
rear	58.3 in.
Tire size	6.40-13
Curb weight	2500 lbs
distribution	54/46
Test weight	2820 lbs
Engine	4 cyl.
Valves	sohc
Bore & stroke	3.35 x 3.29 in.
Displacement	1897 cc
Compression ratio	8.50
Horsepower	120
peaking speed	5700
equivalent mph	104
Torque, ft/lbs	101
peaking speed	3800
equivalent mph	68.1
Mph per 1000 rpm	18.2
Mph at 2500 fpm	82.9
Gear ratios (overall)	
4th	3.89
3rd	5.01
2nd	7.78
1st	13.2
R & T performance factor	39.6

PERFORMANCE

Top speed (avg.)	99.8
best run	102.6
Max. speeds in gears—	
3rd (6000)	85
2nd (6000)	55
1st (6000)	32
Shift points from—	
same as above (see text)	
Mileage	26/31 mpg

ACCELERATION

0-30 mph	4.4 secs
0-40 mph	7.1 secs
0-50 mph	9.3 secs
0-60 mph	13.0 secs
0-70 mph	18.1 secs
0-80 mph	24.0 secs
0-90 mph	33.8 secs
Standing ¼ mile—	
average	19.3
best	19.1

TAPLEY READINGS

Gear	Lbs/ton	Mph	Grade
1st	520 at	21	27%
2nd	370 at	34	1·%
3rd	240 at	50	12%
4th	170 at	65	9%

Total drag at 60 mph, 109 lbs.

SPEEDO ERROR

Indicated	Actual
30 mph	28.2
40 mph	38.0
50 mph	47.6
60 mph	57.4
70 mph	67.0
80 mph	77.0
90 mph	87.0
107 mph	102.6

MERCEDES-BENZ 190SL
Acceleration through the gears

DRIVING AROUND
with WALT WORON

Cooling of brakes is assisted by the fins. Shock mounting is rugged, makes service easy

Putting up the convertible top is absolutely no chore for the owner, even from the driver's seat. Top stows away neatly behind the 2 bucket seats. Altho the factory designates the other version of 190-SL a coupe, in reality it's a convertible with removable metal hardtop and added chrome trim

MERCEDES-BENZ 190-SL

MERCEDES-BENZ has long been a magic name among automotive-minded people, with its mere mention enough to cause goose pimples. Why? The name has always stood for quality, performance, dependability, and a certain aura not to be found in any other car—even for twice the price. It's little wonder then, isn't it, that I've been anxiously awaiting the opportunity to test the new Mercedes-Benz 190-SL?

And just how does this descendant of the long line of Mercedes wonder cars stack up? In a nutshell—more than adequately. Quality is decidedly one of its fortes, while you must, on the other hand, come to the conclusion that the 190-SL is not a sports car in the strictest sense of the word—particularly if you are to thoroughly understand and enjoy the car. It is better that you approach it with the reservation that here is a fine quality, sports-touring car capable of giving you lots of driving pleasure but not many wins in 2-liter competition.

Note single-U-joint swing axle. Suspending rear end in frame keeps unsprung weight low

Shock absorber between frame and pitman arm helps ease steering, smooth out handling

Performance of small engine indicates effectiveness of overhead cam, dual carburetors

photos by Joe Moore

Don't let the horsepower figure of the 116-cubic-inch, 4-cylinder engine fool you, for tho it's a fairly high 120, the overall weight of 2643 pounds (our test car) results in a weight/power ratio of 22 to 1. This is higher (meaning less performance) than the majority of American stock cars. On the other hand, there's no American stock car engine that extracts nearly as much as the 190-SL's one-horsepower-plus for every cubic inch of displacement. It does this by using a highly efficient overhead camshaft arrangement, 8.5 to 1 compression ratio, twin Solex carbs, and by revving high (5700 for peak, 6000 maximum). If you could trim the weight more than is possible now (doors replaced with lighter ones, removing the windshield and bumpers) or up the horsepower with higher compression, you might well go along with the factory's claim of a car in which it is "absolutely possible to participate successfully in automobile racing contests." It *is* possible, but hardly practical.

Now that the contest-minded readers are no longer with us, just what are the 190-SL's attributes? As I said previously, quality is one of the outstanding features. You get the feeling that craftsmen were hard at work, that the artisans who assembled this car are proud of their handiwork. The panels all fit, the finish is good (tho not very inspiring), the bumpers are well made and unusually adequate for such a car. In fact, everything is so well done up that when you come to something like the flimsy decklid and lock, you find it entirely out of keeping with the Mercedes-Benz nameplate. Equally incongruous is the fact that the back of your hand hits the armrest as you crank the window. You're certainly hard put to find any faults

In the driver's seat you are greeted by an array of instruments and controls from an oil pressure gauge always on 90 to a hot engine primer

with the workmanship, tho. It's about as good as you'll see.

Performance-wise you'll show your stop-lights to most of last year's stock cars in the low- and medium-priced fields. Here's what we racked up in standing-start acceleration checks:

0-30 mph, 3.9 secs. (1st gear only)
0-60 mph, 11.6 secs. (1st, 2nd & 3rd)
¼-mile (76 mph), 18.7 secs. (1st, 2nd, & 3rd)

To get maximum acceleration, you wind it up real tight to 6000 rpm in each gear, snapshifting in between. The best times we got in the highway passing ranges were also made by revving up as tight as possible in each gear, for example:

30-50 mph, 4.7 secs. (2nd gear only)
50-80 mph, 13.2 secs. (2nd and 3rd)

I even tried it up a 32 per cent grade, steeper than any you'll find except in Los Angeles and San Francisco. The 1st time I shifted out of 1st gear at 4000 rpm, but it wouldn't take it in 2nd. I repeated the climb, but this time kept it in 1st, cresting the top at 30 mph and 5000 rpm, with plenty of throttle to spare.

You'll have to use the gears a lot in traffic, since you don't get best performance without revving up the engine. You can't go much lower than 40 mph in 3rd gear without bucking or at least lugging the engine; I therefore found it best to use 3rd gear around town. It's easy to whip around in traffic, since the car is small and vision is good; there's no problem in parking.

On the open road, you'll cruise along effortlessly and stably right on up to top speed, which in our case was 103.4 mph (the factory claims 111.8 mph). You won't have to use any corrective action, since the 190-SL keeps a straight-line course, even on crowned roads. There's absolutely no wind wander, nor is the car affected by sharp gusts. The only wheel vibration is over rough roads.

When the road begins to wind you get the general feeling that the 190-SL will handle like a superb sports car, but don't let this lead you to a wrong assumption. As you speed up and begin to push it into the corners, you get a sort of sloshing around (the tires seem to roll under and the car appears to shift sidewise). On a real sharp (90-degree) turn taken fast (30 mph) for its radius, the back end will break, but the steering is so positive you can easily correct without even changing the throttle opening. On faster (40 mph and up) turns, you can take it thru in an easily controlled 4-wheel drift. Body lean is noticeable but not objectionable to the driver, requiring the passenger to hold on.

Coming out of dips or over bumps there's no wallowing. It's no problem keeping control of the car even when you leave the asphalt. Car tracks seem the same as a smooth road, and washboards don't affect it adversely. The ride is a strange combination of soft and firm—it takes dips and bumps in stride, but you do feel the tarstrips. **CONTINUED ON PAGE 40**

JOHN BOLSTER TESTS

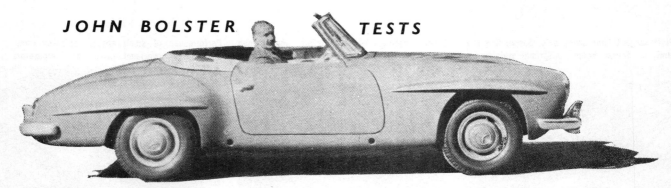

THE MERCEDES-BENZ 190SL

The Mercedes-Benz 190SL is a most unusual car. It is an extremely luxurious two-seater with winding windows, which in this country would be called a drophead coupé. Wide, roomy and with no attempt at weight saving, it is a substantially constructed vehicle of superb finish. This is quite a big car, having the same wheelbase as the famous 300SL and an overall width within 2 ins. of that of the 3-litre.

In this car is placed an engine of only 1,897 c.c. It is a very high output four-cylinder, over-square unit, which can attain 6,000 r.p.m. The compression ratio is no less than 8.5 to 1, and good breathing is assured by fitting two horizontal twin-choke carburetters. This highly tuned single overhead camshaft motor develops 105 b.h.p. at 5,700 r.p.m.

The gearbox has synchromesh on all four speeds and a short central lever. It is mounted in unit with the engine and drives the divided axle through an open propeller shaft. The rear end is designated a "swing axle with low-placed central pivot". The object is to obtain a lower roll centre than normal swing axles provide. It can be described very easily as a conventional axle which has a universal joint interposed, just to the right of the differential.

The two halves of the axle casing are joined at a pivot point beneath the differential housing. It will thus be seen that the two swing axles articulate about this pivot, and the jointed right-hand half shaft gives the necessary flexibility. Naturally, there must be a telescopic joint in the shaft to accommodate end-

FINE LINES (Above) of the smaller sports Mercedes-Benz are shown to advantage in this side view.

★

OFFICE OF WORKS: (Right) The superbly finished interior of the 190SL, showing instrument panel, two-spoke steering wheel and foot controls. The four-speed, all-synchromesh gearbox, says Bolster, "is beyond all praise".

★

OVER 100 B.H.P. is realized by the 1,897 c.c. four-cylinder, single o.h.c. engine (below) of the 190SL. Two horizontal twin-choke Solex carburetters are employed.

wise movement, and this is an elaborate device with recirculating roller bearings. The whole contrivance is rubber-mounted from the central pivot point, and suspended on helical springs with telescopic dampers. The rear suspension is therefore truly independent, but propeller shaft torque is not isolated from the unsprung components.

The front suspension is by wishbones and helical springs, with a recirculating ball steering box. The hydraulic brakes have a vacuum servo, and operate in very large Alfin drums with turbo fins.

A comfortable driving position, which is a feature of all the recent Mercedes-Benz I have tested, makes one feel immediately at home. Most "Mercs" seem a little unusual in their handling characteristics, but this one is an exceptionally easy car to drive. Nothing like as soft as in the other models, the suspension allows the road to be "felt", and controllability is first class. Even if a corner is entered at an impossible speed, the rear end breakaway remains very moderate, quite unlike previous swing axle designs. Under normal conditions, the steering characteristic is neutral.

The steering is accurate and has useful caster return action. It is, I thought, heavy during violent manœuvres, but not objectionably so. The brakes are quite light to apply and very powerful. I completely failed to make them fade on the arduous Montlhéry road circuit, though they tended to judder slightly at the end of a sharp pull up from maximum speed.

Quite the most delightful feature of the car is the gearbox, which is beyond all praise. Although the synchromesh works powerfully on all gears, the lever

CA, C'EST PARIS: (Above) Monique admires the Mercedes-Benz 190SL outside L'Action Automobile.

★

LIKE BIG BROTHER: The frontal aspect of the 190SL (left) is almost indistinguishable from that of the larger 300SL model.

moves easily, and changes can be "snatched" if desired. Personally, I would rather have synchromesh on first speed than on any other gear, for it is such a boon in traffic driving. For those familiar with the 300SL, I would say that the gearbox of the 190SL is just as delectable to handle but much quieter.

It is as well that this car has such a good gearbox, for the engine demands its constant use. It is not a particularly flexible unit, preferring to turn over briskly all the time. The performance is very creditable, especially when one reminds oneself that the capacity is only 1.9 litres. Nevertheless, something must be sacrificed if you are to get a quart from a pint pot, and so that delightful gearbox must be called upon to allow the high-efficiency engine to give of its best. Many sports car drivers prefer to handle this type of power unit because although it will run quite well for any driver it will only reveal its full potential for the man who likes to make proper use of his gear lever.

The maximum speed given in the data panel, 106.34 m.p.h., was the average for a lap of Montlhéry. A banked track tends to reduce the speed a little, and I would expect the car to register nearly 110 m.p.h. on my usual dead level piece of road. The speedometer showed only a very moderate optimism, and I had it round to the 180 k.p.h. mark on occasion. The acceleration figures reveal a lively performance, and the 0-60 m.p.h. time of 11.2 secs. is particularly noteworthy for so substantial a car.

Like the 300SL, this Mercedes-Benz has a very effective silencer. One can cruise fast with only the whistle of the wind for accompaniment, and this is a very effortless proceeding. If the engine is taken up to peak revs. in the gears, however, it becomes more prominent. It has the typically "hard" feeling of a highly tuned four-cylinder, and even the most elaborate silencing cannot entirely mute its powerful hum.

The whole car is built like a watch, and the finish is superb. Such things as the way the doors close, the fit of the hood, and all the detail work, put this machine in the top quality bracket. The under-bonnet installation looks fairly elaborate, but the carburetters, distributor, and valve gear are all highly accessible. As far as major repairs are concerned, there might be one or two problems, but no doubt the average owner would entrust such work to the makers' service department.

The appearance is very effective, and the lines cannot be faulted. "My" car was red, with cream upholstery, and it created something of a furore when I drove it in Paris. Naturally, I went to visit mine host, Harry Schell, at L'Action Automobile in l'Avenue d'Iena, and almost succeeded in emptying his bar, so great was the interest in the latest "Merc". The marked resemblance of the 190SL to its bigger brother is a great attraction, and the makers have been

Acceleration Graph

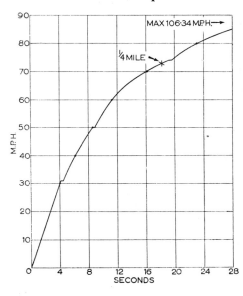

SWING AXLE with a difference—the new Mercedes-Benz system with single, low pivot.

wise to cash in on the glamour that surrounds the 300SL.

The Mercedes-Benz 190SL is not a racing car, though it obviously owes many of its design features to racing experience. It is a luxurious two-seater sports-touring car with winding windows, and a detachable hardtop renders it even more comfortable in winter weather. An elaborate ventilating and heating system is part of the lavish equipment, and the independent four-wheel suspension guards the occupants from bumps in the road. One wonders whether it would be possible to fit the 220 engine to this chassis, and add six-cylinder smoothness to the luxury already provided.

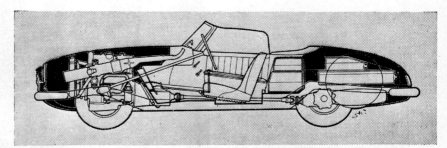

TRANSPARENT view of the smaller sports Mercedes-Benz, showing disposition of components, chassis and body.

SPECIFICATION AND PERFORMANCE DATA

Car Tested: Mercedes-Benz 190SL sports 2-seater, Price £2,776 7s. 0d. including P.T.

Engine: Four-cylinders 85 mm. x 83.6 mm. (1,897 c.c.). Single overhead camshaft, 8.5 to 1 compression ratio. 105 b.h.p. at 5,700 r.p.m. Two twin-choke Solex horizontal carburetters. Bosch coil and distributor.

Transmission: Single dry-plate clutch. Four-speed gearbox with synchromesh on all four speeds and central remote control lever, ratios 3.89, 5.9, 9, and 13.7 to 1. Open propeller shaft. Spiral bevel final drive to low pivoted swing axles.

Chassis: Combined body and chassis. Independent front suspension by wishbones and helical springs. Independent rear suspension by low pivoted swing axles and helical springs. Telescopic dampers. Re-circulating ball steering. Bolt-on disc wheels, fitted 6.40-13 ins. tyres. Hydraulic brakes in turbo-finned Alfin drums, with vacuum servo.

Equipment: 12-volt lighting and starting, speedometer, revolution counter, ammeter, oil pressure, water temperature and fuel gauges. Self-cancelling wipers, heating and demisting, flashing indicators.

Dimensions: Wheelbase, 7 ft. 10½ ins.; track, front 4 ft. 8¼ ins., rear 4 ft. 9¼ ins.; overall length, 13 ft. 10 ins.; overall width 5 ft. 8½ ins. Turning circle, 36 ft. Weight, 23 cwt.

Performance: Maximum speed, 106.34 m.p.h. Speeds in gears, 3rd 74 m.p.h., 2nd 50 m.p.h., 1st 31 m.p.h. Standing quarter-mile, 18.2 secs. Acceleration, 0-30 m.p.h. 4 secs., 0-40 m.p.h. 6.2 secs., 0-50 m.p.h. 8.6 secs., 0-60 m.p.h. 11.2 secs., 0-70 m.p.h. 16.2 secs., 0-80 m.p.h. 23 secs.

Fuel Consumption: 25 m.p.g. (approx.).

CONTINUED FROM PAGE 37
Driving Around

With the 190-SL, you have to be familiar with the somewhat more difficult task of getting in and out of a sports car. There isn't a lot of room between the doorsill and seat, or between the seat and wheel, so you have to wrap yourself in and watch your feet (the column doesn't telescope). You also have to watch your head when the top's up. What a no-concern job putting up the top is! To put it down, you loosen 3 clamps at the windshield, and from the driver's seat push the top to its folded position; reverse the procedure and it's up.

The seats are extremely comfortable; well-padded, contoured to your body, almost wrapping you in place. They adjust back and forth on their track quite easily, and can also be lifted forward to allow access to the rear area. This area takes fitted luggage, or with the removal of a floor covering and addition of a seat cushion can be made usable for an emergency passenger.

The steering wheel is down fairly low, but not quite in your lap. The tach and speedometer are directly in front of the driver, with the other instruments grouped below them. The 190-SL has almost as many controls as a light plane.

There's good room around the foot controls—there's no danger of stepping on your own foot or on the clutch instead of the brake. You can rest your left foot to the left of the clutch pedal, and your right leg against the transmission housing. Your shoulders won't feel cramped, unless your name happens to be Les Bingaman. Headroom is just adequate with top up.

There is some distortion in the sharply radiused corners of the windshield, but vision is otherwise great. The hood slopes forward quite radically and both front fenders are visible. There is no glare and no reflection at night from instruments. The lights themselves are soft.

The electrically operated windshield wipers have an overlapping sweep, but still don't wrap into the upper corners of the windshield. The heat controls are in the center of the panel, accessible to both driver and passenger and altho they are not lit, the map light throws an adequate glow if you get confused. Individual vent controls are on both sides of the panel. You have to grope somewhat for the emergency brake (below the panel) but it's easy to pull on and to release.

It's my feeling that the Mercedes-Benz 190-SL, at its delivered price of around $4000 (plus tax, license, and extras, of course) is a competitor in the personal or luxury car field. You can get such nice extras as a radio with an automatic antenna (for $250) and a removable hardtop that makes it even more weathertight. If you want something different that's dependable to the utmost, the 190-SL could be just your *poisson*.

ON BRITISH ROADS WITH A MERCEDES-BENZ 300SL

Fantastic Speed and Acceleration the Outstanding Features of this Six-Cylinder Fuel-Injection Coupé, Tested over Nearly 1,400 Miles in England and Scotland.

TAKING TO THE WATER.—The Mercedes-Benz 300SL on the Ballachulish Ferry, about to cross Loch Leven, just south of Fort William, during MOTOR SPORT's *extensive test of this remarkable car.*

MOST people will agree that the most fantastic motor car from the performance point of view which is available in the ordinary way is the Mercedes-Benz 300SL from Stuttgart. Produced a few years ago by the famous German firm as an essay in space-frame construction and to discover and subsequently demonstrate how the post-war 3-litre six-cylinder engine designed for the 300 and 300S Mercedes-Benz could be developed into a reliable fuel-injection, semi-competition power unit, the 300SL was successful in finishing first and second at Le Mans in 1952 and 1-2-3 at Berne, and winning the sports-car race (in open form) at Nurburg that year, besides being second in the Mille Miglia to a 4.1-litre Ferrari, after victory in the Carrera Pan-America race the previous year.

Since then this 300SL has been in prestige-production and over 1,000 have been sold, for this exceedingly eye-worthy, fast and, above all, accelerative coupé has proved a ready means of parting wealthy Americans from their dollars. MOTOR SPORT has not been unaware of this fabulous car. In the issue for November, 1954, we published impressions of trying one at Silverstone. In the October issue last year our Continental Correspondent recounted his experiences of motoring to the Arctic Circle in a 300SL, and in August, 1955, R. R. C. Walker described his experiences as the first person to own one of these cars in England. We now have pleasure in presenting a full road-test report on this, the fastest of the production Mercedes-Benz models, with particular reference to motoring on British roads.

IN DETAIL . . .

To remark that wherever it stops the 300SL causes interest and astonishment, from comment by small boys on its 160-m.p.h. speedometer to admiration for its bonnet full of complex machinery, is to state the obvious. The lines of the car are handsome and well blended, and the " gull's wing " doors provide that touch of the futuristic in keeping with its character. In fact, this Mercedes-Benz provides comfortable accommodation for two persons and their holiday luggage, with a maximum speed of 145 to 160+ m.p.h. according to axle ratio, with acceleration " out of this world " and a fuel consumption of 80-octane petrol of at least 15 m.p.g. from an engine developing 190 b.h.p. and running safely up to 6,400 r.p.m.

Access to the interior is through the ingenious doors, which swing up under the action of spring-struts on hinges at the centre of the roof, their pull-out handles being revealed by pressing in a knurled projection on the door. It is necessary to climb in and out over wide door sills, a construction made necessary by the shape of the space-frame tubing, which requires modest lady passengers to wear slacks, shorts or jeans! On the inside, similar pull-out handles release the doors, which swing up automatically, safety-catches being provided for locking them at high speed—the apparent disadvantage being that in the event of an accident unconscious occupants are virtually trapped and that should the driver somehow contrive to get the car onto its roof neither door can be opened—but those who motor fast or fly usually possess an outlook suitably fatalistic not to let such morbid considerations mar their pleasure! The seats of the 300SL are separate, tartan-upholstered, easily-adjustable buckets, one each side of the transmission tunnel; they are hard, a little short in the squab, yet generally very comfortable, more particularly as they hold the occupants securely throughout the " g "-loadings imposed by the car's immense performance. There is good leg room, sitting high with one's feet in wells in the floor.

The dash layout is somewhat " American " in its employment of plating and lots of shining, unlabelled knobs, but these minor controls are of good quality. Spaced right across the plated strip at the base of the dash, from left to right of this left-hand-drive car, are a pair of sliding controls to regulate air supply to left of the windscreen and driver's legs, choke, parking-lights switch, dash-lamp switch, lamps switch (which has four positions : all off, electrics, including " blinkers," other than lamps, side and tail-lamps, head-lamps), Bomora ignition key, which when turned operates the starter, two-speed wiper switch for the self-parking wipers, sliding controls for heater, passenger's horn-button, cigar-lighter, switch to operate heater fan for use in heating or ventilating the car when it is stationary, and sliding controls for passenger's screen and leg-temperature control. Additional controls are the ignition advance and retard (not normally used by the driver), reserve fuel pump switch, which also acts as a means of starting the engine if it is reluctant when hot, together with warning lights for choke-out, " blinkers " in use, headlamps full-beam and dynamo charge. The passenger is reminded of the potentialities of the ride by a " 300SL "

MORE WATER!—Going west, it wasn't long before the Mercedes-Benz " ran out of road " at Land's End—which is where this view of it was secured.

motif in front of him or her, and beside this is an accurate Vdo clock. Immediately before the driver in a hooded upsweep of the dash are the Vdo 4-in. speedometer (reading to 160 m.p.h., with trip and total milometers) and rev.-counter, the latter recording up to 7,000 r.p.m. Both these instruments have steady, clear white needles which move round the dials in the same plane. There are four small Vdo instruments for fuel contents (gauge calibrated in R, ½, F), oil pressure, which varies very considerably with engine speed, oil temperature and water temperature. Normally, oil temperature is about 140 deg. F. and water temperature 175 deg. F. The oil pressure at high r.p.m. is 70/75 lb. sq. in.

The 16½-in. two-spoke steering wheel hinges under for easy access to and exit from the driving seat by pulling a plunger under the boss. In its hub, proudly displaying the Mercedes-Benz three-pointed star, is the push-button for the reasonably-penetrating horn. Vertical grab-handles are placed at each end of the dash and there is a covered ashtray (for smokers of Havanna cigars ?) before the passenger on the off side of the deep dash sill. Further handles enable the doors to be pulled down easily after you have entered. The central mirror has a flick control to obviate dazzle but, mounted on the dash sill, provides a poor view and would probably be better hung from the roof—maybe the excuse is that nothing follows a 300SL for long !

Sitting at the wheel of a 300SL you find yourself well to the left, with a great expanse of motor car to the off side, the more embarrassing because the body is appreciably wider than the track, being, indeed, 5 ft. 10½ in. There is excellent forward visibility over the long but low bonnet with its two " power-bulges," that on the near side to clear the valve cover, but the screen pillars are rather thick. The pedals are close spaced, so that it is possible to " heel-and-toe " when changing gear while braking. The hand-brake, which has an adjacent adjuster, is for parking only, being far forward on the left. The rigid remote-control central gear-lever is rather far back for the right hand; the gear positions are marked on the knob and reverse is well over to the left of the forward gear locations, which are conventional, except that this is a left-hand-drive vehicle, so that top and third are off-side. The lever is not spring-loaded.

Under the dash, from left to right, are the tommy-handle for releasing the bonnet and the screen-squirt knob. The interior lamp is above the screen, between the sun-vizors. Another tommy-handle under the dash opens a scuttle ventilator. At night, with the dash lamp off, all dials save that of the clock remain faintly and very effectively visible. The only warning light which dazzles is that of the " blinkers " reminder.

Luggage accommodation consists of a platform behind the seats which will comfortably accommodate a couple of large suitcases and many smaller objects. The lockable boot lid lifts, and is secured by a prop, to reveal the fuel tank and filler, spare wheel, and tools, but coats can be packed in round the wheel. Some water entered the boot in heavy rain. At the rear of the roof are two open ventilator ducts, so placed aerodynamically that no water or draughts appeared able to enter, and the car never, under any conditions, misted-up screen, side or rear windows. Couple this with a heating and ventilating system the equal in efficiency and adjustment to that of a luxury air-liner, augmented by opening panels, with effective catches, in the side windows—moreover, for summer motoring the whole glass panel of the window is detachable by pulling out a peg—and it will be evident that after lowering yourself into this impressive Mercedes-Benz and locking yourself in, you are

OPENED UP.—The unique construction of the 300SL is emphasised in this picture, showing bonnet, doors and boot-lid all set fully open.

THE ENGINE OF THE MERCEDES-BENZ 300SL.—The semi-horizontally-mounted 3-litre six-cylinder fuel-injection unit develops 190 b.h.p. at 6,400 r.p.m. and runs smoothly and continuously at high speed without fuss. Note the Bosch fuel-injector, the coil ignition distributor and the belt-driven fan. The front of throttled air-intake pipe which runs along the off side or top of the engine can be seen, and the massive valve cover hides the single o.h. camshaft and rocker gear.

certain of comfort. The body is commendably silent and the ingenious doors proved rain-proof in a tropical deluge, save for a little seepage onto one door sill, which didn't reach the occupants, and water which reached the driver's seat *via* the heating ducts. Considerable draught entered round the hand-brake, however, and towards the end of the test the steering column started to squeak. Other sounds were the ventilator fan as it was rotated by the airstream and the loud click of the reserve fuel pump. The driver's door-catch tended to jam, having " picked-up " in its socket. After the car has been running at low speeds in traffic considerable petrol vapour is smelt and the engine " fluffs " until it is cleared by faster driving.

The alligator bonnet hinges at the front, being held open by a strut, to reveal the mysteries of the fuel-injection engine and its equally-mysterious auxiliaries. The engine is inclined to the near side to secure a low bonnet line and the width of the valve cover is impressive, and reminiscent of commercial-vehicle practice. The dip-stick is combined with the oil filler for the dry-sump oil tank and, like the coolant filler for the remote header-tank, is readily accessible.

You are now acquainted with the creature-comforts of the 300SL and require a brief introduction to its technicalities.

The chassis is a multi-tube, longitudinally-stressed, space-frame with the lightweight Sindelfingen body in unit with it. The weight of this structure is quoted as 2,556 lb. Front suspension is by wishbones and coil-springs, rear independent suspension by coil-springs and swing-axles. The 10.23-in. 2LS hydraulic brakes are vacuum-servo assisted and have wide steel drums with alloy turbo-fin coolers. The 3-litre, 88 by 85-mm., 2,996-c.c. engine has a Bosch PES 6KL 70/320 R2 fuel-injection pump and Bosch coil ignition. The overhead valves are actuated by an o.h. camshaft driven by a twin roller chain. A dry-sump lubrication system, with oil cooler, is employed, the oil tank on the near side of the engine having a capacity of 4 gallons. Pressurised pump cooling is used, with a belt-driven four-bladed fan, the total coolant capacity being 4.1 gallons, and a thermostat being incorporated. The balanced crankshaft runs in seven plain bearings. The Bosch injection pump and injectors are not visible from above, being on the near side of the cylinder block, but very imposing is the big air-intake manifold on the off side. The Bosch distributor is at the front of the engine on the near side, supplying the Bosch W280T2 plugs on the same side. The engine develops 240 b.h.p. at the clutch when not driving such auxiliaries as the dynamo, etc., but the more normally quoted output is 190 b.h.p. at 6,400 r.p.m., with 6,000 r.p.m. safe for continuous use; for example in the indirect gears. The compression-ratio is 8.55 to 1. The gearbox has synchromesh of the baulk-ring type on all gears, and axle ratios of 3.42 to 1 and 3.25 to 1 are available on request in addition to the standard ratio of 3.64 to 1, as on the car we had for test. Tyres are 6.50 by 15 and either sports or racing types are fitted. Fuel feed from the 28-gallon fuel tank is by a Bosch FP/KLA22 K1 pump, and the fuel-injector operates at a pressure of 568-682 lb./sq. in. The exhaust system is on the off side, twin clusters merging into a 2⅝-in. tail-pipe.

The air intake at the front of the car incorporates the three-pointed star and the name "Mercedes-Benz" appears on the body on the driver's side only. The wheelbase is 7 ft. 10½ in., ground clearance approximately 5 in., and the turning circle approximately 37¾ ft. The car comes with an excellent instruction book and some intriguing tools, including a gauge and supply of weights for wheel-balancing.

IN ACTION . . .

You have now become familiar with this Mercedes-Benz in the garage and are free to take it out on the road. Even before an opportunity arises to open it up it impresses as a real motor car—decidedly! In second there is a loud, rather rough, gear-noise, which increases to a musical howl in third, which can be held, incidentally, to nearly 100 m.p.h., after changing up at around 70. Engine speed goes up instantly and cleanly as the throttle is opened, sending the needle of the rev.-counter surging round the dial. The acceleration is "out of this world," for apart from the power developed, the power curve is such that the thrust goes on building up without a break, so that even from 100 m.p.h. onwards there is this sense of being hurled forward, the exhaust note remaining constant, until at 5,500 r.p.m. in third gear the noise of gears, engine and exhaust is that of a true competition car. Mere figures cannot convey the vivid, continued acceleration of the 300SL, which enables 90/100 m.p.h. to be reached almost everywhere and 110/125 m.p.h. to come up along short straights. Twice we reached 5,700 r.p.m. in top gear, equal to 126½ m.p.h. with the standard back-axle ratio, once near Salisbury and once on an open road in Scotland. On an arterial road near London, 6,100 r.p.m., or over 135 m.p.h., was recorded. The maximum depends purely on traffic conditions and the driver's disposition, up to an absolute of about 146 m.p.h. In terms of figures, this Mercedes-Benz achieves 0-50 m.p.h. in 5.7 sec., 0-70 m.p.h. in 8.5 sec., and 0-100 m.p.h. or a s.s. ¼-mile in a shade over 16 sec. Even more impressive is its ability to increase speed from 50 to 70 m.p.h. in second gear in a mere 4 sec., or to go from 60 to 80 m.p.h. in third gear in a matter of 5.1 sec., after which 100 m.p.h. is reached, in top gear, after less than 8 sec. have elapsed, and even from "the ton," a velocity of two-miles-a-minute can be achieved after another 9 sec. have gone by.

Yet the acceleration, accompanied by a healthy power-roar from under the broad bonnet, is even more impressive than the sheer speed of the car. Rob Walker aptly compared driving a fast car on English roads with making huffs at draughts, and in a 300SL you have the best means possible of "huffing" in safety. The sense of being propelled forward with undiminished acceleration to two-miles-a-minute if necessary, by the unleashed smooth power of an engine which feels completely reliable, is not only an exhilarating sensation for the occupants, and one which makes passing other vehicles a very fleeting, and therefore safe, operation—it looks exceptionally impressive to those you pass!

At speed the wind noise is very low, unless the ventilator windows are open, while it is possible to converse comfortably when cruising at 100 m.p.h.

The steering is accurate but heavy towards lock, pulling against the castor action, although the latter is not self-centring. There is an element not of lost-motion, for there is none, but rather of sponginess at very low speeds, but in action the steering becomes lighter and, geared 2⅓ turns lock-to-lock, enables the car to be placed accurately. It is rather "dead" steering, hardly any road-wheel motion being transmitted, and no column vibration. The weight distribution is such that this Mercedes-Benz needs concentration to keep it straight, for it tends to wander, and once it departs from the intended course it asks some time before the driver can coax it back. The brakes, while stopping this 24-cwt. car very reasonably from three-figure speeds, especially if aided by changing down, as the handbook recommends, are rather slow, then fierce, in action, as the servo takes effect, and consequently to apply them hard on a slippery surface is a practice to be avoided whenever possible. Too hard an application of the brakes produces a smell of hot lining within the car and tends to cause snaking. The brakes also squeaked slightly at times.

The suspension is quite soft, enabling the car to be driven fast over bad surfaces, but there is a slight penalty to pay in respect of some roll when cornering and over undulations the action of the swing-axle rear suspension could be discerned.

The clutch is light and showed no desire to slip, and the gear change is pleasant but requires decisive (and therefore not lightning-quick) movements, too hurried a cog-swap without correct synchronisation of crankshaft and layshaft speed resulting in an audible "clonk."

The exhaust note is never objectionable and the 300SL can be driven unobtrusively through towns, only the music of the lower gears revealing to the occupants the car's impatience for clear roads.

THREE-POINTED STAR.—The famous Mercedes-Benz motif makes a handsome centre-piece to the frontal aspect of Stuttgart's 160-m.p.h. coupe.

Naturally, with nearly 200 true horse-power available it is necessary to open up with discretion on slippery surfaces, after which that shattering pick-up comes in to propel you relentlessly forward to whatever cruising speed is appropriate.

Power-sliding corners is one of the joys a skilled driver can indulge in with this car, and it is significant that between Glasgow and Fort William, in pouring rain, a gale, and at night, we averaged 54 m.p.h. for an hour's driving on roads so twisting that top gear was seldom if ever engaged, thirty miles being covered in half-an-hour of similar motoring.

Previous to this we had driven from Basingstoke to Land's End at an average speed of better than 56 m.p.h., in spite of much lorry traffic, roads covered in places with melting snow, and a six-minute stop for petrol. The best hour's run accounted for 63 miles and obviously, on clearer occasions, particularly late at night, the 300SL would prove capable of 70-m.p.h. averages in safety on narrow British roads. Yet should Auntie borrow it, she can drive along at 700 r.p.m. in a top gear which gives 22.2 m.p.h. per 1,000 r.p.m. without anxiety on the machinery's part, acceleration, thanks no doubt to fuel injection, being clean as soon as the accelerator is depressed. No doubt, however, she, as we were, would be awed by the width of the car—it is necessary to remember this when taking roundabouts or meeting other vehicles, for the body is appreciably wider than the track and with left-hand drive this is sometimes a little disturbing.

The 7½-in. inbuilt Bosch headlamps are adequate for using the available performance at night; they have a foot dipper.

Apart from the aforementioned "fluffing" and smell of petrol after prolonged slow running, the Mercedes-Benz 300SL functioned with entire reliability while it was in our hands, which was for a matter of 1,348 miles. In this distance five pints of oil were required and the consumption of Esso Extra, in very fast driving, worked out at 15.9 m.p.g. The engine always commenced impeccably with momentary use of the choke, and didn't prove temperamental when hot. The fuel reserve of approximately two gallons is useful and although no warning light is provided the noise of the reserve pump working is sufficient reminder. Apart from the few items listed earlier the only faults were occasional reluctance of the screen wipers to self-park at the first movement of the switch, and momentary blockage of a squirt, which cured itself. The Dunlop tyres proved silent on corners, held their pressure and the racing-pattern treads showed no wear. Incidentally, conditions during the test included dry, wet and snow-ridged roads, torrential rain, mist and gale-force winds, not to mention scores of miles of heavy traffic.

Although no cubby-hole or door pockets are provided, the wide door sills and transmission tunnel provide useful stowage, and so stable is the car that small objects "stay put" in these places reasonably well, although when driven really fast this car is one of the few which, in spite of its comfortable ride, can tire a passenger by the sudden backwards, forwards and sideways movements imposed.

It is truly difficult to convey on paper the fascination, amounting almost to awe, that this car imposes on those who drive it or are driven in it. It is the modern and logical equivalent of the 36/220

SCOTTISH SCENERY near Fort William sets off the imposing side view of the 300SL.

and 38/250 models of the past and therefore is a typical Mercedes-Benz. It is not for Auntie because, although she could drive it slowly without harming it, that would be such a shocking waste. It is not for portly business men with fat stomachs full of good food and wine topped by a layer of beer. It is for experienced drivers who like to motor at speeds upwards of 90 m.p.h. whenever possible. There are some experiences money cannot buy but you can have a Mercedes-Benz 300SL for £4,651 . . .—W. B.

* * *

We follow this road-test report on the 300SL with an account by R. R. C. Walker of his visit to Stuttgart to take delivery of his second of these cars, a modified version with special camshaft, lightweight body, etc. :—

I would strongly recommend this trip to the Daimler-Benz factory to any car enthusiast who is contemplating a short holiday abroad. It is very inexpensive as you can fly there for £16, and most enjoyable, but to get the full pleasure you must buy a 300SL for the journey back or, better still, take a friend with you and buy two.

Our visit took place because the factory had just made two 300SLs with special lightweight bodies, 176 lb. lighter than normal, special camshafts and harder racing springs and shock-absorbers. One was offered to Jack Atkins and one to me, at the normal price, although I believe they cost the firm quite a bit more to produce. We were both already enthusiastic SL owners, and I think this was why we had the first offer. As far as Jack Atkins was concerned, he told me that he had very few vices, he did not drink, nor smoke, and he only had one wife at a time, but he did love beautiful motor cars, and if they were sufficiently good then he liked two of them, so he did not take any time to make up his mind and say yes. Personally I only had one minor problem before I made my decision, and that was how to pay for it. I thought I could raise enough by selling my first 300SL, and if this did not work all I had to do was to mortgage the house, sell my wife's jewellery and borrow all her money, and then all I would have to pay would be the alimony that the judge would award if it came to the Divorce Court. So it took me a good five minutes to make up my mind and accept the offer.

In about ten days' time Owen Williams, of Woking Motors, my Mercedes distributor, rang me up to say the car was ready for collection. We decided that we would fly to Stuttgart and Jack Atkins would take Owen Williams with him, and I was going to take Stan Jolliffe, my manager and late head of our Racing Department and then the secretary of the British Racing Mechanics' Club. We all met at London Airport and found that we were to go by Viscount to Zurich and then change aircraft for the short hop to Stuttgart. I must say that since the war I have never been very keen on flying, but this Viscount was a revelation and I had never felt anything smoother or more comfy. I noticed the odd whine the motors made at the start, so I was not surprised when just before we arrived one of the crew came out with an enormous key about 4 ft. long and proceeded to tear up the floorboards and start winding. I naturally thought that we were running on clockwork and that it needed winding up, but not a bit of it. It turned out that one of the flaps refused to go down and the key was for winding it down by hand. When I used to pilot an aircraft, if one flap came down on its own

---

THE MERCEDES-BENZ 300SL COUPE

Engine : Type M198. Six-cylinder, 85 by 88 mm. (2,996 c.c.). Overhead valves operated by single o.h. camshaft. 8.55 to 1 compression ratio. Bosch fuel injection. 190 b.h.p. at 6,400 r.p.m. (250 S.A.E. h.p.)
Gear ratios : First, 12.3 to 1; second, 7.17 to 1; third, 5.04 to 1; top, 3.64 to 1.
Tyres : 6.50-15 Dunlop Extra Super Sport on bolt-on steel disc wheels.
Weight : 1 ton 4 cwt. 2 qtr. 21 lb., without occupants but ready for the road with approximately three gallons of fuel.
Steering ratio : 2⅓ turns, lock-to-lock.
Fuel capacity : 28 gallons (two gallons in reserve). Range approx. 445 miles.
Wheelbase : 7 ft. 10½ in.
Track : Front, 4 ft. 6½ in.; rear, 4 ft. 8½ in.
Dimensions : 14 ft. 10 in. by 5 ft. 10½ in. by 4 ft. 3 in. (high).
Price : £3,100 (£4,651 7s., inclusive of p.t. and import duty in this country).
Concessionaires : Mercedes-Benz (Great Britain) Ltd., Mercedes-Benz House, 58, Camberwell New Road, London, S.E.5.

---

the aeroplane usually turned upside down, but now apparently nothing so entertaining happens.

After a short stop at Zurich, where you can buy almost anything in the world in the airport, and for any currency, we took off for Stuttgart and arrived 45 minutes later, to be greeted by Herr Rapp, the Daimler-Benz Export Manager for Great Britain, New Zealand, Australia, Siam and all stations East. Herr Rapp was in West Africa before the war and during the war he had been interned, eventually ending up in the Isle of Man, where he had learnt the British tea habit. We had been warned that tea in Germany cost £1 a pound, so we had all come armed with some as gifts. For myself, I can't stand the stuff and when, just after the war, I was posted by the Admiralty to the Ministry of Aircraft Production, I was totally at a loss as to how to pass my time, as a non-tea-drinker is entirely misplaced in a Ministry.

On our arrival Herr Rapp packed us all into his 180 diesel, and drove us straight to the Daimler-Benz disposal factory about 10 miles out of Stuttgart, where our cars had just completed their final tests, and were awaiting us. They were not clean, I may say; this was the only black mark we awarded the factory. Although we both had 300SLs already, we had to go through each point and check all equipment before we were allowed out of the works with our cars, from whence we drove straight to our hotel, which had been previously reserved for us by Daimler-Benz.

We had an excellent dinner in the hotel and after a few beers in the bar, Jack and I decided to go to bed, whilst the other two thought they would sample the night life of Stuttgart. About 2.30 a.m. I heard somebody slip outside and, amidst shouts of " the favourite's down," I knew the English contingent was once more at full strength, or at any rate more or less, and above proof I guessed.

At 9 a.m. sharp the next morning Herr Rapp came to collect us and we followed him with our two cars to the Unterturkheim factory in Stuttgart, where we were to start by being allowed an interview with Herr Uhlenhaut, who is the Technical Director and manages all the racing side ; although only a young man he was with the Racing Department some time before the war, and is also quite good enough to be one of the works racing drivers, but he is considered too valuable to the firm to allow him to get up to such pranks. Herr Uhlenhaut was born in England and so he speaks perfect English. He more or less started by saying " Right, shoot, ask me anything you like and I will try to answer," and I must say he really was extremely frank in his replies.

We asked many things but I have just picked out three of them that I consider of interest. We started off on tyres, as we found our cars fitted with Continentals and we wanted to know more about them. He told us that they would take a set on a 300SL and test it on the Autobahn, and they would then cut the tyre themselves to make the car behave just as they wanted it to, and when satisfied they would return the tyres to Continental and tell them to make their tyres to this pattern; and from my experience it certainly seems to be extremely successful, as they really handle beautifully, especially in the rain. I next asked Herr Uhlenhaut why Mercedes did not use disc brakes for racing and why they preferred the rather impractical wind brake. He replied that in the first place the Germans were not nearly as far ahead as the British with disc brakes and, secondly, even if they were they would still prefer the wind brake as it had added advantages of control. For instance, he said that if you were to take a course like the Swedish Grand Prix, where there was one corner which started as a very fast one, then suddenly tightened up on you; if you braked hard in the middle of the corner where it tightened up, with disc brakes, it would naturally tend to send the car out of control, but if you used your wind brake in the same position it would tend to give you more control and hold the tail down, rather than making it difficult; in fact it generally helped the cornering ability of the car. I must say this put quite a new light on the whole affair to me and I found it very interesting.

Our next question was could we buy a 300SLR? Personally I did not want to buy one, as I should not know what to do with it, and I don't want piles of suggestions, either! But Jack Atkins reckoned he knew exactly what to do with it, and he was ready to fork out the lolly on the spot almost, if he could have one, but the reply was emphatically " No." When we pressed for a reason, Uhlenhaut told us that it had a roller-bearing crankshaft and after roughly 2,000 miles this would be worn out and would probably need renewing; naturally, Daimler-Benz could not have their cars in private hands needing new crankshafts every few weeks. It rather emphasises the big difference between the 300SLR and the D-type Jaguar and DB3S Aston Martin, both of which can be sold on the open market to private owners. Also, I believe that prototypes at Le Mans are intended to be sold to the public in time, so this may be one of the reasons Mercedes are giving up racing, but I think the real ones are that they have got all the advertising they need for the moment from racing and if they continued winning for another year the public would probably get fed up with their continual successes and say they were spoiling the competition in racing, which would be bad advertising, instead of good. Also, to maintain their present superiority they would obviously need a new model and this would be very costly.

We were next taken around some of the factory and the Racing Department, and also given some interesting facts. After the war the factory was 87 per cent. demolished, but all the skilled workers came back there and said that, as their fathers and grandfathers had worked there, they wished to continue to do so and would not go anywhere else. So they were given one square meal a day for themselves and their families and a small retaining fee, and, although they were mechanics and not builders, they set to to rebuild the place. They took a year to clear away the rubble and then they rebuilt a wonderful new factory, and now they turn out 260 cars a day. They are very particular that their metal comes exactly up to their specification, so it is carefully examined and 50 per cent. is returned; also every nut and bolt is crack tested and a large percentage not accepted. Everybody has started work by 7 a.m., including the directors, and Herr Rapp told me that although he was supposed to start work at 7 a.m. he was always in his office before, because he had so much work to do. If I had to get up at that hour I should not feel it was worth going to bed at all. We were proudly shown a picture of the late Managing Director, who had died, aged 52, of overwork; I am rather surprised he lasted that long!

Our last visit was to their wonderful museum, where they have all their famous machinery dating back to 1886. It starts with Daimlers ranged on one side and Benz on the other and later, of course, they amalgamate. They started up an 1896 Benz and drove us each in turn around the museum in it; the driver was rather old and looked as if he had been in charge of the car since its birth. There is too much in the museum to try to describe it and it just must be seen to be believed.

We were then taken to lunch with Herr Willhelm, one of the Directors, and we went to the Senior Executives' luncheon room, which is situated right on the roof of the factory with a wonderful view of the surrounding hills. When we walked in we found about 50 tables, but at ours there was a tiny flagstaff in the middle with a Union Jack flying from it, a most pleasing and thoughtful gesture, and just such a one that you might expect from this company. We discussed various subjects at luncheon, but one remark Herr Willhelm made particularly struck me, showing what an extreme regard they had for Stirling Moss and his judgment. It was during the time that it was rumoured that Stirling was going to drive for B.R.M., and Herr Willhelm said that until then he had always thought that the B.R.M. was a joke, at which we all stared rather hard at our soup plates and someone muttered that if it was a joke it was a pretty poor one; but Herr Willhelm continued, saying that if Stirling was going to drive for them, then undoubtedly the car must be a good one. Well of course it turned out that Stirling is not going to drive for them, and we will have to await this season to see if the car *is* any good.

After lunch we followed Herr Rapp and he led us about ten miles out to the start of the Autobahn, where we said our final farewells and then set out, remembering our running-in figures, which worked out on my "clock" at 100 m.p.h. maximum for the first 300 miles and 125 m.p.h. for the next 600 miles; after that you work up the speed towards maximum.

It was decided that I should lead all the way, but I don't speak one word of German; in fact, Owen Williams was the only one in the party who did. The most frequent and important signs were *Ein Faht* and *Frei Faht*, one-way and free-for-all, and Owen said I must not misinterpret this. At one stage I did and the atmosphere got very bad when I shot into a garage because it said *Ein Faht*, which I later realised only referred to one way into the garage, so I shot out the other side back on to the Autobahn with the other SL faithfully following behind.

We covered the first 210 miles in exactly three hours, averaging 70 m.p.h., and I must say it was one of the most tiring drives I have had. These Autobahns are very good but they carry an enormous amount of traffic, mostly lorries and trailers, and when you are approaching them at 100 m.p.h. they will put out their "wanger" without looking behind and pull out to pass right in front of you. We found several times we had to put on "the lot" to stop in time, and were fortunate it did not happen on some of the icy patches. We arrived at Cologne soon after dark and I handed over to Stan Jolliffe; Jack was muttering about it being time to call it a day as he wanted a bath, but I reckoned we should push on to Aachen as we had quite some mileage to do the following morning to catch the boat at Ostend. We spent a very pleasant night at Aachen and got on the road at about 9.30 a.m. the following morning. The last part of the journey was absolute heaven along the Brussels-Ostend road, which must be the best in Europe, and although it was raining we averaged 100 m.p.h. for the last 50 miles, and the only reason the average was not higher was because of the restricted speed owing to running-in the cars. Jack, in fact, got fed up for a short time with basking in my spray, and he came by flat-out. I was cruising along at about 120 m.p.h. and he came past at about 140 m.p.h., and the sight and sound was most impressive until I was suddenly obliterated in the spray. We arrived in Ostend at 1.30 p.m., just in good time to get the cars on board and have lunch. When we got back to England we were greeted by the usual November fog, so our average of 40 m.p.h. back to London seemed very slow after what had gone before. But I find these cars are really excellent in a very thick fog because, sitting on the left or near side, you can open your door upwards and feel your way along the pavement with your hand; perhaps they were especially designed for fog.

I had no choice with the colour of my car as it had been painted before it was offered to me, and it is rather a bright red. The other morning my wife was helping me wash the car when she suddenly said that it made her feel sick to look at the colour for a long time, and didn't I feel the same? Well I always feel sick in the morning so I didn't really feel any different, but we are having it painted white now, with dark blue underneath like the last one, and I find it makes it look much smaller and lower.

The only real "dice" I have had in the car went on for about twenty miles or more with a helicopter. Actually he cheated a bit because he would keep cutting the corners, but to make up for this he would go ahead at the major cross-roads, turn around and wait at about 10 ft. and beckon me on, then he would turn around and we would get at it again. But, try as I would, I could not beat him, either on acceleration or top speed, which surprised me as I was at times hitting quite high spots around the 120s, but it was when we came to the corners that he really made me feel a dissatisfied owner; but I bet I could beat him in a thick fog.—R.C.C.W.

DRIVING AROUND
with WALT WORON

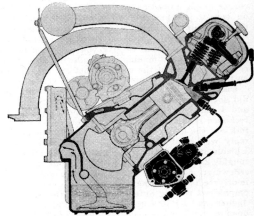

The tilted engine gets its fuel from the injection pump, tucked below the block. Air temperature and atmospheric density are compensated for by a thermostat built into the pump

The Mercedes 300-SL is one car that deserves whatever superlatives may be heaped upon it

AMONG SPORTS CAR ENTHUSIASTS 2 cars stand head and shoulders above all others: the Mercedes and the Ferrari. My nod would definitely go to the Mercedes 300-SL, mainly because it's genteel on city streets and yet in the country it becomes a raging, loping cheetah after a kill. The Ferrari, on the other hand, isn't tame enough for the restrictive boundaries of the city.

If there's a better production sports car in the world than the 300-SL, show me the way to it! Only then could the biggest automotive thrill of my life be equalled. I wouldn't mind going thru that quite often; in fact, anytime.

Why so much enthusiasm? Here's why: Drive it, and you'll be spoiled for all other cars until you again twist and turn yourself over the side rail, behind the "broken" wheel, and into the firmly contoured bucket seat. Command it—at any speed and in any of its 4 forward gears—and you'll get the pleasurable sensation of being *pressed* back in your seat.

The biggest surprise you'll get from the SL's performance is the fact that there seems to be no end to the acceleration: it's there from the screeching rubber takeoff, in the "tweek" of gear changes from 1st to 2nd and 2nd to 3rd, in the slap in the back of the neck when the 182-cubic-inch engine revs to around 3500, then *surges* to 6000. At 100 mph, when you would normally expect the rate of acceleration to drop off, you hook onto a passing jet and zoom on up to the top speed in a matter of seconds. It actually feels hotter from 80 mph on up to 135 mph than it does from zero to 80.

In the matter of actual acceleration times, the 300-SL was a trifle disappointing in its comparison to some other cars. For example, its time of 4.2 seconds to go from a true 30 (indicated 34) to a true 50 (indicated 56) in 2nd gear, is just slightly faster than a '56 Oldsmobile; its best time from scratch to 60 mph (indicated 67) of 8.5 seconds was but 0.7 second quicker than the Studebaker Golden Hawk with Ultramatic. The faster it goes, the better it seems to accelerate, getting to 84 mph and the end of a quarter-mile in 16.1 seconds, and going from a true 50 to a true 100 (or an indicated 108) in 14.9 seconds.

The tighter you wind it in each gear the better, too, instead of jumping on it in a lower gear and waiting for it to rev up. The best 50 to 80 times were made by winding tight in 2nd, then snapshifting to 3rd, while the same applied to the 50 to 100 times, except that it was necessary to drop into 4th.

The clutch is quite stiff and with those 220 horses straining to move, it's hard to get off the mark without burning rubber. It takes a concrete or asphaltic concrete surface and exactly the right coordination between engine revs and clutch engagement to keep from leaving tread behind you for yards. Fourth gear is mostly for high speed cruising, altho you can lug down to about 30 mph in top gear without the engine bucking in protest. The gearshift itself is close to your right hand and there's plenty of room to move it; it's

Here shown in upright position, the engine has a dry sump lubrication system and a large oil cooler. Driven by a twin roller chain, the camshaft rests on the cylinder head. Cams are extra steep

cam installed for $120—this will up the horsepower to 240.

A Top of 134.73 Mph

Top speed runs were made on the caked mud surface of El Mirage Dry Lake on a clear, windless day with the temperature hovering near 75° F. To enable us to get extremely accurate times, the National Hot Rod Association set up their official timing device, consisting of electronic timing lights, electronic meter and the necessary wiring. The approach to the actual trap was laid out in a somewhat zig-zag fashion to avoid rough spots and wet patches. On the 1st run I had to change my direction to stay on course, at one time even correcting a drift at 120 mph; the car did no more than go where I aimed it. On the 2nd run I hit a soft patch and the tach dropped off, but otherwise nothing happened. The speed was 133.72 mph at a tach reading of 6100 rpm. On the 3rd run I hit a rough surface which I thought would throw me around a bit, but it was like going over a smooth railroad crossing. I must have had it flat out, for the tach would not climb above 6200 rpm; the time was 134.73 mph, which surely could be upped to 138-140 on a good asphalt or concrete surface.

This particular 300-SL had the lowest of 3 gear ratios available—3.64 to 1. The Daimler-Benz factory claims 9 mph more top speed with the 3.42 to 1 rear axle and 15 more with the highest available ratio of 3.25 to 1.

almost like writing a big letter H off to one side of your body.

Where it Gets its Go

What's so fantastic about the 300-SL's go-ability is that it comes from an engine that gives much more than one horsepower from each cubic inch, yet is smaller than anything produced in Detroit. The inclined 6-cylinder engine (to get a lower hood line) gets much of its power from an inherently good overhead valve design with chain-driven overhead camshaft and fuel injection pump that provides the right fuel-air ratio for all conditions. It breathes right at all engine speeds, with no valve float. Everything is designed for high revs, including the balanced, 7-main-bearing crankshaft. And if you want more from the engine you can have a high lift

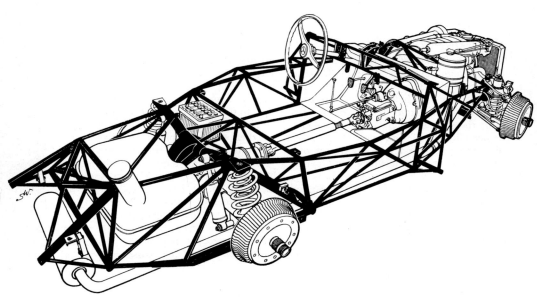

The lightweight body bolts as a unit to this torsionally rigid, tubular frame, which plays its part in the 300-SL's roadability. Individual struts are stressed only longitudinally. Steel-lined aluminum brakedrums efficiently dissipate heat with the aid of strong air turbulence. The now-traditional Mercedes swing axle takes only a little getting-used-to. Note lateral muffler at rear

Formidable trail of rubber is laid by 300-SL at the Willow Springs course, where violent wind gusts can perturb lesser cars. Pointing this car is all there is to it; it does the rest. Note the roof ventilators, clearly visible in this rear view

passenger, you're immensely confident in the car, with no fear that you'll get tossed about no matter what the road surface. Here's a case too, of the rigid tubular frame and its waist-high sides giving you the feeling that you have a contact with the ground that can't be broken.

The combination of true steering, fantastic roadability, and comfortable ride are wrapped up in these things: hydraulically dampened steering; front wheels independently sprung by twin wishbones and coil springs; rear wheels suspended by swing axles and coil springs; and, double shocks all around.

Behind the Wheel

The 1st time or 2, I found it awkward climbing into the 300-SL, once bumping my head and another time banging my knee on the wheel. When I learned that you get in by sitting on the siderail and swinging your legs over, making sure that the top is full up, I had no more trouble. In fact, it was even more convenient than a regular door in tight parking spots. Regardless of the disadvantages of such an arrangement, once you were behind the

What Can Go Must Stop

Never was any trouble encountered with the power brakes; they clamp down at any speed, stopping you in real short order with slight foot pressure. Over mountainous roads and many times around the Willow Springs Road Course the brakes never faded, largely due to plenty of lining surface and radial fins to help cool the drums. Pitching forward on sudden stops is notable by its absence.

How it Handles and Rides

The roadability of the 300-SL was well demonstrated in the '52 Mexican Road Race, swept 1-2 by the Mercedes team. Driven on a straight road, it goes straight as an arrow shot from the bow of Howard Hill; there is absolutely no wind wander or side effect from wind gusts. On a snake-like road you'll find it holds the groove when you just point it where you want to go. The steering is stiff so you really get your exercise thru a turn; it's not a car for a woman.

Pushing it to its fullest thru a turn, you might find that the back end will begin to come around; the best thing is not to let it get into this position in the 1st place. If you do, you handle it pretty much the way you do a Porsche—and that is, feather off the throttle and slightly turn the wheel to bring yourself in line, coordinating the 2 as closely as possible. You'll feel it coming back onto the curve's radius, then you feather down on the throttle again. You don't want to either punch it in such a case, or back off, for you'll increase your tendency to spin.

Tony Anthony, at the Mercedes-Benz distributors in Hollywood (who loaned the car), tells me that drivers in Europe treat them rough in the turns, really mauling them thru, whereas most drivers here sort-of saw the wheel around corners. If you haven't driven a swing-axle car or one with a rear engine, you'll have to get used to the different feel of the 300-SL.

There's no weaving on washboard, whether dirt or asphalt. Streetcar tracks and ruts cause slight sidewise movement.

Many other cars tend to soften dips and bumps, while the 300-SL just squashes them. You hit a bad one and there's no floating sensation and absolutely no wallowing—you're over it and that's all.

Body lean—even at speeds up to 80 mph—is certainly not of any magnitude to bother driver or passenger. As a

Cockpit has no meaningless fripperies, just everything where you need it, plus pungent leather and flawless chrome. Windows are removable

48

Electronic timing light, official device of National Hot Rod Association, awaits coming of the 300-SL. Even top speed runs, a frequent strain, were easy with the instant response of this car. Rough surfaces and soft patches did no more than drop the tachometer a little from its firm high of 6200 rpm. Top recorded speed was nearly 135 mph, with much greater safety than in many cars driven at half that impressive speed

wheel, you would feel such pride that the trouble getting in would be completely forgotten.

The bucket seats are well-shaped, deeply padded, cloth-covered (or optional leather), and provide much comfort on short or long trips. There's good headroom and legroom for a 6-foot driver and passenger—for taller persons the space begins to get cramped.

There's nothing to hinder your view to front, sides, or rear. The windshield posts are thin and the quarter panels don't blank out a large area. There is some distortion in the corners of the windshield, where the glass curves quite sharply. There's no glare from any spot.

What Else Makes it Good

From immaculately chromed front bumper to finely finished rear bumper, from hand-rubbed top to road-hugging tread, the 300-SL is *built!* The manufacturers didn't quit with just the design of one of the nicest-appearing hunks of machinery—they made certain that it was *assembled* with the care of a German camera. Airplane-canopy-type doors clunk softly into place, chrome trim of classic era quality is fitted where it's supposed to be, gaps between panels and openings (doors, deck, hood) are all uniform, there are no rough spots in bodywork or paint, no loose threads dangling from the upholstery or headlining, no screwdriver scratches anywhere, and no sealing compound oozing out of joints.

Here is truly a car that deserves all the superlatives that can be heaped upon it. For the individualist who would have a sports car that is a giraffe's head above the crowd, there is but *one* excuse for not owning a 300-SL—and that is not having the wherewithal ($7500-$9000) to buy it.

Getting out isn't as awkward as you might imagine. To begin with, door folds up out of the way for tight parking places, leaving entranceway unobstructed. Doorsill is upholstered, clean

Hardest part is hoisting yourself up onto the broad doorsill. Once there, swing the legs over and you're on your way. Getting in is easy, since sill is a good height, even beside a curbing

ROAD TEST

Gordon Wilkins with one of the fastest cars in the world, and certainly the fastest car ever road tested by the press. This view emphasises the sleek low lines of the Mercedes-Benz 300SLR Coupe. With coupe body, panelled in magnesium-alloy, car is only 43½ in. high, and weighs, in road trim with full tanks, 2175 lb. Racing weight dry is 1964 lb.

GORDON WILKINS TESTS
The 300 SLR Coupe

With the co-operation of Daimler-Benz this coupe version of the car which won the World Sports Car Championship in 1955 was tested extensively by Gordon Wilkins on the track, autobahn, and in the Alps.

For a few privileged visitors to the Frankfurt Motor Show early in 1956, all other impressions were overshadowed by the memory of a few minutes spent sitting beside Rudolf Uhlenhaut while he demonstrated with superb skill the fantastic qualities of the special 300 SLR Mercedes-Benz coupe which he uses for fast long-distance journeys.

As one sat there in an inferno of blaring sound, with Uhlenhaut calm and relaxed, changing gear up and down continuously, with the car rarely seeming to do less than 100 mph, yet always slowing down under perfect control where others would still be accelerating, it was obvious that this was performance on a scale that is probably matched by no other car licensed for road use. Yet Uhlenhaut himself had never had an opportunity to check this performance in detail, and the absolute maximum speed of the car remained a subject for calculation and speculation.

This started a train of thought and a series of negotiations which culminated in a long-distance telephone call from my friend Robert Braunschweig, Editor of the Automobil Review of Switzerland, a few weeks later. The directors of Daimler-Benz had agreed to make the car available for a full and complete road test, problems of registration and insurance had been overcome, and the car would be available during several weeks of the summer. We were to share the driving, using the normal equipment of the Automobil Review technical bureau for performance testing. All except for the maximum speed tests, which would be run on the Munich-Eching autobahn,

specially closed for us, and timed by the official German timekeepers with the collaboration of the local automobile clubs.

That was the prelude to an unforgettable series of long-distance runs in the most varied weather conditions, using this priceless car as one would for normal business or pleasure motoring, but at average speeds which are right outside everyday experience. It was by no means the first time we had tested fast cars together; we did our first Ferrari road test together, but the SLR opened up a new stratum of experience, not only in acceleration and speed, but in braking, and steering and road holding, and all those factors which allow high performance to be exploited safely.

Here is a car which did 180 miles an hour over the flying kilometre and was still accelerating at the end of five kilometres; which flashed from a standstill to 50 mph in 5.2 seconds; went from 0 to 100 mph in 13.6 seconds; it is a car which runs as easily at 140 mph as it does at 100 mph; indeed when the speed drops to 100 it is time to think about changing down, from fifth to fourth gear, for this speed coincides with peak torque in fourth, and with this gear engaged the car will flash up again from 100 to 120 in 6 seconds as soon as the slightest opportunity presents itself.

For normal road running and the acceleration tests, the combination of crown wheel and pinion and gears in the all-indirect gearbox gave overall ratios of 4.89 to 1 for fourth and 3.81 to 1 for fifth speed. At 7450 rpm, the revs for maximum power, equivalent speeds in the gears were: first, 50 mph; second, 77 mph; third, 95 mph;

fourth, 127 mph; and fifth, 163.

It was possible to run up to 100 mph in third gear without exceeding the absolute rev limit of 8000, which is permissible for short periods.

With the gearing used for the maximum speed tests, fourth was 4.32 to 1 and fifth 3.48 to 1. Speeds on gear at maximum power were: first, 71 mph; second, 88 mph; third, 107 mph; fourth, 144 mph; and fifth, 179 mph. In fact the mean of four runs over the measured distance, timed electrically, was 176.47 mph, and the car was still accelerating slightly. With the exception of the special Dessau record track now in the Russian zone, it seems that there is nowhere in Europe where its absolute maximum can be established, but its behaviour on the ordinary autobahn used for the tests vividly illustrated the progress in controllability which has resulted from the latest Daimler-Benz racing programme. The outward approaches to the timing stretch are by no means straight. I had previously been timed over this stretch in a 300 SL at 154 mph, and there was one curve which required considerable concentration at this speed. The SLR was no more difficult to handle at a speed 25 mph higher.

Total duration of the test was over 2000 miles, and it included every kind of weather and road condition that can be found in Western Europe. My first acquaintance with the car was driving it from Stuttgart down the autobahn to Munich in a cloudburst. Another day we roared over the Susten Pass, necks straining to the acceleration, twitching the wheel to hold the tail as it slid on traces of ice and melting snow.

180 mph in the 300 SLR Coupe is officially timed on the autobahn at Munich—the highest speed ever recorded on a car in a press road test. For this run the external silencer was removed, as was also the plastic bug deflector on the bonnet.

We went storming down to Wassen, up through Goschenen to Andermatt, and then off over the rough and rocky tracks to the Oberalp, then down to Disentis, for a double reverse round the narrow hairpin in the little village street, then up and over the 6000 ft Lukmanier, and on to Biasca and Bellinzona.

We spent a blistering hot day at Monza recording the acceleration and braking figures, and averaged 120 mph from Milan to Como in a dawn reconnaissance to investigate the maximum speed with touring equipment and the low axle ratio. Then back over the St Gotthard and over to Locarno and Ascona, through the heaviest of the summer holiday traffic.

With such fantastic acceleration on tap, achieved without any trace of wheelspin, overtaking is possible in complete safety on short stretches of road where one would never normally dream of it. A quick snatch to pull the gear lever into second, a quick flick left and right on the steering wheel, and the car ahead is overtaken in less time than it takes to read this sentence. Where vision permits, the car will go rocketing up past six or eight others, roaring up to 75 in second between two hairpins, before slowing to a crawl under the action of its fabulous brakes, to take the next corner.

Such performance obviously requires a period of initiation before it can be used safely, but the first few hundred miles brought many surprises. The mental picture of the over-powered racing car, ready to spin round with smoking tyres at the slightest indiscretion with the throttle on the getaway rapidly disappeared. By painstaking study of suspension design, weight distribution, transmission, and all the elements of a chassis designed for sheer performance, the Daimler-Benz engineers have produced a car which has almost unbelievable traction, and an amazing disinclination to spin its wheels no matter how vigorously the throttle is used.

The only special instruction with regard to driving methods was a request to avoid slipping the clutch. It was therefore treated gently in the acceleration tests, and there was a distinct pause in the initial getaway, for maximum torque does not come in until the engine is doing nearly 6000 rpm. The standing start acceleration figures, excellent as they are, could therefore be bettered by a driver making a one-off start in racing conditions. As the engine starts producing its full torque, things happen at a terrific pace, but the combination of low-pivot swing axle, ZF self-locking differential and a weight distribution which puts 60 per cent. of the total weight on the rear with tanks full and two persons on board, simply eliminates wheelspin as a factor in the proceedings.

The gear change is superb, despite a complicated series of interlocking stops which make the gate look like a combination lock. First, forward on the left is used only for racing starts, and is reached by depressing the button on the gear lever. Reverse, opposite to it, is obtained by lifting up a guard on the gate. Second is back in the centre and third is forward in the centre. Another sliding guard closes the right hand part of the gate and prevents the lever passing through from second to fifth, instead of into third.

The Porsche servo ring synchromesh on the top four ratios allows changes to be made just as fast as one can move the lever. The travel is fairly long, and after a morning of acceleration testing at Monza, my elbow was bruised from repeated contact with the edge of the seat. I was changing as fast as I could move the lever, but I was not surprised when Grupp, the Daimler-Benz racing mechanic, told me that Fangio got them in even faster. As there are two gear changes between a standstill and 100 mph, there is another point where a fraction of a second could be carved off.

The unerring wheel grip, and those enormous chassis-mounted inboard brakes at front and rear, produced braking results that have never before been recorded so far as I am aware. The Tapley meter showed 100 per cent. efficiency with monotonous regularity, even when the brakes were slammed full on for a crash stop from 75 mph. That was an experiment I would care to make on very few cars, but on the SLR it produced a perfect straight-line stop, with four neat black lines on the concrete. Fifth wheel and Hasler recorder, already used for the acceleration figures, were brought into service again to render these performances in terms of deceleration times and stopping distances, with the results shown.

Pedal pressure is fairly high for maximum results, but a light pressure brings adequate results for normal fast motoring, thanks to the hydraulic servo fed by a pump driven from the gearbox. The brakes were memorable not only for these test results. They were used mercilessly on the road, as we roared down Alpine passes, accelerating to 50 and 60 mph between hairpin bends, and braking hard for the corners in a way that would be suicide on any normal car. After half an hour of this sort of thing they would still be capable of doing a perfect straight line crash stop without a trace of grab or fade.

Steering is disconcerting at first. It is

Maximum Speed, Mean of 4 runs ... 176.47 mph. Best run ... 180 mph.

SPEED IN GEARS in mph

RPM	1st	2nd	3rd	4th	5th
Road test axle, 3.81 to 1					
1000	6.8	10.5	12.4	16.7	21.7
5950 (max. torque)	40.3	61	75	100	137.7
7450 (max. power)	50.3	77	95	127	163.4
8000 (short period max. revs.)	54	83	102	136	(174)*
Maximum speed test axle 3.48 to 1					
1000	9.3	11.8	14.3	19.2	23.6
5950	57	71	86	115	143
7450	71	88	107	144	179
8000	76	95	116	154.7	(190)*

*Not obtained in practice—figure theoretical, allowing for tyre growth.

ACCELERATION IN GEARS (with driver and passenger)

Speed (mph)	1st gear secs	2nd gear secs	3rd gear secs	4th gear secs	5th gear secs
10– 30	2.3	—	—	—	—
20– 40	2.1	3.4	—	—	—
30– 50	3.0	3.2	4.0	5.6	8.6
40– 60	—	2.8	3.3	4.8	8.4
50– 70	—	2.5	2.9	5.6	8.3
60– 80	—	—	3.1	5.3	8.1
70– 90	—	—	—	5.1	8.0
80–100	—	—	—	4.8	8.2
90–110	—	—	—	5.4	8.9
100–120	—	—	—	5.8	9.4

BRAKING EFFICIENCY

Speed (mph)	Distance to stop	Tapley reading
31	39 ft	100 per cent
50	104 ft	100 per cent
75	207 ft	100 per cent

ACCELERATION THROUGH GEARS

Speed (mph)	Gears	Seconds
0– 30	1st	3.3
0– 50	1st	5.2
0– 60	1 & 2nd	6.8
0–100	1st, 2nd & 3rd	13.6
0–120	1st, 2nd, 3rd & 4th	20.3

FUEL CONSUMPTION... At 75 mph average on autobahn 16.5 mpg. At 40 mph average in mountainous country 12.8 mpg.

ENGINE.—Eight cylinders in line. 78 × 78 mm. 2976 cc. Compression ratio 9 to 1. Maximum power 296 hp at 7450 rpm. Maximum torque 228 lb ft at 5950 rpm. Fuel, 90 octane research, 83 octane Motor method.

ENGINE CONSTRUCTION.—Two blocks of four cylinders with integral heads, in Silumin-Gamma. Chromium plated bores. Roller bearing mains and big ends. Desmodromic valve gear with two rockers per valve. (Valve clearance taken up by engine compression.) Bosch injection pump. Dry sump lubrication with full flow filter. Bosch twin magneto ignition. Pressure cooling system with thermostat, but no fan.

TRANSMISSION.—Central power take-off to single plate dry clutch in unit with engine. Two-piece propeller shaft. Five speed and reverse all-indirect gearbox behind rear axle, with Porsche servo-ring synchromesh on top four forward ratios. ZF differential. Various axle, and crown wheel/pinion ratios available.

OVERALL TEST RATIOS.—Road use and acceleration tests. 1st—12.4 to 1, 2nd—8.00 to 1, 3rd—6.53 to 1, 4th—4.89 to 1, 5th—3.81 to 1.
For Maximum Speed Runs.—1st—8.62 to 1, 2nd—6.95 to 1, 3rd—5.77 to 1, 4th—4.32 to 1, 5th—3.48 to 1.

CHASSIS.—Welded tubular space frame. Independent front suspension by double wishbones, torsion bars and anti-roll bar. Independent rear suspension by low pivot swing axle, longitudinal location by Watt linkages, torsion bar springing. Telescopic dampers. Hydraulic brakes inboard, with turbo cooling fins. Parallel-action shoes. Ate hydraulic servo. Total brake lining area: 294.5 sq. in. Fuel tank at rear: 33–44 gallons. Centre lock wire wheels. Tyres 6.00–16 front. 7.00–16 rear.

DIMENSIONS.—Wheelbase 93.3 in. Track front 52.3 in. Rear 54.3 in. Length 171.25 in. Width 68.9 in. Height 43.5 in. Ground clearance 6.2 in. Turning circle (at tyres) 38.9 ft. Weight dry in racing trim 1964 lb. As tested, with silencers, two spare wheels and full tanks, 2175 lb.

Gordon Wilkins suitably attired for the speed tests.

Accessory before the fact. Accelerations and decelerations were recorded by a fifth wheel driving a Hasler accelerometer, which automatically recorded speed and time elapsed.

Steering wheel removes for easy entry, a customary Mercedes racing car feature. Below the column is a reminder about tyre pressures. Grouped in the centre, below main cut-out switch are controls for direction indicators, bonnet lock, fuel cut off, screen washer, screen wiper, lights, ignition and electric fuel pump. Instruments are rev-counter calibrated to 11,000 rpm, speedometer up to 300 km/h, oil and water thermometers, and oil pressure gauge.

light and direct (2½ turns from lock to lock) and transmits some road shock at low speeds, but as the speed rises, it becomes instinctive, and above 100 mph the car almost seems to sense the wishes of the driver, responding with complete accuracy to the slightest pressure on the wheel. At low speeds the ride is harsh enough to set one glancing apprehensively upwards at the padded fairings over the hinges of the gull-wing doors. When the car gets into its stride the bumps are controlled but the ride is never really smooth.

As the photographs show, the car looks like a longer, leaner 300 SL. It has similar gull-wing doors, but unlike the SL the steering wheel comes off, so that one can step over the high sill into the tartan-covered driving seat, where one sits with feet 30 inches apart in wells flanking the big cover over the clutch housing. The passenger has a narrower seat and less foot room.

On switching on there is a whine from the electric fuel pump at the rear, but as soon as one touches the starter button, there is a shattering noise from the engine which momentarily numbs the senses. It is compounded of the whine of gears, the clatter

Darkness before the dawn. Gordon Wilkins and Robert Braunschweig discuss coming maximum speed tests, while mechanics fit new racing plugs, using long-handled forceps and spanners through a hole in the body side. There are two 300 SLR Coupes. Here they are on the Munich Autobahn before a dawn try-out with (l to r) Rudolf Uhlenhaut (director of passenger car research at Daimler-Benz), Robert Braunschweig and Gordon Wilkins.

The eight-cylinder 2976 cc engine lies at an angle of 60 degrees in the frame. The inlet manifold has a butterfly throttle at the front, and air connection from the venturi to the injection pump control unit. Equi-length pipes connect injection pumps and injectors in head, which is integral with block. A remarkable feature of the engine is its fuel economy. (Below) On a Swiss mountain pass a Ford Fairlane is overtaken. We had to make allowances for the silencer and exhaust pipes overhanging on the passenger's side.

of the desmodromic valve gear and the injection pump, and a variety of grinding noises from the region of the clutch housing. Plastic ear plugs are normal wear for both driver and passenger.

Remember that this car is not for sale, and in this form never will be; it is a racing car adapted for road use with certain experimental objectives in view; it is neither quiet nor docile in city streets, especially in view of the prohibition on slipping the clutch. It has to be mastered like a mettlesome horse. Hung on the outside is a vast silencer, with twin exit stubs, which adds about nine inches to the overall width and has to be remembered when passing stationary cars, or taking tight corners in the Alps.

The really amazing thing is the confidence the car gives the driver, so that after a relatively brief acquaintance one is really using its unique performance, and throwing it into corners in a way one would hesitate to employ with lesser machines. It points the way to vast improvements in performance, controllability and safety, which will render existing conceptions obsolete. To have driven it has eclipsed all previous experiences in 20 years of test driving on the world's finest cars, and I do not expect to find its match for a long time to come.

In just one season the fabulous Mercedes-Benz 300SLR managed to mop up virtually every important sports car race in the world. Here, in an SCI exclusive, are the full details and driver's report on

GERMANY'S

FOR years the Italian sports cars had dominated the international racing picture, with Jaguar occasionally upsetting the scheme. Then Mercedes uncorked their 300SLR sports car, and the scene changed with stunning impact.

Realizing that wins in international competition would produce prestige for German products on the potential world market, the Daimler-Benz organization invested a bundle of cash, in the neighborhood of $2,500,000, and the whole of their bountiful engineering brains in designing, building and racing the finest machines the world has ever seen in competition. Suddenly all other makes were "also rans," and the Unterturkheim plant in Stuttgart lost no time in announcing to the world the latest Mercedes wins.

The blitz was headed by Juan Manuel Fangio, who ran away with the World Championship Grand Prix driving title in the Mercedes G.P. cars, and 26 year-old Stirling Moss, the youthful British driver who shadowed the great Fangio in Grand Prix events, and who whipped all comers in the sports car competitions with a 300SLR.

Every sports car fan in the world has wondered what made this fabulous car go. Opportunities to roadtest a Mercedes 300SLR are nonexistent, the cars have been retired and are not for sale. However, after months of postal bombardment, the factory sent to SCI a set of special prerelease SLR specifications, and with the aid of Stirling Moss we have put together the first full report of this latest Mercedes masterpiece.

When I showed Stirling the "specs" he exclaimed "God, it's fantastic!" Several minutes later, as he read on, he murmured "Oh what a wonderful car" and "Thank God it's not for sale, I'd hate to have to run against it!" From the man who drove the machine all last season, blasting the records of Europe's major roadraces, this gives some idea of

Mercedes 300 SLR cockpit is clean and simple; every item is laid out for the driver's convenience alone. Four knobs below the dash control injectors which squirt thin oil into break drums to prevent seizing or sticking after repeated application.

By BOB ROLOFSON

SILVER SCREAMERS

how closely guarded these figures have been. He knew very little about the technical aspects of the car, but knows better than anyone in the world how it handles and performs in the thick of battle.

One of the most amazing aspects of the SLR is the engine, an item guaranteed to leave armchair engineers the world over scratching their heads and choking on their own words. This potent plant is of a design considered dead and buried with the in-line Buick — a straight eight, theoretically with all of the disadvantages of the design coupled to the small displacement limit of 181.9 cubic inches. Yet this "obsolete" engine slams out almost two brake horsepower per cubic inch, a rating scarcely approached by other manufacturers with the help of a blower and almost unbelievable in an unblown machine. Further, its peaking speed, 7400 rpm, which was constantly reached, and used for considerable periods, would tear any other straight-eight to pieces from sheer crank whip alone. One can hardly blame the manufacturer for boasting that the car had never dropped out or lost a race through mechanical failure.

How can such a mill stand such treatment? The answer lies only partially in the square bore and stroke ratio of 3-1/16 inches for each dimension and the 10 main bearing crank. A good part of the answer lies in the way these engines are put together. The engine assembly room at the Unterturkheim plant is held at a constant temperature, winter and summer. No component is matched to another

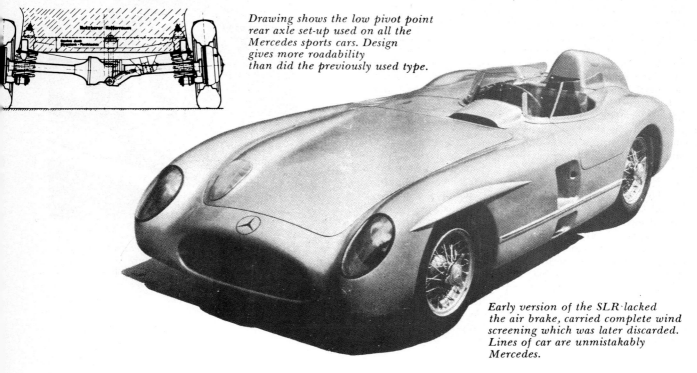

Drawing shows the low pivot point rear axle set-up used on all the Mercedes sports cars. Design gives more roadability than did the previously used type.

Early version of the SLR lacked the air brake, carried complete wind screening which was later discarded. Lines of car are unmistakably Mercedes.

the Mercedes-Benz 300 SLR
(continued)

SPECIFICATIONS 300 SLR

GENERAL
- List price .... not for sale
- Wheelbase .... 93-5/16 inches
- Tread: front .... 52-3/8 inches
- Tread: rear .... 54-5/16 inches
- Tire size .... front: 6.00 x 16
-                              rear: 7.00 x 16
- Dry weight .... 1940 pounds
- Curb weight .... 2491.2 pounds
- Weight distribution ...... front: 41.5%
-                              rear: 58.5%
- Over-all length .... 171-5/16 inches
- Over-all width .... 68-7/8 inches
- Over-all height .... 43-1/2 inches

ENGINE
- Cylinders .... 8 cylinders in-line
- Valves .... Desmodromic valve timing

until the temperature of each and every micro-finished part is equalized. In storing, every finished part is carefully wrapped in soft, oily flannel to prevent even the smallest scratch. In short, nothing at Mercedes is left to chance. Assembly methods resemble those on a fine Swiss watch. It is this slavish devotion to the smallest detail which makes the machine so nearly unbeatable.

Another factor is the engine's seemingly inexhaustible abililty to wind up is the desmodromic valve layout in which the valves are not only opened but closed by mechanical means at exactly the right time without depending on springs and completely eliminating valve bounce or float. The result is fantastic volumetric efficiency at any speed.

Packed under the hood, along with the engine, are the enormous inboard front brakes which Mercedes perfected after Lancia (who pioneered them in 1953 sports cars) had abandoned them in their G.P. and sports cars. With the engine and injection equipment, inboard brakes, coolers, steering, and torsion-bar suspension all packed like a three dimensional blue-print under the low, silver hood, the German engineers have created a new high in totally functional construction, leaving absolutely no waste space. As if this thorough engineering job were not enough, each and every part has been finely machined to the point where maximum strength, per ounce of weight, makes it unnecessary to cut or drill holes for lightness!

Hefty gear shift lever works through double-H gate in six positions including a reverse which, with low, is locked out in normal operations.

Various motoring publications have periodically referred to the 300SLR as nothing more than a W196 Grand Prix car in "thin disguise." This statement ruffles the famed Moss calm and he defends the sports car by maintaining that although the general construction and layout follows the Grand Prix car, the SLR is definitely a breed alone. He points out that the 132-pound frame (20% lighter than the 300SL) is a development of the space-type frame of the SL, using exceptionally small diameter tubing. It handles differently from the G.P. car, and was (for Stirling) more difficult to drive. One major difference was the shifting of balance caused by loss of weight in the rear as the fuel was consumed. In the G.P. car it was possible to adjust the angle of the rear wheels from the cockpit, maintaining the same rear-end characteristics throughout the race.

The car was at its best in open road racing, Moss says, and riding qualities were properly stiff for good handling but "much softer and more comfortable than I had expected." Ride, roadability and handling qualities are difficult to measure specifically, but in his estimation the SLR riding qualities are good despite the fifty-odd pounds of tire pressure required in competition. The car corners very flat, is extremely responsive and settles down to hug the road in straight line driving. Cruising speed can be maintained anywhere between 80 and 160, depending on road conditions. In the wet the car is excellent to a point, "But when it goes, you notice its size." The booster actuated, hydraulic, inboard brakes with their compound drums and parallel shoes are extremely efficient and stop the car

Wire wheels used on Mercedes make others look like rolling gear taken from a tricycle. Wheels are triple-spoked, with tremendous lateral strength. Note deep alloy rims.

SPECIFICATIONS 300 SLR

Cylinder bore..............3-1/16 inches
Stroke........................3-1/16 inches
Displacement.............181.99 cubic inches
Compression ratio.....1:9
Maximum b.h.p..........345 h.p. (SAE) at 7400 r.p.m.
Maximum torque........217 ft. lbs. at 5620 r.p.m.
No. of main bearings..10
Carburetion................4 stroke, gasoline injection
Ignition......................dual
Lubrication................Dry sump
Fuel consumption.......30 litres per 100 km (Le Mans)

TRANSMISSION
No. of forward speeds..Daimler-Benz mechanical 5 speed
No. of speeds
  synchomesh..............2nd through 5th gear
Clutch........................Daimler-Benz single dry disk
Type gears.................Spur gears, involute
Standard ratios...........1:3.963-0.2524 (Le Mans)
Reduction in engine
  between crank-
  shaft and flywheel....1:1.0606

PERFORMANCE
Over-all ratios   (top speeds)
5th gear 1:3.5..............180.2 m.p.h. (Le Mans)
4th gear 1:4.513...........1399 m.p.h.
3rd gear 1:6.004...........104 m.p.h.
2nd gear 1:8.123...........77   m.p.h.
1st gear 1:10.02............62   m.p.h.

CHASSIS
Frame.........................Torsionally-rigid, three dimensional (space frame) tubular steel.
Front suspension........Daimler-Benz independent, torsion-bar springing with F&S shocks.
Rear suspension.........Daimler-Benz swing-axle with low-placed pivot for axle and shafts. Torsion-bar springing with S&F shocks.
Brakes........................Hydraulic 4-wheel brakes with "Teves" booster, compound drums and parallel shoes. All mounted inboard.
Fuel tank....................44 gallons
Electrical system.........12 volts
Wheels.......................Light metal, with drop center rim 5.50 x 16
Body..........................Open streamlined light metal, two seater.
Top speed..................180.2 m.p.h. (Le Mans)

AIR BRAKES
(Data included in text)

Despite several severe contacts with immovable objects, Moss and Collins kept the fabulous Mercedes going on to win the rugged 1955 Targa Florio.

Side mounted exhausts protrude like a pair of gun muzzles. Screaming note makes conversation impossible in cockpit when underway.

straight, with little or no "fish-tailing." The only time he experienced brake fade was in Argentina, where it was so hot that drivers, brakes and engines were *ALL* "fading!"

At this point it is interesting to note that the Stuttgart engineers discarded the tried and proven De Dion rear axle, which Daimler-Benz pioneered on their competition cars in 1937. Instead, they used the racing machines to "prove" a new type of swing axle, which they were considering for their production cars. Daimler-Benz has been using swing axles in production cars since 1930, and welcomed the opportunity to try their latest innovation. The new system embodies a low-placed pivot for axle and shaft, providing slight, easily controllable, oversteer, which permitted maximum speeds in turns. Combined with the swing axle advantage of reducing unsprung weight, this new feature improved the car's road-holding, riding qualities, and increased stability. Stirling is convinced that it is the best handling rear suspension in the business and backs his bet by wheeling his 220 Mercedes-Benz around the English countryside — full bore!

With all equipment in good shape, the weakest link in the chain of possible failures in race slike the Mille Miglia, is the endurance of the driver. To this end, the Daimler-Benz organization goes out of its way to afford the driver

Here is the powerhouse. Out of 181.9 cubic inches comes 345 bhp, an almost unbelievable rating of nearly two horsepower per cubic inch. Note the huge inboard brakes between engine and radiator.

Tech. Report: Mercedes Benz 300SLR

every possible advantage by making him comfortable and providing large, simple, easy to operate controls. Basic among these considerations is the driving position. A "mock-up" is made, identical with the driving position in the car. The driver is seated in the "mock-up," where he assumes his most comfortable driving position. The seat is measured to fit the driver so that it will give full support to the back, shoulders, legs and hips. The next time the driver jumps into the car he settles down to discover that he has literally "put the car on."

The second innovation in the SLR "office" is the special Mercedes steering wheel. This is instantly removable by pressing a button in the center of the hub and pulling the wheel off, giving the driver plenty of room to jump in and out of the car (wheel in hand) at quick pit stops. Steering characteristics can be varied to suit every driver's personal preference. Stirling isn't positive, but thinks that five stock steering ratios were available, and if none of these were suitable "Mercedes would make one to fit."

The steering is slightly oversteer, or as Moss says "just about neutral," and sufficiently "hard" to enable the driver to hold the car straight at high speeds. The instruments are large, well hooded from reflections and are equipped with a rheostat for night driving. The oil, water and tachometer are placed so the driver can read them instantly, without taking his eyes from the road for more than an instant. The tachometer is red-lined at 7000 rpm but Moss exceeded this in the Mille Miglia (to 7600) with no apparent damage or strain on the engine. The only instrument Stirling would like to add to the car is an odometer on the right side, for the navigator's use on long races like the Mille Miglia.

As in the Grand Prix car, the driver straddles the drive shaft, with legs spread wide apart, giving as Moss says, "Three point suspension" to the driver. I had the rare privilege of sitting in one of the Mercedes Grand Prix cars during my recent visit to the Stuttgart plant, and can say without any reservations, that the driving position is unbelievably comfortable and inspires confidence. I wanted to turn the engine over and "go" the instant I settled into the machine. The tunnel and seat combine to hold the legs in driving position, automatically guiding the feet onto the pedals. There is plenty of footroom, and the pedals are serrated to keep the driver's feet from slipping off. The starter is incorporated into the ignition switch, which aids in fast get-aways at Le Mans-type starts.

The clutch is smooth, but can't be slipped too much because it is of the single plate variety. The fully adjustable gearbox is fast, strong, and foolproof. The right hand falls naturally into position on the husky floor-

New airbrake was completely successful.

mounted shift lever, which clicks into each position with a precise solid feeling. Reverse is locked out (by a gate) as is first gear (spring loaded) so that accidentally dropping into first instead of third is difficult. Shifting positions are reversed: starting at the left of the double H, down is reverse, straight up is first (62 mph), to the right and down is second (77 mph), straight up is third (104 mph), to the right and down is fourth (139 mph), and straight up is fifth (180.2 mph). Stirling missed his shift numerous times during his record breaking run in the Mille Miglia and the box stood the abuse with no breakage.

Brake is raised, lowered hydraulically.

I asked Stirling if the light metal body rumbled or creaked at speed. He couldn't say because the side-mounted exhaust pipes, roaring wind, and transmission noise drowned out any other sound. All conversation between driver and navigator must be carried out by hand signals, or printed code numbers on small cards.

The most controversial feature of the SLR is the air-brake. A refinement of the experimental brakes used on the SL's several years ago at Le Mans, the perfected version was completely manageable and successful. Designed to assist the shoe brakes when stopping at high speeds, the flaps furnish amazing deceleration when used at speeds over one hundred miles per hour. The working cylinder of the air brake is connected to the oil circuit of a pump which is flanged to the rear-mounted transmission. By manual operation of a control slide in the cockpit, the plunger is moved in either direction, thus engaging or disengaging the aerodynamic brake. Stirling is enthusiastic about the device and says "It feels as if a giant hand had reached down and grabbed the car by the rear end."

With the spare wheels, the car carries a comprehensive set of tools, jack and special plug wrenches. Practicing for the Mille Miglia, Stirling and his navigator Dennis Jenkinson had the wheel change down to one minute and thirty seven seconds: from their seats, wheel change, and back into the seats! It is possible to drive the car "fussily" in normal traffic, but with no fan it would boil if held behind a line of cars for too long.

The 300SLR blasted all competition in its first (and probably last) racing season, confounding the theory that new designs need a season of conditioning before crowding the winners' circle. The Daimler-Benz engineers have retired their magical talents into the super-secret confines of the Mercedes experimental section, while rumors crowd the motoring world about such things as airbrakes on Grand Prix turbo cars and other strange and wonderful possibilities from Stuttgart. Meanwhile, in Stirling Moss' opinion, the "old" 300SLR is the ultimate in out-and-out sports car competition. #

Bearing marked resemblance to 300SL at the front, it lacks performance of bigger brother, but holds road better.

Mercedes 190SL

A MIGHTY MACHINE

Our road test finds the 190SL an ideal road car, handles better than the 300SL, but is too slow for competition work.

Instruments on 190SL are joy to behold. Everything is layed out with typical efficiency.

Making the long, hard descent from an automotive Nirvana back to plain hack iron is always a jolt, and you learn to expect it — especially with Daimler-Benz products. There's a kind of monotony to testing cars marked with the three-pointed star. D-B technicians have a way of grasping the guts of a problem and solving it with such success and apparent ease that the result is downright intoxicating for the appreciative driver. The post-Mercedes withdrawal pains are tougher to take than most.

But I wasn't expecting them with the 190SL. After living with a 300SL, I made the mistake of assuming that the "lesser" car would be a letdown. I was wrong. The 190SL is just as exciting, in a quieter, more subtle way, as the 300SL, and it's my feeling that for most mortals it's actually a more desirable car.

In the 300SL you're over-gunned

for the road. In the 190SL you're armed just right. It corners more securely than the 300SL, it has the same excellent steering, a similar full-synchro gearbox, the same quality finish throughout, and better rear suspension. Its beauty of line and many of its dimensions approach those of the 300SL.

But it's a car that you might not mind turning your wife loose with — something not many 300SL owners are doing, you can bet. For a sports-touring car—not a competition car—the 190SL is about as close an approach to perfection as any of us are likely to see, and for the kind of connoisseur's car it is, it's not expensive. But if you want a car for winning Class E races, keep looking; this is not the machine.

The 190SL is a high-performance *luxury* two-seater, built to the highest standards of quality and finish. The way it's made is just about flawless, its behavior is impeccable. It's a car that steers, stops and goes precisely as you want it to. It has no surprising little tricks when the going gets exciting. It's totally on the side of the driver, protecting him, keeping him covered, keeping him out of trouble. It's sound and safe as a car can be. You've heard people speak of cars as "sweet." This is a real sweet one.

Our test car had a glaring fault shared by other 190SL's we've seen. The paint job was completely out of character with the quality of every other part of the car. The paint had been rubbed, all right, but only on the obvious high spots; the orange-peel effect elsewhere was bad. The only other flaws in the car were in the speedometer. One was infinitesimal: the paint had chipped off the needle at the point where it contacts the zero peg. The other was that the instrument was fast—to a point. All the way up to 90 it had a healthy percentage of optimism. But at an indicated 100 m.p.h., it suddenly became conservatively accurate. We doubted our readings, re-ran the calibration runs, got the same results.

With a normal windshield and with top and windows up we clocked an easy 104.5 m.p.h., meaning that the engine had to be turning about 5,750 r.p.m. At this time, the test car had been driven just about 482 miles, and even though 190SL engines are fully broken in at the factory, some of the horsepower was getting used to break in bearing surfaces in the drive line and wheels. The car definitely has a higher potential top speed. However, if the tach could be red-lined at 6,000 this would give 108.8 m.p.h. and to get up to 111 you'd have to wind out to 6,120 r.p.m., which this engine is not yearning to do in top cog.

The 190SL engine is much like the 300SL's. It has the same single overhead camshaft, the same big bore and short stroke, and most of the same details of design. It has two cylinders less, though, and while the longer 300SL crankshaft is supported by a main bearing at each side of each throw, seven in all, the shorter 190SL crank gets along nicely with its three mains. Both engines have oil coolers, but the 190's instrument panel has no oil temperature gauge. Some drivers will probably be unenthusiastic about the fact that the 190SL's oil pressure gauge spends most of the time riding the high peg at 90 psi, will have visions of jammed by-pass valves and washed-out bearings. But those acquainted with aircraft practice are likely to nod approvingly and conclude that the engine is built to last. At or near 90 is where this engine's pressure is intended to stay, except in the low-rev range.

The induction system occupies about half the engine space, and the pair of intricate, costly twin-throat Solexes and their massive intake duct are more impressive to look upon than any fuel injection setup. If you leaf through the magnificent parts book that comes with the 190SL, you'll see two distinct types of carburettors pictured. Those with the flat-bottomed ports are the ones in current use. The change was made chiefly in the interest of venting "puddled" fuel away from the engine.

The engine is awfully strong. You don't have to use first to make a getaway from standstill. You

Two twin choke carbies are fitted to 190SL, not fuel injection. Air goes via large cleaner. Is virtually four cylinder version of 300SL.

MERCEDES 190SL
A MIGHTY MACHINE

can let the clutch right out and pull away in second. You can slip the clutch a little and pull away in third. You can slip it more and pull out without bucking in fourth —pretty good for 1897 c.c. The engine doesn't vibrate, doesn't have throb you learn to expect from a four. It's quieter, in spite of the overhead cam, except above about 80 m.p.h., when it begins to emit a powerful lovely moan. There's not the pronounced sag and then the sudden rise in output that you get with radical valve timing, although the engine begins to run at its smoothest at about 2,500 r.p.m.

An important part of the 190SL's "sweet" character comes from its clutch and gearbox. The clutch is very soft and gentle yet it bites with absolute firmness. The transmission has baulk-ring synchromesh even on bottom gear, and the synchronisation never fails. We felt a pronounced heaviness to the gear-change mechanism that we're assured diminishes with accumulated miles, but part of this heaviness is deliberately built in.

You can't force a shift with this box. Try to make a fast, slicing gear change and you meet unyielding resistance—until gear speeds are equalised, which takes a half-second or so, and then the lever slips right into its gate. On downshifts you can spare the synchro mechanism and make quicker changes with the double-clutch technique. The transmission is foolproof, one of the nicest there is, and the shift lever is ideally located, right at hand in all positions.

An interesting point is that if you shift to fourth at 50 m.p.h. or so, letting the clutch out fast and hitting the throttle, you'll hear a pretty little squeak from the rear tyres. This is not so much a result of engine torque as it is of the 190SL's fine single-pivot swing axle, which it shares in modified form with the 2.5 litre grand prix car and the 300SLR sports-racing car. When we asked factory technicians to account for the fact that the 190SL's cornering manners are superior to the 300SL's, they said immediately, "Why, it's the new rear end, of course." Oddly enough, the 300SL still makes do with the older, more complicated double-pivot axle, which has a higher centre of gravity.

The total axle assembly is mounted to the chassis at three points. One point is the central pivot bracket at the bottom of which is the pivot journal or shaft. This bracket is bolted to a frame cross member but is insulated from the frame by a laminated rubber bushing. Each of the half axles is mounted on the pivot shaft and is free to rock vertically on it. Rubber buffers limit vertical axle travel and torque arms anchored to the frame side members provide the other two mounting points of the rear axle assembly. These arms carry the springs and control fore and aft axle motion and torque reactions.

The rest of the 190SL chassis derives largely from the 180, in which the frame and floor form a unit and a separate, very stiff U-section cross member carries the front of the engine, all of the front coil spring-and-wishbone suspension, and the bulk of the steering mechanism. Rubber pads lie between the cross member and the frame floor. The main purpose of this arrangement at the front end is to

Occasional rear seat will carry one full sized adult, or two children. Foot-well is provided for rear rider.

Brake drums are cast iron, with turbo fins on front. Stopping power is good.

Car takes test curve at 60 m.p.h. Body gives flat ride, whole unit has well braced feel on turns.

provide the best possible suspension and steering geometry while also insulating the rest of the car against suspension vibrations.

It performs this job very effectively, but so do the suspension systems in quite a few other makes. Where the 190SL chassis really shines is in road holding on curves and straightaways at high speeds. It squats close to the ground and tracks true on the straights like the 300SL. It stays glued in the turns better and its resistance to power slides is far, far greater. You'd have to be driving way beyond the limits of commonsense to get into trouble with the 190SL.

The steering is typical Mercedes-Benz. That means it's on the heavy side, quick and free of backlash. The gearing is of the recirculating ball type, probably the costliest and best there is. The pitman arm is a forging massive enough to go on a 20-ton truck. A tubular shock absorber is built into the linkage to absorb road vibrations, and in the steering is self-centreing. There is no wander or wobble at high speeds.

Just as the 190SL's available power, road holding and steering inspire a profound sense of security, so do its brakes. However, although these resemble the brakes of the 300SL, they have about 108 sq. ins. less lining area and are therefore just extremely adequate in performance, rather than fantastic. They have two leading shoes at the front and the smoothly progressive action that this implies. The price you pay for this convenience is that when you back down a steep hill, only the rear brakes are operative; it takes strong pedal pressure to slow the car. Our test car was equipped with the optionally - available vacuum booster and Al-fin front drums. During the standard ten-stop fade test there was a ten per cent. loss of braking power in the first five stops; after these braking power remained constant.

Daimler - Benz, unlike other manufacturers, is willing to admit that a car is occasionally a cranky device, and that it will perform better and last longer when you face the fact and take appropriate steps. With other new cars, for example, the makers urge you to turn the key and take off without a moment's concern for the innards. In the 190SL handbook, on the other hand, D-B advises, with some sternness and much honesty:

"*Attention!* In order to check lubrication of the engine, every vehicle and every engine which has been laid up for more than three weeks or which has been transported for such a period should be started as follows: 1. Take off distributor cap. 2. Declutch and turn the engine with closed throttle by means of outside or own battery until oil pressure is indicated. Note—the battery must be fully charged; do not exhaust it completely, but allow to recuperate. 3. Replace the distributor cap.

4. Pull the choke and start as usual."

The theory behind all these directions and the elaborately w o r k e d - o u t maintenance programme is that if the owner will follow them, he'll never have a moment's trouble with his car. In the 190SL this contributes on a more or less subtle psychological level to a sense of security and perfection that grows on you every hour you drive the car. It's more than just pleasant; it's habit-forming.

Stripped for competition, the Mercedes has light doors, bonnet and areo screen, is not rapid enough to win anything big.

PERFORMANCE

TOP SPEED:
Two-way average 103.6
Fastest one-way run 104.5

ACCELERATION:
From zero to—
30 m.p.h. 3.7
40 m.p.h. 6.1
50 m.p.h. 7.8
60 m.p.h. 11.0
70 m.p.h. 15.1
80 m.p.h. 23.3
90 m.p.h. 32.0
100 m.p.h. 52.1
Standing half mile 18.1
Standing mile 48.6

CHASSIS:
Wheelbase .... 94.5ins.
Front tread .... 56ins.
Rear tread .... 58ins.
Suspension, front—
  Independent, coil springs and wishbones.
Suspension, rear—
  Independent, coil springs and single - pivot swing axle.
Shock absorbers—
  Double - acting hydraulic.
Steering type Recirculating ball
Steering wheel turns L to L 3.23
Turning diameter .... 36ft.
Brake type—
  Hydraulic, "turbo-cooled" drums 2 leading shoes at front
Brake lining area .... 150 sq. ins.
Tyre size .... 6.40 x 13

GENERAL:
Length .... 165ins.
Width .... 68ins.
Weight, test car—
Height .. 52ins. with top up
  2550lbs. (full fuel tank)
Weight distribution, F/R .. 52.5/47.5
Weight distribution, F/R, with driver .... Same
Fuel capacity ... ...

RATING FACTORS:
B.h.p. per sq. in. piston area ... 3.42
Pounds per b.h.p.—test car   21.4
Piston speed at 60 m.p.h. 1815 fpm
Piston speed at max. b.h.p. 3125 fpm
Brake lining area per ton
  (test car) .... 118 sq. in.

SPEED RANGES IN GEARS:
I 0-30
II 0-50
III 11-70
IV .... 13-max.

SPEEDOMETER CORRECTION:
Indicated   Actual
30 28
40 37
50 46
60 55
70 65
80 74
90 83
100 99

FUEL CONSUMPTION:
Hard driving, 20.0 during speed tests
Average driving (under 60 m.p.h.)—
  34.4

BRAKING EFFICIENCY:
(Ten successive emergency stops from 60 m.p.h., just short of locking wheels, using Perfometer)—   Per cent.
1st stop 55
2nd stop 54
3rd stop 50
4th stop 49
5th stop 45
6th stop 45
7th stop 44
8th stop 45
9th stop 45
10th stop 44

SPECIFICATIONS
POWER UNIT:
Type .... In-line four
Valve arrangement—
  Single overhead camshaft, vertical valves
Bore and stroke ..... 85 x 83.6 mm
Bore/stroke ratio .... 0.98 to one
Displacement .... 1897 c.c.
Compression ratio 8.50
Carburetion by—
  Dual twin - throat Solex side drafts
Max. b.h.p. at r.p.m. .... 120 at 5700
Max. torque at r.p.m. .... 101 at 3800
Idle speed—
  Cool 900 r.p.m.;
  warm 1350 rp.m.

With neat stowage for the hood, the 190SL has clean, elegant lines. As tested the car was fitted with Continental RS tyres; the independently-sprung rear wheels have negative camber in their static condition

Autocar ROAD TESTS 1668

Mercedes-Benz 190SL
ROADSTER

WHEN the Mercedes 190SL was introduced in February 1954, it was a little overshadowed by the more exotic 300SL coupé announced at the same time, and so suffered by comparison. Several Continental journalists who tested the 190SL soon after this date considered it to be rather sluggish and lacking in the performance expected from such a car, but these views were not confirmed by a recent road test by *The Autocar*. Since the car's introduction power has been increased by approximately 10 b.h.p. by raising the compression ratio from 8 to 8.5 to 1, so that the net horse-power is now 105 b.h.p. (gross 120 b.h.p.) at 5,700 r.p.m. This is a commendable output from an engine of 1,897 c.c.; it is achieved at a higher point in the revolution range than that of many cars, but this does not result in any roughness.

This test, undertaken wholly on the Continent, covered nearly 1,200 miles, mostly at average speeds unattainable in Britain. The overall impression was one of comfort and of sparkling performance with a very reassuring level of safety. It is necessary to make full use of the well-designed four-speed gear box if maximum performance is to be obtained, and there are reservations on the degree of visibility and comfort of the seats.

The car tested was a left-hand-drive roadster, but it is also available as a fixed-head coupé or a convertible coupé. In each form it is a two-seater, and makes no pretence of carrying more. Such a seating arrangement in a comparatively large car gives ample luggage space. Behind the seats two medium-sized suitcases and a large quantity of soft baggage can be placed without encroaching on the stowage space for the hood. In addition, the tail luggage compartment will accommodate two large suitcases beside the vertically-mounted spare wheel. Thus the car is well equipped for two people for high-speed long-distance touring. In character with this is a fuel tank which has a capacity sufficient for 300 miles between replenishments, even in hard driving.

With a laden weight of nearly 25 cwt, and geared to give 18½ m.p.h. per 1,000 r.p.m. in top, frequent use must be made of the intermediate ratios if more than 50 miles are to be put into each hour on other than the *autobahn* type of road. To meet these conditions third gear is an ideal ratio which gives a maximum speed of 76 m.p.h. In this gear the engine proverbially puts its neck into the collar, to record a time under 14sec from 30 m.p.h. to 70 m.p.h. Even in top gear the car has plenty of bite and the best speed of 109.2 m.p.h. was achieved from rest in a little under two miles. For town driving top gear cannot be employed usefully below 15 m.p.h., but this is no criticism in a car of this character.

Frequent use of the intermediate gears does not appear to have an adverse effect on fuel consumption. During one period of the test, which involved a run from Germany to Italy through Switzerland, with a climb over the Alps, an average running speed of 47.5 m.p.h. was maintained and the fuel consumption was 21.7 m.p.g.—slightly better than when cruising on the *autobahn*, mostly in excess of 100 m.p.h., for nearly two hours. Driving in more leisurely fashion on the motor road, and keeping maximum speed down to below 80 m.p.h., a fuel consumption of 24 m.p.g. was recorded.

Absolute smoothness may never be attained with a four-

The Mercedes three-pointed star is a dominant feature of front end styling. The degree of encroachment of the steering wheel on vision is apparent. Head lamps provide good penetration for fast driving, with a wide spread of light in their dipped position

Mercedes-Benz 190SL . . .

Protection from wind buffeting in the open condition is afforded by wind-up door windows. Wheels are of the bolt-on type

Bodywork is well protected by substantial bumpers which wrap round the extremities of front and rear wings. The hood gives good weather protection without impeding entry, and is completely draughtproof (below)

cylinder engine, but the 190SL reaches a high standard. Engine speed is limited to 6,000 r.p.m., with a warning quadrant on the rev counter between this and 5,750 r.p.m. The maximum speeds quoted in the gears were taken at the upper limit, and the rotational speed of the engine at the highest figure recorded in top was 5,600 r.p.m.

Starting is by means of the ignition key; although different keys are required for the doors and luggage locker, they are of different shapes and immediately recognizable for their respective purposes.

Really cold weather was not experienced during the test, but on several mornings the air temperature was as low as 40 deg F. In such circumstances, and using Continental premium grade fuel, the engine started instantaneously and the choke could be dispensed with almost immediately. If full throttle was used too soon an occasional misfire occurred, but slight use of the choke eliminated this tendency. Should the choke control be left in operation inadvertently, a warning light is seen as soon as the engine reaches its normal running temperature.

The engine has two double-choke carburettors arranged so that one choke in each operates over the low-engine-speed range, and the second stages are brought into operation by vacuum control in the upper speed range. It was impossible to detect the point of change-over, and no flat spot could be noticed in any part of the range.

This carburettor arrangement can result in some difficulties in hot starting, but a special control is provided for such circumstances. When restarting with the engine at maximum temperature a control knob, on the lower edge of the facia, is pulled out after the throttle pedal has been fully depressed; the effect is to open up all the carburettor passageways to atmosphere, to ventilate the system and disperse trapped fuel vapour. Provided the maker's instructions are followed in this respect no difficulties are encountered.

Synchromesh of the baulk-ring type is provided on each of the four forward ratios, and straight-through snap changes can be obtained at any time. Full throttle upward changes were unrewarding because of clutch slip. This was particularly noticeable during tests from a standing start and undoubtedly affected the performance figures.

Clutch operating loads are light and pedal travel is not excessive; when changing gear with the car in motion only a slight depression of the pedal was necessary for clean changes. Fore and aft movements of the change-speed lever in the gate are short but the cross travel greater, calling for a long reach with the right hand (the car tested had left-hand drive) and there was some interference with the passenger if he was sitting a little towards the centre of the car. A slightly stiffer gear lever would eliminate surplus springiness. Gear noise on all ratios was virtually non-existent and no vibrations were evident in the transmission.

The suspension is a good compromise to achieve safety for fast cornering without too much harshness over indifferent surfaces. It is firm, but no violent vertical motions are suffered by the passenger. Over cobbled streets, with the tyres at the recommended pressures for fast driving, there was at times a high-frequency pitching. This was particularly evident after fast runs when the tyre pressures rose to 35 lb sq in from their normal cold setting of 28 lb sq in. In such conditions a scuttle and windscreen shake also became apparent, and this was more noticeable with the hood lowered.

A fairly stiff front anti-roll bar gave a noticeable freedom from roll under the most severe cornering conditions. At such times the steering had to be wound on just a little, indicating a trace of understeer, but for all normal motoring the characteristics could be rated as neutral. In tricky situations, such as approaching an unknown bend too fast, the car will help the driver out of a mistake—it will break

Rear luggage space is sufficient for two large suitcases. The well-equipped tool roll is stowed beside the spare wheel. The large diameter filler takes the full flow from a refuelling pump without blow-back

away at the rear and for an instant may appear to go out of control, but immediately corrects itself without any help from the driver. Except in the wet, power is insufficient to slide the rear wheels, but the most stable cornering conditions are achieved with power on through the bend.

Steering is precise at all times, with just a trace of feed-back over bad surfaces, despite the use of a hydraulic damper in the linkage. There are 3½ turns from lock to lock and at the extremes of travel noticeable effort is needed, which shows up a trace of springiness in the mechanism. At the same time, there is a desirable degree of self-centring and the wheel can be allowed to spin through the hands to the straight-ahead position without any overrun.

Cross winds have no effect on stability either with the hood erected or folded away, but a momentary snake is noticed when crossing tram lines or a joining strip on a concrete road at a narrow angle. This was less noticeable than with earlier Mercedes cars such as the 300SL coupé, which had an orthodox—not a low pivot—swing axle at the rear, but is a characteristic which cannot be completely eliminated with independently sprung rear wheels.

Braking power fully matches the car's performance. The light alloy drums are of relatively small diameter, heavily finned for heat dissipation, and the necessary braking area is recovered with wide shoes. These operate in conjunction with a vacuum-servo giving pedal pressures which are low and consistent. Automatic adjustment is a feature, but seems to result in a peculiarity of pedal movement. After several applications have given rise to high drum temperatures, followed by an interval which allows them to cool down, the first application results in a noticeably longer pedal travel, but a quick second jab restores the normal pedal movement. A deliberately fast run down a pass in the Alps failed to induce any fade, and at the foot only a slight increase in pedal load could be detected. At all times braking between each wheel was balanced and there was never deviation from a straight line.

The driving position could be improved. For a person of normal height, the top of the steering wheel rim is in the line of vision, while a short person may find it necessary to look through the wheel at times. This defect could be overcome by lowering the steering wheel, for there is ample room between the seat cushion and the wheel rim for even the most portly driver. The seats are firmly upholstered— there is a divergence of opinion among designers about the desirability of this feature—but a little more support for the back in the seat squab, to avoid lateral movement, would have been appreciated. A wide range of seat adjustment is provided, sufficient for the passenger to stretch his legs fully and doze in comfort on long journeys.

The main instruments, immediately in front of the driver, are clearly visible through the two-spoked steering wheel. An exception is the temperature gauge, which is almost entirely hidden by the wheel hub. On the lower edge of the facia, equally spaced on either side of the steering wheel, are the control knobs. Those most frequently required, such as the light switch, are easily reached, but others involve a rather awkward movement of the arm under the steering wheel and would be more convenient if grouped in the centre of the panel.

Included among the instruments is a control for altering the ignition timing according to the grade of petrol used; it can be set to obtain optimum fuel consumption by advancing the timing when cruising at low throttle openings. A full horn ring serves also, with rotary motion, to operate the winking turn indicators, but it is not self-cancelling. Beneath the steering wheel is a lever which automatically flashes the head lights on and off in a repeating sequence—a warning in common use on the Continent and often superior to a horn.

Two-speed windscreen wipers are a standard fitting, as is the windscreen washer. The control for this, operated by the left foot, is above the head-lamp dip switch, and it brings the wipers into operation at the same time even though their main control switch is out of circuit—a thoughtful arrangement. There is ample foot room around the pedals, and the clutch and throttle pedals are arranged for simple heel-and-toe manipulation. On the left-hand-

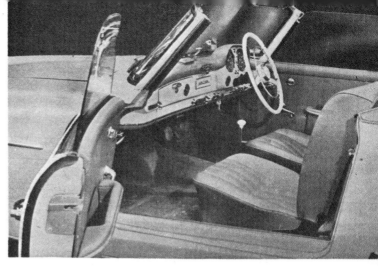

Right-hand drive is available without extra cost. Matching leather covers the top of the facia, which has a centrally mounted ash tray and a map-reading light. Seat backs are adjustable to three positions

drive car the gear-box tunnel is so shaped as to act as a guide and rest for the throttle foot.

Space for small personal effects is provided by a deep, lockable glove compartment, on the lid of which is mounted a luminous electric clock. Additional accommodation for small objects is provided in door pockets which are combined with the arm rests and door pulls.

Heating is regulated by a centrally mounted control with two levers, one for each side of the car. It is augmented by a blower which was very silent in operation, and there is a separate control to divert all the heat to the screen for defrosting. Overriding this heating system is an independent fresh-air inlet for the driver and passenger. As with the ventilator control there are two levers, the upper one regulating the flow of air to the screen and the lower one to the leg area. By suitable balancing of the fresh air and heating controls, comfort is afforded over a wide range of climatic conditions.

Wide, front-hinged doors with a large opening angle make entry very easy, and there is no complication when the hood is raised. The seat backs hinge forward to permit easy stowage of luggage in the space behind the seats. The folding top can be raised and lowered quickly and with very little effort by one person. It is fixed by a quick-action clamp on each side where the pillar joins the screen top rail. When folded, the hood nestles in a recess and is covered by a flush-fitting canvas cover to give a very neat appearance. Each door has a wind-down frameless window without separate ventilating panels. In the open position some wind buffeting is experienced if these windows are lowered, but in their raised position protection is extremely good.

When the hood is raised it is very free from drumming even at maximum speed and the wind noise is negligible. There is a high-pitched whistle if a side window is opened. Even at speeds approaching the maximum, the noise transmitted from the engine with the hood up is such as not to

A real bonnetful, yet the items requiring frequent attention are reasonably accessible. The vacuum booster for the brakes can be seen beyond the oilbath air cleaner

Mercedes-Benz 190SL . . .

interfere with normal conversation. The luggage locker lid, like the bonnet, is held in the raised position by a manually fixed stay; it is opened with a key, but is self-locking when closed. A wind-up jack is provided with a single mounting point at each side of the chassis.

Under the bonnet the engine compartment is a little crowded, but all points which need regular attention are readily accessible. From our experience the dipstick would not need to be used often, for the car used but two pints of oil throughout the 1,200 miles. One particularly noteworthy feature is the use of individual fuses for each electrical circuit so that any fault can be traced quickly. On the debit side there are as many as 34 points which need regular greasing or replenishing with oil.

The 190SL was approached with keen expectation, knowing the reputation of its makers for quality and workmanship. It proved to be fast and tireless, exhilarating to drive, and was obviously created with long distance, comfortable travel in mind rather than competition work. Naturally its powers of acceleration do not approach those of the larger engined SL (Super Leicht) type. In all aspects of handling and control it is certainly one of the safest cars tested by this journal.

MERCEDES-BENZ 190SL

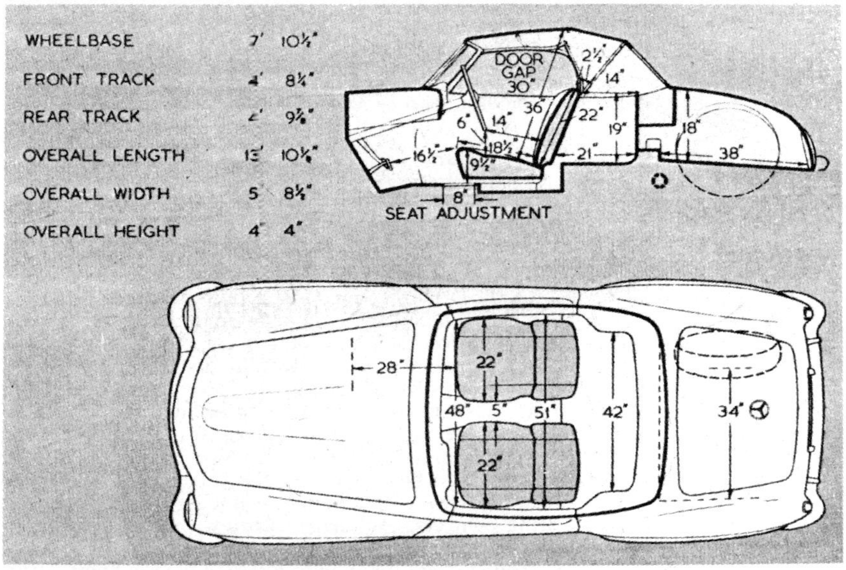

Measurements in these ½in to 1ft scale body diagrams are taken with the driving seat in the central position of fore and aft adjustment and with the seat cushions uncompressed

PERFORMANCE

ACCELERATION: from constant speeds. Speed Range, Gear Ratios and Time in sec.

M.P.H.	3.89 to 1	5.92 to 1	9.02 to 1	13.7 to 1
10—30 ..	—	7.5	4.5	4.0
20—40 ..	11.9	7.2	4.9	—
30—50 ..	11.7	7.2	—	—
40—60 ..	11.3	6.9	—	—
50—70 ..	12.9	6.7	—	—
60—80 ..	15.2	—	—	—
70—90 ..	18.4	—	—	—

From rest through gears to:

M.P.H.	sec.
30	4.9
50	10.3
60	13.3
70	17.5
80	24.4
90	33.9

Standing quarter mile, 17.8 sec.

SPEEDS ON GEARS:

Gear	M.P.H. (normal and max.)	K.P.H. (normal and max.)
Top (mean)	106.8	172
(best)	109.2	176
3rd	57—76	92—122
2nd	36—47	58—76
1st	23—31	37—50

TRACTIVE RESISTANCE: 39 lb per ton at 10 M.P.H.

TRACTIVE EFFORT:

	Pull (lb per ton)	Equivalent Gradient
Top	219	1 in 10.1
Third	381	1 in 5.8
Second	585	1 in 3.8

BRAKES (in neutral at 30 m.p.h.):

Efficiency	Pedal Pressure (lb)
56 per cent	25
72 per cent	50
91 per cent	65

FUEL CONSUMPTION:

22.4 m.p.g. overall for 1,187 miles (12.6 litres per 100 km).
Approximate normal range 20-26 m.p.g. (14.1 to 10.9 litres per 100 km).
Fuel, premium.

WEATHER:

Air temperature 50 deg F, dry, cross-wind 5-10 m.p.h., concrete surface.
Acceleration figures are the means of several runs in opposite directions.
Tractive effort and resistance obtained by Tapley meter.
Model described in *The Autocar* of 12 February, 1954.

SPEEDOMETER CORRECTION: M.P.H.

Car speedometer	10	20	30	40	50	60	70	80	90	100
True speed	12	22	31	42	52	63	73	82	92	102

DATA

PRICE (basic), including heater, with roadster body, **£1,930.**
British purchase tax, **£966 7s.**
Total (in Great Britain), **£2,896 7s.**

ENGINE: Capacity: 1,897 c.c. (115.74 cu in).
Number of cylinders: 4.
Bore and stroke: 85 × 83.6 mm (3.35 × 3.30in).
Valve gear: single overhead camshaft.
Compression ratio: 8.5 to 1.
B.H.P.: 120 (gross) at 5,700 r.p.m. (B.H.P. per ton laden 97).
Torque: 107 lb ft at 2,800 r.p.m.
M.P.H. per 1,000 r.p.m. on top gear, 18.4.

WEIGHT (with 5 gals fuel): 21¾ cwt (2,425 lb).
Weight distribution (per cent): F, 51; R, 49.
Laden as tested: 24¾ cwt (2,761 lb).
Lb per c.c. (laden): 1.46.

BRAKES: Type: hydraulic, with A.T.E. vacuum servo.
Drum dimensions: F, 9.05in diameter; 2.56in wide.
R, 9.05in diameter; 2.36in wide.
Lining area: 165 sq in (133 sq in per ton laden).

TYRES: 6.40—13in.
Pressures cold (lb sq in): F, 24; R, 25.5 (normal). F, 27; R, 28.5 (for fast driving).

TANK CAPACITY: 14.3 Imperial gallons (including 1.3 gals reserve).
Oil sump, 7 pints.
Cooling system, 16 pints (including heater).

TURNING CIRCLE: 34½ft (L and R).
Steering wheel turns (lock to lock): 3½.

DIMENSIONS: Wheelbase: 7ft 10½in.
Track: F, 4ft 8¼in; R, 4ft 9⅞in.
Length (overall): 13ft 10⅛in.
Height: 4ft 4in.
Width: 5ft 8½in.
Ground clearance: 6⅛in.

ELECTRICAL SYSTEM: 12-volt; 56 ampère-hour battery.
Head lights: Double dip; 42 watt bulbs.

SUSPENSION: Front, wishbone and coil with telescopic dampers and anti-roll bar. Rear, coil and single low pivot swing axle with telescopic dampers.

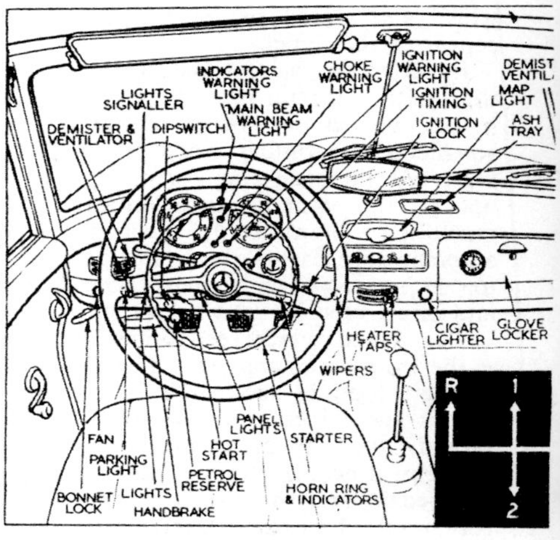

MERCEDES 190 SL ROAD TEST

BODY LEAN IS QUITE NOTICEABLE, DURING TEST AT RIVERSIDE RACEWAY, BUT CAR STICKS LIKE GLUE, DUE TO FINE SUSPENSION.

THE MERCEDES 190SL is a car in a class by itself. There are automobiles that will match its price, quality, performance and handling, but none have these qualities combined so as to be classed as a direct competitor to the 190SL.

The SL designation (an abbreviation for Super Licht, which translated means super light) is a misnomer as the curb weight of the "SL" is 2,515 lbs. and the weight of the car as tested was over 3,000 lbs. Not exactly "super licht."

Technically, the 190 is a sports car, actually it is a touring car, and a good one. Its four-cylinder engine is the smoothest one we've seen and a person driving the 190 for the first time would not be able to determine how many cylinders the engine had without being told, or looking under the hood, the engine is that smooth.

The test was made on the car in two sessions, about two weeks apart, and we found the car to be more enjoyable the second time than it was the first.

The car is powered by a four-cylinder, single overhead cam engine of 116 cubic inches. Rated horsepower is 120 at 5,700 rpm, torque is 107 ft/lbs. at 2,700 rpm. The car is surprisingly quick for the power-to-weight ratio and could be an indication that the engine is slightly underrated. Theoretical safe cruising speed with the 3.9-to-1 rear-end gear ratio, which is standard for the car, is about 80 mph and therefore gives a good safety margin for long engine life.

An integral body-frame construction is used and independent front suspension with unequal length wishbones and coil springs. The rear suspension is the well proven low pivot swing axle setup with coil springs as used on all Mercedes cars in some form. The transmission is a four-speed manual, floor-mounted shift unit with synchromesh on all four gears.

Quality of the car, as mentioned on the previous pages, is evident to a degree that is almost unknown in modern automobile construction. It is not just surface quality, but can be seen everywhere on the car. Upholstery, paint, fit of the body panels, trim, chrome, accessories and the way things work.

Impressive as this quality is, the roadability is even more outstanding. Winding roads are actually fun to drive in the 190. Rough roads are smoothed out, due to the magnificent suspension, and the integral body-frame construction makes for a rattle-free ride, even on the roughest roads.

Driving through mountains, the heavy steering becomes

Mercedes Test Data

Test Car: Mercedes 190SL roadster
Basic Price: $5,547.46 (delivered as equipped)
Engine: Four-cylinder, single overhead cam, 115.74 cubic inches, liquid-cooled.
Compression Ratio: 8.5-to-1
Horsepower: 120 @ 5,700 rpm
Torque: 107 ft/lbs. @ 2,700 rpm
Curb Weight: 2515 lbs.
Transmission: Four-speed, floor shift with synchromesh on all four gears
Acceleration: 0-30 mph 4.4 seconds, 0-45 mph 8.0 seconds, 0-60 mph 14.2 seconds
Speedometer Corrections: Indicated 30, 45 and 60 mph was actual 28.4, 42.8 and 57 mph
Gas Mileage: 25 mpg at steady 60 mph cruising, 19.6 mpg on tank which included acceleration runs and fast trip through mountains to test cornering

SINGLE OVERHEAD CAM four-cylinder engine is modified version of the 190 sedan engine. In the SL it has 8.5-to-1 compression ratio, dual two-throat Solex side draft carburetors and is rated at 120 bhp at 5,700 rpm. Engine is extremely smooth, for four cylinders.

STABILIZER LINK, in white, is attached to chassis by rubber bushings and by a yoke to the swing axle center section. Its purpose is to give a triangulated (lateral) mounting to the vertical post which supports the low pivot-bracket for the swing axle assembly.

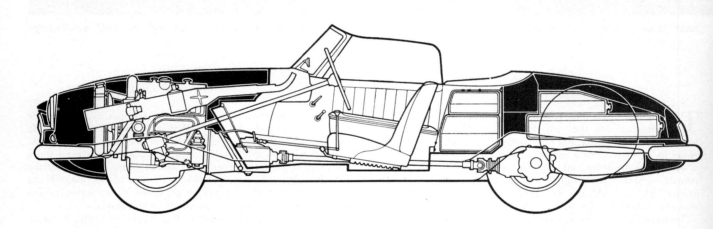

LINE DRAWING of 190SL shows location of major components. The 190 is available with either retracting soft top, hard top, or both.

INSTRUMENT PANEL layout is both attractive and practical. Instruments are placed in front of driver where they should be, and all controls are within easy reach. Seats are adjustable fore and aft and seat backs have three positions of angularity, suiting most occasions.

TUBULAR SHOCK ABSORBER is attached to the steering tie rod to absorb road shock in the steering mechanism before it gets to steering wheel. Crankcase and bell housing are aluminum, brackets behind shock absorber are rear engine mount supports.

FRONT A-ARMS are not unusual. They are of unequal lengths and inner pivot axis are parallel. End of stabilizer bar can be seen and just barely noticeable are some of the small holes in the lower edge of the backing plate to allow water to escape.

evident. The steering is actually a little stiff at all times but is not too noticeable until sharp bends are encountered. This "heavy" feel may be due in part to the shock absorber attached to the tie rod, which is put there to absorb road shock before it gets to the steering wheel.

While the car has no difficulty climbing hills, the moderate power does not allow the driver to "power slide" corners as he might in a sports car, especially going uphill. On downhill corners, the car will take them in its stride but a great amount of tire squeal is noticed in the process.

The 190 seems to display its handling qualities best on long sweeping bends or over extremely rough roads. On freeways it is no different than a multitude of other vehicles.

Acceleration tests were the average of runs made in opposite directions, keeping the tach below the rev limit indicated by the manufacturer. 0-to-30 mph 4.4 seconds. 0-to-45 mph 8.0 seconds and 0-to-60 mph 14.2 seconds. No top speed runs were made.

Economy during the test showed the car to be better than most cars, but not as good as the factory claims. For a short distance at a steady 60 mph we did manage to get 25 mpg but the overall tank test resulted in a mileage of 19.6. It should be noted here, in all fairness, that during this tankful the acceleration tests were conducted with two people in the car, and a very fast trip through the hills was made to check handling (using the shift lever liberally), none of which is conducive to economy.

The 190SL should not be promoted in this country as an economy car anyway. Advertising should emphasize quality, handling and comfort, with adequate performance and economy a bonus effect.

Driver's and passenger's comfort are well attended to. The individual bucket seats are comfortable, and wide enough to suit a person of wide girth. The test crew found that safety belts would be a welcome addition to the car (over and above their value to the occupants in case of impact) to help hold the driver and passenger in place on winding roads.

Both seats are adjustable, fore and aft, and have three positions for the angle of the backrest. Seating position is a sort of compromise between a domestic car and the feet-straight-out attitude of most sports cars.

It might be of interest to note here that while the factory description for this car is a roadster (like the new 300SL roadster) it is actually a convertible coupe by U.S. standard, complete with folding top and roll-down windows.

Noise level at all times is low, and is achieved by precision engineering and much attention to sound insulation.

On examining the trunk space, it was found to be adequate and actually is rather large if the car is to be considered by sports car standards. In addition to the space in the rear compartment, there is a large area behind the seats that could hold almost as much as the trunk. An interesting feature was noticed, when the car was put on a hoist so we could examine the underside, and that was the presence of a second tire well, below the trunk floor. This is not noticeable from the top as a cover is placed over the well to make the trunk floor flat. Two spares could be carried, possibly for international touring, where service is at a minimum.

Speaking of service, included with each car is a first-rate owner's manual, a complete parts list for the car, and a listing of all service and parts stores for Mercedes Benz throughout the world. This could prove invaluable if stranded in the wilds.

Who would buy the 190SL? Only those who appreciate quality, its compact size and/or a person who wants better than average handling. The desire for these features has to be strong enough to lay out over $5,000 for them, too.

Those who wouldn't buy the car probably would choose another make with more performance, or one for less money, and be willing to sacrifice these qualities for what *they* consider to be more important. •

ROAD TEST 300-SL ROADSTER

IT HAS BEEN almost three years since we were fortunate enough to have one of the very first Mercedes-Benz 300-SL coupes for testing purposes. Since that time, only very minor changes had been made in the model—at least, until the roadster model was announced last summer.

The new car is designated by the factory as the 300-SL roadster and should not be called the 300-SLR, which is, of course, the straight-8 factory racing type. Actually the new body is a true convertible coupe with frameless wind-up windows and a folding cloth top.

Mechanically, the detail changes made in some of the later (but now discontinued) hard-top coupes are included in the convertible: principally a higher compression ratio and the so-called competition camshaft. The multi-tube frame has been extensively redesigned to retain its original rigidity and yet allow lower-cut doors of conventional front-hinged pattern. The rear suspension is the low-pivot type, as now standardized on all Mercedes passenger cars. The net result is a more powerful but somewhat heavier car. Accordingly, the standard axle ratio for the American market has been changed from 3.64 to 3.89:1.

Since comparisons are bound to be made between the present and the previous model, these figures will help.

PERFORMANCE COMPARISON

	roadster	coupe
Year built	1957	1954
Weight (no fuel)	2920	2710
Test weight, lb	3375	3060
Axle ratio	3.89	3.64
Compression ratio	9.50	8.55
Bhp	250	240
Torque, lb-ft	228	202
Acceleration, sec.		
0-40	4.3	4.0
0-60	7.0	7.4
0-80	11.6	11.6
0-100	18.9	17.2
ss 1/4, avg.	15.5	15.2

Incidentally, all our tests were made with the top up and windows closed. Not incidentally, one of the nation's best drivers was at the wheel. Paul O'Shea, National point champion for 1957 and well known for his proficiency at the wheel of a 300-SL, was our test driver.

The car itself was in perfect tune and required no attention at any time, whereas our 1955 test car had required a plug change. The shift from 3rd to 4th had a tendency to crunch

Huge induction pipes: trademark of Mercedes fuel injection system.

Mechanical top can be erected with one hand in a matter of seconds.

a little and O'Shea felt that the control lever needed a slight adjustment on its serrations. Conditions at the test strip we use were almost perfect, and it was a terrible temptation to try just one high-speed run, but we had promised the Holly-

Turn right at the Valkyrie, and drive straight to Valhalla

wood Mercedes-Benz people that we would not. Obviously the car will exceed 130 mph at 6200 rpm. The official factory data for top-speed capability are as follows:

AXLE RATIO	MAXIMUM MPH
3.25	155
3.42	150
3.64	146
3.89	137
4.11	129

We spent two days at the wheel of this magnificent machine, with enjoyment because of the car's combination of qualities but with some trepidation over the responsibility of its six-figure valuation. The ride is somewhat firm around town but improves considerably if the standard Michelin-X tires are kept at 24 pounds per square inch. However, control feels a little mushy at this pressure; we much preferred 30 psi in front and 32 psi at the rear. This combination was perfect for high-speed cruising, the slower steering now supplied (3 turns lock to lock) feeling much safer than before. The former ratio of 2 turns was slightly heavy at low speed and much too sensitive at high speed for the average driver.

With the low-pivot rear suspension and more adhesive tires, the car handles beautifully under all conditions. This is a tremendous improvement over the hard-top models, which had a tendency to oversteer rather violently if pressed too hard. The roadster appears to be absolutely neutral-steering, though eventually the rear end will break away rather suddenly.

The car is very easy to drive and to control. The seats hold you firmly in place, but the rear edge of the cushion feels a little harsh after an hour or two. The steering wheel is placed very far forward, which some, but not all, drivers will like. The clutch is light and the gearbox control is almost ideal. The servo-ring synchronizers sometimes make selection of first gear a little trying, and a 6-foot driver may object to hitting his elbow on the seat when pulling the lever into 2nd gear. The brakes are tremendous, as before, with Al-Fin drums, a vacuum booster and 257 square inches of lining area.

The engine idles steadily at 800 rpm and is one of the most flexible units ever. Neither the indirect gears nor the engine are entirely silent when pushing hard, yet you can tootle through town smoothly and quietly at 20 mph in high gear, if you wish.

While the price asked seems almost astronomical, there is no doubt that the 300-SL roadster is a truly great dual-purpose sports car, equally at home in traffic and the open road, or on the track.

ROAD & TRACK ROAD TEST NO. 154

MERCEDES-BENZ 300-SL ROADSTER

SPECIFICATIONS
List price	$10,970
Wheelbase, in.	94.5
Tread, f/r	55.0/57.0
Tire size	6.70-15
Curb weight, lb	3075
distribution, %	48.5/51.5
Test weight	3375
Engine	6 cyl, sohc
Bore & stroke	3.35 x 3.46
Displacement, cu in.	182.8
cu cm.	2996
Compression ratio	9.50
Horsepower	250
peaking speed	6200
equivalent mph	128
Torque, lb-ft	228
peaking speed	5000
equivalent mph	103
Gear ratios, overall	
4th	3.89
3rd	5.40
2nd	7.66
1st	13.0

CALCULATED DATA
Lb/hp (test wt)	13.5
Cu ft/ton mile	91.6
Engine revs/mile	2920
Piston travel, ft/mile	1685
Mph @ 2500 ft/min.	89.0

PERFORMANCE, Mph
Top speed	130
3rd (6500)	96
2nd (6500)	68
1st (6500)	40
see chart for shift points	
Mileage range	15/21 mpg

ACCELERATION, Sec.
0-30 mph	2.9
0-40 mph	4.3
0-50 mph	5.7
0-60 mph	7.0
0-70 mph	9.0
0-80 mph	11.6
0-90 mph	14.8
0-100 mph	18.9
Standing start ¼ mile, avg.	15.5
best run	15.1

TAPLEY DATA, Lb/ton
4th	290 @ 92 mph
3rd	430 @ 73 mph
2nd	600 @ 55 mph
1st	off scale
Total drag at 60 mph, 102 lb	

SPEEDOMETER ERROR
Indicated	Actual
30 mph	29.9
40 mph	39.0
50 mph	47.9
60 mph	57.7
70 mph	67.5
80 mph	77.2
90 mph	86.7
100 mph	95.1

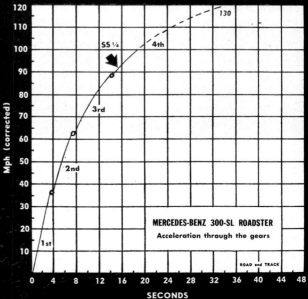

MERCEDES-BENZ 300-SL ROADSTER
Acceleration through the gears

SCI ROAD TEST:

MERCEDES-BENZ 190SL

Photos by Don Typond

Generously lent to the staff for over a month by Wolfgang Robinow, the 190 SL served faithfully and faultlessly.

THE STOCKY MAN in the immaculate white shop coat patted the hood of the immaculate black convertible. "Take it up to six t'ousand in all gears — you have to wind it up for full power," he said in an accent redolent of *bier, wurst* and other forms of *gemutlichkeit.* "Don't worry," he added, "you won't break it."

We did wind it up to 6000 rpm in every gear but Fourth and we didn't break it. Daimler-Benz products have a worldwide reputation for absolute reliability and the reputation is deserved if the 190SL which we were privileged to treat as our own for a full month was any criterion.

Everything about the 190SL is designed to coddle its possessor. From a top that can be raised or lowered with one hand while cruising at 30 mph down the parkway to its rock-solid steering at *any* speed, there isn't one piece of shoddy or make-do workmanship in this neat sports-touring machine. Mind you, this is no racing car — though it could probably be made into one if the factory were inclined to peel off a few hundred pounds in weight, close up the ratios in the gearbox and stiffen up the springs and shocks. True, 190SLs *have* on occasion distinguished themselves in competition, Macau and the Nassau Islander's races for example, but these are rare instances and the circumstances involved could hardly be considered normal.

No, it's no racing car but it comes near to being the ideal car for going to and coming from races — which is just exactly what we used it for. At least one of these trips was an eleven-hour haul each way and the others ranged from six down to two hours. Further, virtually every sort of of weather — springtime in Virginia to a minor hurricane in southern Maryland — was encountered and not once did we get that aching fatigue handed out by more prosaic transportation under similar circumstances.

Lest we be accused of being too lyrical, it might be pointed out that others who have lived with the 190SL share our opinions. One such is well qualified to talk. He is "Red" Byron, *quondam* professional race driver of considerable note in both pure racing cars and modified stocks and now a shop owner, foreign car dealer and *scuderia* chief. Red has owned a 190SL for some three years and his enthusiasm for the car as a method of getting from here to there approaches reverence. During this time he has averaged well over 20 thousand miles a year and during all of this has had to adjust the carburetion once, change plugs twice, replace tires once and fit a new top once. The last item was added primarily because he preferred tan material to the original black that came with the car.

In the past many people have complained bitterly about the two mammoth twin-choke Solex carburetors hung on the side of the engine. Rather than feed a separate port per throat as might be expected from such a set-up, these are compound units, one throat in each case acting as a secondary carburetor for high speed operation. Both throats feed into one large manifold port which in turn feeds two ports in the head which is a true four-port. This has caused a lot of comment from armchair purists who would prefer to see a four-port be a four-port all the way through. Byron differs with this opinion and we're inclined now to agree with him.

"It would be different if this were a competition machine, but it's not," he says. "This is a touring machine and it's set up that way. Most people who get a 190SL feel immediately that they have to fool around with those carburetors and as a result they completely ruin the setting. There's only one way to do it — have a good Solex man set them up and then leave them strictly alone. The only playing around you should do is to move the cut-in point for the secondaries to the speed you want. After that you don't touch them."

When we first picked up our test car from Wolfgang Robinow, Daimler-Benz executive with the New York office of the company — it was his personal car — the carbs were not right and Mr. Robinow told us they weren't. He suggested we take it to the service department and have Otto Vogeler, their service chief, make things right.

Before servicing, the car would barely touch 95 miles an hour and there was a most disconcerting feeling that the throttle was sticking at that point. Actually it was an air velocity increase as the

primary butterflies closed that was the villain. This increase actually opened the secondaries a little further as the throttle pedal was backed off and there was a momentary increase in revs. When Otto got through, however, there was none of this. Instead, there seemed to be no limit to the revs in the lower three gears and when the throttle was backed off the revs dropped immediately. It was like having an entirely different engine. At one point we actually edged the somewhat optimistic speedometer past the 115 mark, a point which can probably best be correctly pronounced as 109 miles an hour. With a little more space it might have squeezed a mile or two more into the hour.

Which brings us to the only real complaint we could find on the car. In a product that otherwise stands head and shoulders above other touring machinery for quality it seems strange that a full six-miles-an-hour discrepancy would be allowed in the speedometer. With everything else so letter-perfect this relatively minor fault becomes almost glaring. True, it does allow one to apparently nudge the legal speed limit and still avoid summonses but for all other purposes it requires a sort of constant mental conversion as though it had been calibrated in kilos instead of miles. Owners who are sticklers for accuracy, however, can send the instrument to VDO in Detroit, the American branch of the German concern that makes it, and have them insert a measure of pessimism to bring it down to a point of reasonable accuracy.

About the only other complaint we could dredge up in the space of a month was one that only a purist would find. For our personal reasons we felt that the ratios in the gearbox were a bit widely spaced for our liking, especially between Third and Fourth gears. Top speed in Third, with the engine literally screaming was 75 or a little better which meant that really quick passing of a vehicle moving along at 60 or better was out, at least if we wanted to downshift to Third for the job. A ratio that provided another ten miles an hour or even fifteen in Third would be welcome. Second gear with a top of 50 mph is about ideal and low is good for anything from 30 mph down to pulling stumps and climbing walls. But that 30 to 35 mph differential between Third and top gear bothered us personally. It showed up more under circumstances that would normally not be encountered by the average owner, however. On the road it was no bother, long smooth, fast passes were made in every instance with ease. On all other counts the gearbox scores perfectly. It's butter-smooth, fast and the lever is exactly where you can reach it with a minimum of grabbing.

Everything else about the car's handling was impeccable. Daimler-Benz engineers have long felt that a car should have a small understeer tendency built in that gradually decreases up to a point then, through a fairly long transitional period of dead neutrality, passes on to a gentle oversteer. While none of this can actually be experienced by the driver its effect can be readily felt. Up to about 60 or 70 mph one must crank the wheel into a corner. As the speed rises the car has a tendency to move slightly sideways with almost an equal slip from both bow and stern — actually the true slip angle is a bit more at front than rear at this point — and then as more poke is fed to the throttle the rear end starts to move out. This last can be aggravated by horsing the throttle, a practice not recommended with the old 300SL coupes or even the new 300SL roadsters. All in all it's a very safe feeling — you know what's happening and when and if things get a bit disconcerting it's easy enough to back off and correct.

Another thing about the 190SL's handling is it's feeling of *wanting* to cruise fast. Delightful as the car is at low speeds, the upper reaches of the speed range become sheer sensual pleasure. Everything lightens up and the whole car seems to live. The steering becomes seemingly lighter and more positive if such a thing is possible; throttle response gets a pinpoint accuracy and, strangely enough wind-blast lessens in the cockpit. As with all Daimler-Benz products the builders know that their cars are strong and they don't have to announce the fact with a ripping exhaust note. So it is with the 190SL; at low speeds there is at most a gentle swish and at high speeds there is a hard machine-like hum and that's all. The hum is very much a part of the feeling of liveness mentioned above.

John Christy

Leaving Lime Rock's famous ess-bend, the gleaming black roadster grips the road firmly, the swing axle's presence evident only to those outside the car.

Wearing a crash helmet belies tremendous confidence which the stable M-B inspires.

SPEED IN EVERY LINE: The appearance of the Roadster will please the most severe critic of modern styling.

AMERICAN ROAD TEST
The Mercedes-Benz 300SL Roadster

by Gregor Grant

WITHOUT a doubt, one of the world's most important prestige cars is the Mercedes-Benz 300SL Roadster, a development of the world-famous "gullwing" with which Daimler-Benz successfully re-entered motor racing in 1952. As a luxurious fast-tourer it has a rather special appeal to connoisseurs who do not count cost when it comes to acquiring the vehicle of their choice. It is a car which possesses near-racing car performance, with almost unbelievable tractability in normal traffic. Its lines will please the most harsh critic of modern styling, and it has an individuality which immediately commands attention, even on hard-bitten Broadway, or sophisticated Fifth Avenue.

During my visit to New York, Larry Richards of Mercedes-Benz offered me the loan of his own Roadster, which had been used as a demonstrator for several months. Naturally I accepted, and in due course took over temporary ownership of the beautifully finished light blue car. Apart from the fitting of a slightly higher-lift camshaft, the 300SL was standard in every way, having the U.S.A. rear-axle ratio of 3.89 to 1.

This Mercedes-Benz offers an entirely new conception of motoring. The engine is so smooth and effortless that it is difficult to imagine that there is over 240 b.h.p. waiting to be unleashed under that sleek bonnet. Beyond a highly satisfying purr from the exhaust, and the joyous whine of gears invariably associated with the more expensive type of motor-car, the 300SL is completely silent. Bodywork does not have a single rattle anywhere; windows wind up or down on perfectly balanced mechanism; the top is surely the finest example of convertible equipment to be found anywhere. Absurdly simple to raise or lower, when stowed it disappears under a hinged panel behind the seat squab. The facia panel will please the most fastidious, with its fairly simple treatment and easy-to-read instruments. Every detail has been thought out; for example the "horn" ring actuates the traffic blinkers, the warning instrument itself being controlled by a flick-switch on the steering column. The dash is padded as are the sun-visors; on the scuttle beside the passenger there is even the refinement of a combined ash-tray and lighter.

Comfort has been studied to the nth degree, and I would like to compliment the genius who designed and made those wonderful seats. Hundreds of miles can be reeled off without the slightest sign of discomfort; arm-rests are exactly in the right position, and even with the side-windows down, there is no evidence of back-draughts. Visibility is excellent, although a panoramic mirror of larger dimensions would be more desirable in a country where "speed-cop-spotting" has of necessity been brought to a fine art. The outside mirror is useful in traffic lanes, and is of the streamlined pattern introduced by Daimler-Benz and marketed in Great Britain as the Walpress Continental Speed Mirror.

Being a sporting vehicle of great character, one does not think in terms of automatic transmission. The all-synchromesh gearbox is a delight to use, and is so efficient in operation that it is virtually impossible to beat the synchromesh mechanism. Brakes are probably the highest development of the drum pattern, and the booster or servo makes them very light to use. There was, however, a slight tendency to judder when braking from high speeds, but this may have been a sign that adjustment was required. An inclination to pull to the right was cured by equalizing tyre pressures; in point of fact, the 300SL is particularly sensitive to pressures. The wheels were shod with Michelin "X" covers, and there was a warning on the speedometer that on no account was 125 m.p.h. to be exceeded. Presumably racing tyres would be necessary if one wished to achieve the 136 m.p.h. of which the car is easily capable with the 3.89 to 1 axle. I understand that 155 m.p.h. is achievable with a 3.25 to 1 ratio, and I recall that John Bolster managed to get over 140 m.p.h. with the standard European 3.64 to 1 axle, in the 1955 "gull-wing".

I can state quite categorically that driving the 300SL requires experience of fast cars. Everything is achieved with so little fuss, that one can approach bends far faster than is realized, and cruise at very high speeds indeed quite unknowingly. Although the car possesses great road adhesion, and can be cornered at very high speeds, any sudden "ham-handedness" can quite easily provoke rear-end breakaway. The correct word for driving the Mercedes-Benz

STUDIED REFINEMENT: The facia panel is both simple and elegant: the top disappears beneath the hinged flap behind the seat squab. The dashboard and sun visors are heavily padded.

Specification and Performance Data

Car tested: Mercedes-Benz 300SL Roadster. Approximate price in U.S.A. $11,000.

Engine: Six cylinders, 85 x 88 mm. (2,996 c.c.), single o.h.c. 8.55 to 1 compression ratio, 240 b.h.p. at 6,100 r.p.m. Bosch direct injection, Bosch ignition (coil and distributor). Cooling system includes heat exchanger.

Transmission: Single dry-plate clutch with steel reinforced inserts. Four-speed all-synchromesh gearbox, ratios 1, 1.39, 1.97 and 3.34 to 1. Reverse, 2.73 to 1. Central remote gear lever. Hypoid final drive.

Chassis: Welded multi-tubed triangular frame. I.f.s. by unequal length wishbones, helical springs and anti-roll bars; i.r.s. by swing axles (helical springs). Fichtel-Sachs dampers. D-B recirculating ball steering. Bolt-on pierced wheels with 6.50 x 15 ins. tyres. Hydraulic brakes (2ls in front) with bimetal turbo drums and vacuum servo operation.

Equipment: 12-volt lighting and starting (Bosch). Speedometer, tachometer, ammeter, oil, water and fuel gauges; clock, two-speed wipers with washer, flashing indicators, cigarette lighter, etc. Dual heating and ventilating equipment.

Dimensions: Wheelbase, 7 ft. 10½ ins.; track, front 4 ft. 7 ins., rear 4 ft. 9 ins.; overall length, 14 ft. 7 ins.; overall width, 5 ft. 10 ins.; turning circle, 38 ft.; ground clearance, 5 in.; weight (dry) 24 cwt.

Performance: Maximum speed (est.) 136 m.p.h.

Fuel consumption: 16 m.p.g. (U.S.).

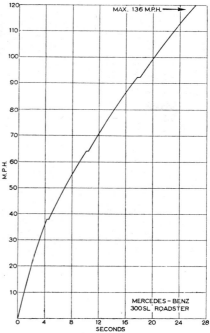

at all times is put so aptly by the French, *doucement*.

Steering is high-geared and very lively after one becomes used to the hydraulic damping. There is no reaction from bumps, but I did find that a slight shimmy developed at about 80 m.p.h., which was only momentary, and disappeared completely above that speed. The car is primarily a top-gear vehicle, but going through the gears will show a shapely tail to any of the products of Detroit. Wheelspin is completely absent, one of the merits of the very fine, low pivot-point swing-axle rear suspension—but it is so easy to leave a couple of wicked-looking black marks on the highway when making a really dashing getaway. The long-travel clutch is inclined to be awkward at first, but one soon becomes used to it.

One of the most exciting things about the 300SL is that the acceleration is practically constant up to 120 m.p.h. With this car, the engine torque is such that when one changes up, the machine still surges forward, and goes on accelerating in top gear till one heeds the 125 m.p.h. warning. The power is positively immense from about 3,000 r.p.m., when presumably the efficient Bosch fuel injection system really comes into its own. The absence of roar from the induction system is the only indication that a p.i. system is employed. There are no flat spots throughout the speed range, and the engine ticks over sweetly at about 500 r.p.m.

Accompanied by Mike Porter, the Koni importer in U.S.A., and formerly with the Reynolds Chain Co. as racing manager, I took the 300SL into the Catskill mountains in New York State. The roads in these parts are atrocious in places, with large potholes left by winter snow and ice. On several sections, big American cars were being driven at about 15 m.p.h., the suspension receiving a tremendous battering. The Mercedes-Benz could be driven at well over 50 m.p.h., without a tremor. The independent springing was perfectly damped, and never at any time was there a sign of grounding. We found many sections which would have made ideal speed hill-climbs, but inevitably there was slow-moving traffic and double white lines on every bend. Whenever the dotted line was in our favour, a quick change to third and the 300SL streaked ahead of all other traffic.

It was the same story on the "thruway", where lanes of traffic move along at around the 60 m.p.h. limit. However, other drivers did not seem to object to being overtaken by a Mercedes-Benz. In spite of going well over the legal limit on many occasions, we never went through a radar trap and were not chased by the Highway Patrol—it must have been our lucky day!

Fuel consumption was not inordinately high for such a fast and powerful car, the average being about 16 m.p. U.S. gallon, giving a range of around 460 miles with the reserve tankage, at 60-70 m.p.h. cruising. The lights for U.S.A. are nothing like as powerful as those

Acceleration Graph

used in Europe, owing to rigid regulations regarding bulb wattage.

The "Mexico" station-searching radio was excellent, but oddly enough one could hear much better with the top down. With all-weather equipment raised, wind noise was emphasized, and there was also a certain amount of flapping from the fabric. Heating and ventilation equipment is of the high standard associated with Unterturkheim; the instruments were more than usually accurate, although the fuel gauge gave some peculiar readings on occasion.

The bonnet is, of course, simply packed with engine, and shows the typical Daimler-Benz thoroughness in dealing with components and accessories. The power-unit has been virtually unchanged for several years; of 85 x 88 mm. (2,996 c.c.) the valves are operated from a single overhead camshaft. Power-output with 8.55 to 1 pistons is 240 b.h.p. at 6,100 r.p.m. The M 198 11 (9.5 to 1) gives 250 b.h.p. at 6,200 r.p.m.

Steering has been revised since the "gull-wing" was introduced, and now employs Daimler-Benz recirculating ball-type in place of the ZF assembly. The car is heavier than the earlier coupés, dry weight being about 24 cwt.

On the whole, driving this superb machine was an exhilarating experience. Only a race-bred machine could behave like the 300SL, and although there may be a few faster cars, it would be difficult to imagine anything else which could compete as regards sheer perfection of engineering and a remarkably high standard of finish. During the past few years, the famous "ringed three-pointed star" has become something rather more than a manufacturer's trade mark in U.S.A., and is associated at once with that aim of all who are concerned with the production of top-flight machinery—quality.

CORNERING ABILITY is very high. The 300SL is seen here on a country road at Ashokan Reservoir, near Phoenicia, N.Y.

ROAD TEST

MERCEDES 190-SL

A deluxe touring car for the quasi-sporting

To EVALUATE the Mercedes-Benz 190-SL properly, one must first put the car into its proper category.

First, this is not a sports car—as far as we know, no one has entered a 190-SL in a sports car race in several years.

Second, the factory calls it a roadster, and with wind-up windows this is very obviously a true convertible coupe, with the folding cloth top; and a perfectly normal, standard hard-top coupe body style as tested.

Third, for a 2-liter car, the 190-SL is certainly not particularly light—it weighs 2550 lb and, while that's not bad for a very deluxe convertible coupe, it's not light, let alone *super* light.

So, what is the 190-SL? With some considerable experience with it during the period of 5 years since its introduction, we can state unequivocally that this machine is one of the finest 2-seater coupes on the market today. The first production cars came into this country during the summer of 1955 and our first road test appeared in October of that year. A technical description of the car was carried as far back as the April 1954 R&T. As a tribute to the excellent all-around, well-balanced design, no really large changes have been made since our first test of the car. Minor changes in the rather complex carburetion system give slightly more torque lower down and the 3rd gear ratio was revised some time ago so that it would be more useful in traffic. Beginning in 1960 the optional hardtop was given a new shape—more in conformance with that of its larger running mate, the 300-SL. Other than that there have been no changes, nor will there be any changes for 1961.

Having put the 190-SL in its place, the question arises as to whether 5 years has made it any different to drive, or is there any difference in performance? For a quick answer, there is no difference in driving impressions or in performance.

Though we have driven several different 190-SL models since the original test, getting behind the wheel is always impressive. The steep price tag seems a little more plausible when one looks over the details and sees the

quality of this car's interior. The seats are quite firm, but very beautiful and well designed to give the best possible comfort on long runs. The instrument panel layout is somewhat unique and best described as typical of the marque—neither American-flamboyant nor sports-car-stark. A pair of large dials give road speed and engine rpm. They are well located and cowled to avoid reflections. Two small instruments are for engine temperature and fuel level while warning lights indicate such things as low oil pressure, generator not charging, choke on, direction signals on, and high beam. Two special controls merit attention; a hot-start knob which can be pulled out if the engine shows signs of being flooded, and a manual spark adjustment. This latter is not normally used, but it can be useful on those occasions when a tankful of low grade fuel is encountered (premium grade is recommended but the engine will run on regular in an emergency because of this control).

Our test car was still a little tight (1650 miles on the odometer) and while the steering felt natural for the make, the shift lever worked very stiffly. The lever is correctly placed and the synchromesh on all 4 gears could not be beaten, no matter how quickly the lever was moved. First is a very low gear and starts could be effected in 2nd gear if the car was barely rolling. However, 2nd gear starts from a dead stop are not recommended and, actually, are not too comfortable because this rather high output 4-cyl engine wasn't meant to lug at low rpm. Nevertheless, it will pull in high gear remarkably well; as a test we dropped down to 12 mph (only 650 rpm) and were able to move off smoothly by not using full throttle. This test also produces a fair amount of torque reaction or shake and, between 20 and 25 mph, a strange acoustical disturbance. The point is that this is, after all, a fairly large high performance 4, and driven properly, 3rd gear is always engaged at below 30 mph.

Likewise the performance of the 190-SL is a function of intelligent use of the gearbox. Driven vigorously through the gears it gets out and moves. A 0 to 60 acceleration time of 13.5 sec is not slow, even today. During the acceleration tests we used 6000 rpm as an absolute rev limit though the unit will go higher. Again, driven properly through the gears, it is difficult to tell that this is a 4, but there is some engine noise (but no vibration) at 4000 rpm and up. For most driving conditions a 4000 rpm limit gives more than enough performance, this corresponding to 32 mph in 2nd, 48 mph in 3rd and 74 mph in high.

On the highway an 80 mph cruising speed is extremely comfortable and well within the car's capabilities, both as to engine durability and roadability. (Note that the theoretical safe cruising speed is 84.5 mph at a piston speed of 2500 ft/min.) As a matter of fact, the Mercedes line of single overhead camshaft engines is designed for, and capable of, a continuous 6000 rpm—if one wanted to push that hard and had the Indianapolis track to use for the purpose. At any rate, the power peak and the true top speed very nearly coincide (5700 rpm and 105.5 mph). This indicates a well chosen compromise in gear ratio and one which, combined with the product's well known reputation for stamina, insures the car a long life—when driven as fast as the law allows.

The steering ratio requires 3.5 turns lock to lock and this is an excellent compromise for parking effort, quick control and easy high-speed cruising. The steering characteristic is moderate understeer and this feature makes for one of the best, and safest, high speed touring cars we know. Really vigorous corners at lower speeds produce fairly loud protests from the tires and the normal understeer changes to a neutral characteristic. There is some roll, but the angle is not excessive for a machine such as this, designed for safe high speed travel in comfort, and not for road-racing. In short, the riding and

handling qualities are excellent for the uses to which this car is suited.

The braking system is excellent, with a vacuum booster which is completely innocuous, yet gives a light pedal with a progressive action or feel that is readily controlled by the driver without conscious effort or special techniques. The drums are Al-fin and of small diameter (9.05 in., because of 13-in. wheels), but very wide linings give an ample 165 sq in. of lining surface. The parking brake is nearly concealed under the left hand side of the cowl, but is effective and convenient.

Fuel economy varies a great deal and exactly in accordance with driving methods. A low of 15 mpg was recorded during our performance tests and our best figure was 20 mpg, obtained at a steady cruising speed of 60-65 mph.

A fair criticism, we feel, can be made regarding the very large speedometer error quoted in the data panel. This latest car is definitely faster than our original test car and while it may be impressive to see the needle at 120 mph it seems to us that such optimism is hardly necessary in a car of this type and category. This error may possibly not be typical, as other published tests we have seen noted very little optimism in the instrument and one example even read slow.

Another criticism, which several 190-SL owner-friends specifically asked us to make, concerns the rubber boots which surround each rear universal joint (on each side of the differential). The Germans were the first to synthesize rubber but still seem reluctant to use one of the oil and ozone-proof materials such as Neoprene, Thiokol, or the like. The boots supplied fail in less than 2 years and if not noticed the differential runs dry—a very expensive failure which doesn't make for owner loyalty. The factory supplied boots should be replaced at least once a year to be on the safe side.

The list price of $5129 quoted in the data panel is a bare car; local taxes and license are extra, of course. Our test car had the expensive Becker Mexico radio, genuine leather upholstery and both tops. It lists for $5758, so equipped. This seems like, and certainly is, a lot of money. We could dwell at great length over the really superb quality that goes into the products of Mercedes-Benz and it would be true, but boring. The best way to determine value is to look the car over carefully, both inside and out, give it a good test drive, and form your own opinion.

We say it's well worth the money.

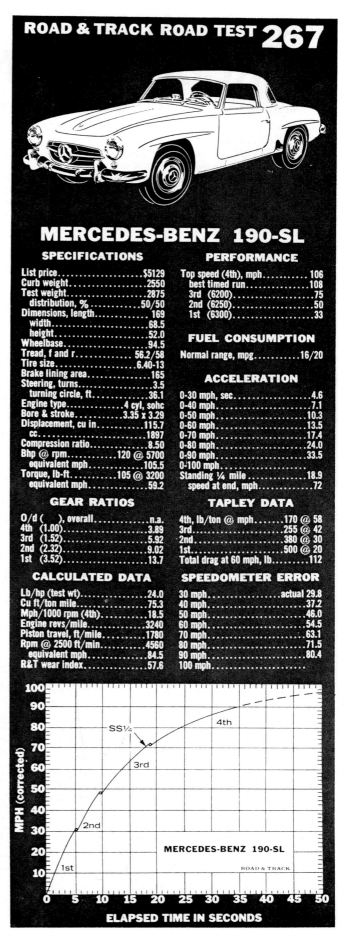

ROAD & TRACK ROAD TEST 267

MERCEDES-BENZ 190-SL

SPECIFICATIONS
List price	$5129
Curb weight	2550
Test weight	2875
distribution, %	50/50
Dimensions, length	169
width	68.5
height	52.0
Wheelbase	94.5
Tread, f and r	56.2/58
Tire size	6.40-13
Brake lining area	165
Steering, turns	3.5
turning circle, ft	36.1
Engine type	4 cyl, sohc
Bore & stroke	3.35 x 3.29
Displacement, cu in	115.7
cc	1897
Compression ratio	8.50
Bhp @ rpm	120 @ 5700
equivalent mph	105.5
Torque, lb-ft	105 @ 3200
equivalent mph	59.2

GEAR RATIOS
O/d ( ), overall	n.a.
4th (1.00)	3.89
3rd (1.52)	5.92
2nd (2.32)	9.02
1st (3.52)	13.7

CALCULATED DATA
Lb/hp (test wt)	24.0
Cu ft/ton mile	75.3
Mph/1000 rpm (4th)	18.5
Engine revs/mile	3240
Piston travel, ft/mile	1780
Rpm @ 2500 ft/min	4560
equivalent mph	84.5
R&T wear index	57.6

PERFORMANCE
Top speed (4th), mph	106
best timed run	108
3rd (6200)	75
2nd (6250)	50
1st (6300)	33

FUEL CONSUMPTION
Normal range, mpg	16/20

ACCELERATION
0-30 mph, sec	4.6
0-40 mph	7.1
0-50 mph	10.3
0-60 mph	13.5
0-70 mph	17.4
0-80 mph	24.0
0-90 mph	33.5
0-100 mph	
Standing ¼ mile	18.9
speed at end, mph	72

TAPLEY DATA
4th, lb/ton @ mph	170 @ 58
3rd	255 @ 42
2nd	380 @ 30
1st	500 @ 20
Total drag at 60 mph, lb	112

SPEEDOMETER ERROR
30 mph	actual 29.8
40 mph	37.2
50 mph	46.0
60 mph	54.5
70 mph	63.1
80 mph	71.5
90 mph	80.4
100 mph	

ROAD TEST/31-61
MERCEDES-BENZ 190SL
Fine for rallies and touring, it's not built for the race course.

ALTHOUGH WE'VE BEEN ENTHUSIASTIC over several Mercedes models and lavished well-deserved praise on them, the only way we find the 190SL even likeable is if we constantly rationalize that it is a prestige "personal car," no more, no less. A description for it that one knowledgeable person advanced was: "An old man's roadster." This, perhaps, is a bit severe but does accurately nail down the car's concept. It's been three years since we road-tested the 190SL and, though there have been many improvements, our impressions remained unaltered; it's a dull-but-expensive piece of transportation in sports car clothing. While this opinion may infuriate some proud 190 owners, we doubt it will even raise an eyebrow at the factory, as we suspect this is exactly what they had in mind.

One thing there's no question about — typical Mercedes-Benz quality of workmanship and materials have gone into the car. We may have some quarrel with design innovations, but it's put together as well as any machine we've ever driven. With a few annoying exceptions, it's every bit as durable as its price tag would dictate. Even microscopic examination of the entire car will fail to unearth anything but the most minor flaws. We could wish for a more distortion-free windshield, for example, but it wasn't really objectionable.

From a driving impression standpoint, let's start from the beginning. The thick doors open easy enough and provide wide access by sports car standards. The seat upholstery is beautiful to look at, but the pleasantry ends there. In a fairly new unit the leather smell is almost overpowering. One wag remarked, "Why doesn't someone tell them they have to *wash* the cows?" But our complaint was directed at the seating comfort, or lack of it. First, they're supposed to be bucket types, but have less lateral support for the torso than many bench designs. This is magnified by what seems to be an extra firmness over previous models. The seat backs have an elaborate and beautifully-chromed adjustable hinge, but damned if we could come up with a comfortable angle. This singular complaint was voiced by others of varied heights who sat in the car, and those over 5' 8" complained that the top of the windshield frame cut well into their field of vision. It should be emphasized that this is apparently a recent "improvement"; seating in earlier versions being vastly more comfortable.

As for the steering, it's rubbery in feel — typical of the entire Mercedes line. The wheel on the 190SL, however, seems big enough to mount on their express busses. Distance and angle are argumentative, but steering pressure was moderately light if the car was moving at all. While the basic instruments are well-placed and legible, the remainder of the dash will appeal to those that get their jollies knob-twisting and lever-pulling, or to a kid playing "rocket-ship." We suspect it takes the average owner two months with handbook open before he memorizes all the controls placed there in front of him.

The floor-mounted shift handle is relatively stiff, but comfortable to shift IF you use the nice-and-easy method. Otherwise, the baulk-ring synchronizers argue with you. This is especially true in the lower gears. Because of somewhat weak gradeability, the transmission ratios are widely-spaced. Another reason for the change from the closer-ratio box, circa 1955, was that M-B found many

PHOTOS: PAT BROLLIER

High-speed shenanigans over the brow of a reverse-camber hill (above and right) accented stability of the roadster, but it was a handful to hold on the road. Below, we pass through the Standing-¼-Mile. Times and speeds as recorded during acceleration runs were "sedate" but car has other attributes.

Left: "Get the manual, Gertrude. I've lost the choke again!" The control knobs are drawback in otherwise functional cockpit. Top, above, is excellent in both design and ease-of-operation.

Jam-packed engine compartment is due mainly to compound carburetion and its linkage and air-intake. Cast airbox has tendency to absorb under-hood heat and rarify fuel mixture in traffic but we encountered no difficulty during test.

Trunk is modest in size, but well finished. Workable complement of tools is supplied. Extreme left is the rubber-bushed mount suspending differential.

MERCEDES-BENZ 190SL

ROAD TEST/31-61

customers were lugging the engine in 2nd and 3rd speeds.

While critical to proper adjustment, the little 1.9-liter engine (we consider it little for a 2558-lb. car) is a workhorse. There's some valve-gear noise from the overhead-cam and rocker-arm setup, but things are otherwise very quiet in the engine compartment. We had, for years, engaged in verbal battles with factory reps over the tandem-staged Solex carburetors — concerned with the difficulty of getting the second stage to cut in correctly. This is stating the problem very simply, but let's just say that these carbs had many a tuner, including the factory mechanics, beating their heads against the wall. The majority of this problem seems to be eliminated. It still gets quite hot under the hood and that big cast airbox is still there, yet the car idles well in traffic, doesn't burn spark plugs, doesn't over-run, doesn't vapor-lock. In short, the engine runs well and starts easily under all types of *normal* operating conditions and holds its tune for a reasonably long period.

The brake department of the 190SL is first-rate. They still, however, use the same "soft" lining that absorbs heat faster than the finned-alloy drums can dissipate it, so that fade is easy to encounter if a cool-off period between hard applications isn't allowed. A booster was installed on our test car to relieve a normally firm pedal pressure required to actuate the wide brake shoes. The car stops straight and fast. There is some nose-dive, but not an annoying amount.

Despite the seats, ride is excellent. The car has a heavy "feel" that exceeds even its ample poundage. It rolls over freeways or back roads smoothly, transmitting an absolute minimum of bump deflection or surface deviations to those aboard. Where the car really shines is over dips or railroad tracks. These it negotiates in true Mercedes tradition. The same split-axle-housing setup used on the 220 series gives the car a full-independent suspension and the large coil springs at the four corners are rated ideally for maximum comfort.

While normal road handling of the 190SL is likeable and normal enough, any attempt at cornering at near competition velocities is *very* discouraging. The car develops a *strong* understeer and, if "dirt-tracked" to compensate, it just plain slides out.

There have been a few attempts by hardy souls to make the 190 raceworthy. Though considerable improvements can be made within the realm of "legality" to both handling and performance, it's an uphill battle that, at best, makes the car an also-ran in competition. It's widely used, however, as a rally machine and is very popular as such because of its ride and all-weather characteristics. In the latter department, the elaborate heater-ventilation system is very effective. Our test car was the soft-top model and the top is extremely well-made, can be operated with ease, and forms a tight seal that's impervious to the elements. Only Porsche makes one that's equal in quality.

The car's biggest success is its public impression, even though it's been around long enough to be fairly common in appearance. Driving a 190SL, you LOOK like a sport and we had to fight off one member of another Petersen publication who constantly wanted to borrow the car for girl-baiting tours down Sunset Blvd. Which, if we may say so, is indulging in what can be an already expensive hobby. However, as this same colleague put it: "You may not be king of the road in a 190SL but you sure *feel* like a prince of the parkway."

—*Jerry Titus*

TEST DATA

VEHICLE .... Mercedes-Benz   MODEL 190SL
PRICE (as tested) $5809 .... POE L.A.   OPTIONS .... FM Radio, WW tires, leather uph., bumper guards

ENGINE
Type: .... Iron-sleeve, alloy block, in-line, 4-cyl.
Head: .... Removable, alloy
Valves: .... OHC, rockers
Max. bhp .... 120 @ 5800 rpms
Max. Torque .... 137.4 lbs./ft. @ 3500 rpms
Bore .... 3.34 in. 85 mm.
Stroke .... 3.29 in. 83.6 mm.
Displacement .... 115.7 cu. in 1897 cc.
Compression Ratio .... 8.8 to 1
Induction System: .... 2 dual-throat, staged Solex carbs. Type 44PHH
Exhaust System: .... Cast manifold into single pipe
Electrical System: .... 12V Bosch single distributor

CLUTCH: .... single disc, dry   DIFFERENTIAL:
Diameter: .... N.A.   Ratio: .... 3.9 to 1
Actuation: .... Mechanical   Drive Axles (type) .... enclosed, swing offset pivot
TRANSMISSION: .... 4-speed D-B   STEERING: ... Recirculating ball sector
                        full-synchro   Turns Lock to Lock: 3½
Ratios: 1st .... 3.52 to 1   Turn Circle: .... 36 ft.
        2nd .... 2.32 to 1   BRAKES: .... Booster Brakes
        3rd .... 1.52 to 1   Drum Diameter .... 9 in.
        4th .... 1.0 to 1   Swept Area .... 163.88 sq. in.

CHASSIS:
Frame: .... Oval tube, single modified X
Body: .... Steel, semi-unit panels
Front Suspension: .... I.F.S. unequal arm, coilsprings, tube shocks
Rear Suspension: .... Split, enclosed swing, coilspring, tube shocks
Tire Size & Type: .... 6:40 x 13 Continental Ribord

WEIGHTS AND MEASURES
Wheelbase: .... 94.5 in.   Ground Clearance .... 7 in.
Front Track: .... 56.2 in.   Curb Weight .... 2558 lbs.
Rear Track: .... 58.0 in.   Test Weight .... 2833 lbs.
Overall Height .... 52 in.   Crankcase .... 4.5 qts.
Overall Width .... 68.5 in.   Cooling System .... 11 qts.
Overall Length .... 168 in.   Gas Tank .... 17.2 gals.

PERFORMANCE
0-30 .... 3.5 sec.   0-60 .... 12.0 sec.
0-40 .... 5.8 sec.   0-70 .... 16.1 sec.
0-50 .... 9.0 sec.   0-80 .... 21.5 sec.
Standing ¼ mile 21.5 sec. @ 80 mph   Top Speed (av. two-way run) 101 mph
Speed Error   30 40 50 60 70 80 90
Actual   31 39 50 58 68 78 88
Fuel Consumption Test: ...... 15 mpg   RPM Red-line .... 6000 rpm
Average .... 20 mpg   Speed Ranges in gears:
Recommended Shift Points   1st .... 0 to 30 mph
Max. 1st .... 28 mph   2nd .... 15 to 47 mph
Max. 2nd .... 45 mph   3rd .... 35 to 74 mph
Max. 3rd .... 70 mph   4th .... 48 to top mph
Brake Test: 74 Average % G. over 10 stops.
Fade encountered on 7th stop.

REFERENCE FACTORS:
Bhp. per Cubic Inch 1.03
Lbs. per bhp. 21.3
Piston Speed @ Peak rpm .... 3189 ft./min.
Sq. In. Swept Brake area per Lb. 0.048

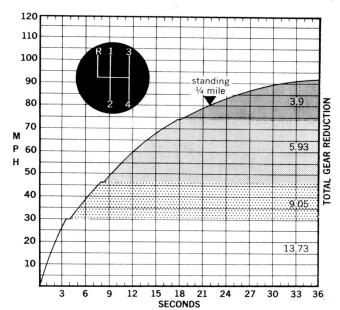

MERCEDES 300-SL

Race bred for road use, combining speed, comfort and safety

Ask any sports car enthusiast what he considers to be the best, most desirable sports car in the world, and chances are better than even that he'll say Mercedes 300-SL without hesitation. This answer will, naturally, bring on cries of dismay and snorts of indignation from Ferrari and/or Aston Martin boosters.

The basis for each person's argument is, to a certain extent, one of personal taste or preference, and *may* have been based on personal contact with one or more of the best-ranked cars, but more likely it is the result of company prestige and reputation. For no matter what racing does or does not do to improve the breed, it does build prestige for a company with a successful racing department, viz., Ferrari, Porsche and Daimler-Benz. And who's to say that racing hasn't improved these cars?

This is the third example of the 300-SL series to be tested by *Road & Track:* the 300-SL "gullwing" coupe in 1955, the 300-SL roadster in 1958 and now the 300-SL roadster with removable hardtop.

Changes and improvements have been minor (on the surface) in the last three years, but have made a good car better by constant refinement and attention to detail. Exterior appearance and interior appointments are virtually identical to the car tested three years ago.

Speaking of appearance, few will quarrel with the businesslike looks of the 300-SL. The lines are "soft," yet leave no doubt as to the car's purpose. It signifies power and speed as few designs do, and the appearance seems to appeal equally to men and women, even though it is a man's car (more on this later). We prefer the older "gullwing" coupe to the roadster, but this is strictly a matter of personal choice, as there's little *real* difference in over-all appearance.

In designing the roadster, the complex space frame of the coupe was retained but was altered around the cockpit area so lower doorsills could be utilized. This makes getting in and out a bit easier, especially for members of the fair sex, who sometimes wear skirts, even in sports cars, and who don't seem to have any trouble in getting the owners of these cars to take them for a ride. *We* still found it to be somewhat awkward getting into the 300-SL (old age?), but very much worth the effort.

The 4-wheel independent suspension—unequal length A-arms in front, low-pivot swing axle in the rear—is unchanged from our test car of three years ago and is similar to that of all 300-SLs built since 1952. The major change has been in the rear suspension where the low-pivot design was adopted at the same time as the body change from coupe to roadster. Springs are coil all around and shock dampers are tubular hydraulic.

The interior appointments of the 300-SL are in keeping with the five figure price tag and have successfully separated this car from the category of stark functionalism fitting the die-hard sports car enthusiast's ideas of what a sports car should be. Due to the car's de luxe interior, and the relatively heavy weight (which is rather ar afield from the company's designation of SL, meaning Super Light) we would actually classify the 300 as a Grand Touring car, rather than a sports car. And what grand touring it is!

The individual, uphosltered-in-leather, bucket seats are comfortable almost to a fault, very successfully limiting side movement of driver and passenger. A time or two, during our more exuberant dashes through the mountains, we felt the need for seat belts, but then both members of the test crew have belts in their own cars and are used to them.

A pleasant touch, which more cars should have, and a result of the competition experience of Daimler-Benz, was the perforated upholstery which allows a certain amount of air circulation through the seat cushion, thereby cooling the driver's derriere. Some upholstery material does not "breathe" and on a hot day the car's occupants end up sitting in wet seats.

The loudest noise to be heard from this ultra silent car is the whir of the injector pump as the ignition key is turned on. A few additional degrees of rotation (of the key) actuates the starter and the engine bursts into life. We had some trouble starting the car after it had been sitting all night, but this was largely due to inexperience with the car and its fuel injection system. Normal starts were made with no trouble at all and we know of no owner who has regular trouble starting his own car unless he has let it get badly out of tune.

Getting underway in ordinary traffic or striving for maximum acceleration proved to be easy and the clutch always had a firm, smooth bite. Never during our test did we experience difficulty with the clutch in any way. Even after the acceleration tests it was still smooth and positive.

The transmission also proved to be as we remembered it: quick, positive and easy to shift with the lever falling conveniently to hand. All four well-spaced ratios have synchromesh, and shifting up or down was accomplished with a minimum of fuss and effort.

The steering is another matter. To be sure, it is positive and direct, and the wheel is positioned in such a manner that most drivers can find a seating position to

suit themselves, but the steering is incredibly stiff. Getting the car in or out of a parking place was real work. Leaving town and driving on an expressway eased the burden and the steering seemed to lighten up. From the thruways onto rural roads, and finally into hilly country, brought out the stiffness of the steering once again.

There are few cars in the world that can match the feeling of confidence one gets from driving the 300-SL.

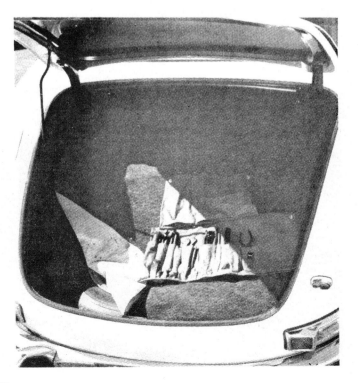

Curves can be taken at what seem impossible speeds, and although we did provoke a good deal of oversteer on some curves, it was only due to the car being driven at close to its limit. Under ordinary, or merely fast, driving conditions the attitude of the car is virtually that of a neutral steerer. The wonderful suspension and roadability of the 300-SL make its hard steering even more regrettable.

One of the most important requirements of any car, and particularly a car built for high sustained speeds, as the Mercedes is, is that of adequate brakes. Obviously a car can't, or shouldn't anyway, be driven faster than its brakes will allow it to be driven safely. In this respect the 300-SL scores very well. We found it almost impossible to fade the brakes and believe that it would take very brutal treatment to cause the car to run out of brakes. The new Mercedes-Benz 220-SE is equipped with Girling disc brakes on the front, the first car from Mercedes to be so equipped, and recent news has been received from Daimler-Benz to the effect that the front drums on the 300-SL will be replaced with Dunlop discs.

Our test car's drums were of aluminum with cast-iron liners. The drums are radially finned, more for strength than for cooling, although the fins would help to dissipate heat to some extent. Brakes are outboard all around in contrast to the 300-SLR and W-196 racing cars where they were mounted inboard to further reduce unsprung weight.

Our acceleration times were just a shade slower than the times we recorded during the previous 300-SL test which we're sure is partly due to the fact that Paul O'Shea drove the car on the previous test runs. He was better able to extract the most the car had to offer. Any driver, however, novice or pro, can wring enough performance from the 300-SL to astound his friends (and probably himself).

Aside from the heavy steering, the only objectionable feature we found was the limited headroom under the hard top. Only one person on our staff could sit up straight in the driver's seat without his head touching the top lining. The top does have its advantages, however. It is removable, albeit not quickly, and it is vented at the back, over the rear window, so the interior temperature can be controlled by the fresh air intake and/or the heater without opening the side windows.

The 300-SL is an expensive car and its value in relation to its cost can only be balanced by the purchaser's desire/ability-to-pay ratio. To those who can afford the initial cost it offers a car they can be proud of, and they will be secure in the knowledge that not many cars on the road are better built or can cover ground faster with as much safety.

ROAD TEST
MERCEDES 300-SL

SCALE: 10" DIVISIONS

DIMENSIONS
Wheelbase, in 94.5
Tread, f and r 55.0/57.0
Over-all length, in 180
   width 70.5
   height 51.0
   equivalent vol, cu ft 375
Frontal area, sq ft 20.0
Ground clearance, in 5.0
Steering ratio, o/a 19.8
   turns, lock to lock 3.0
   turning circle, ft 37
Hip room, front 46
Hip room, rear ....
Pedal to seat back 40
Floor to ground 8.0

CALCULATED DATA
Lb/hp (test wt) 13.6
Cu ft/ton mile 90.5
Mph/1000 rpm (4th) 20.8
Engine revs/mile 2890
Piston travel, ft/mile ... 1678
Rpm @ 2500 ft/min 4340
   equivalent mph 90.4
R&T wear index 48.4

SPECIFICATIONS
List price $11,128
Curb weight, lb 3050
Test weight 3390
   distribution, % 49/51
Tire size 6.70–15
Brake swept area 456
Engine type ..... 6 cyl, sohc
Bore & stroke .... 3.35 x 3.46
Displacement, cc 2996
   cu in 182.8
Compression ratio 9.5
Bhp @ rpm .... 250 @ 6200
   equivalent mph 129
Torque, lb-ft .... 228 @ 5000
   equivalent mph 104

GEAR RATIOS
4th (1.00) 3.89
3rd (1.39) 5.40
2nd (1.97) 7.66
1st (3.34) 13.0

SPEEDOMETER ERROR
30 mph .... actual, 27.4
60 mph 53.7

PERFORMANCE
Top speed (4th), mph ... 130
   best timed run .... n.a.
3rd (6500) 96
2nd (6500) 68
1st (6500) 40

FUEL CONSUMPTION
Normal range, mpg 15/21

ACCELERATION
0-30 mph, sec 3.6
0-40 .... 5.0
0-50 .... 6.2
0-60 .... 7.6
0-70 .... 9.9
0-80 .... 12.5
0-100 .... 20.5
Standing ¼ mile 16.2
   speed at end 91.2

TAPLEY DATA
4th, lb/ton @ mph .. 290 @ 92
3rd .... 430 @ 73
2nd .... 500 @ 55
Total drag at 60 mph, lb ... 105

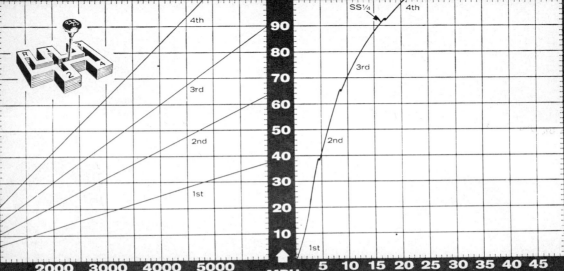

MERCEDES 190-SL ROADSTER

ENGINE CAPACITY: 116.02 cu in, 1897 cu cm;
FUEL CONSUMPTION: 21.6 m/imp gal, 25.9 m/US gal, 10.9 l x 100 km;
SEATS: 2; MAX SPEED: 108.7 mph, 175 km/h;
PRICE: list £ 2,033, total £ 2,457.

ENGINE: front, 4 stroke; cylinders: 4, in line; bore and stroke: 3.35 x 3.29 in, 85 x 83.6 mm; engine capacity: 116.02 cu in, 1897 cu cm; compression ratio: 8.8 : 1; max power (SAE): 120 hp at 5800 rpm; max torque (SAE): 114 lb ft, 15.8 kgm at 3800 rpm; max number of engine rpm: 6000; specific power: 63.3 hp/l; cylinder block: light alloy; cylinder head: light alloy; crankshaft bearings: 3; valves: 2 per cylinder, overhead, finger lever; camshaft: 1, overhead; lubrication gear pump, oil-water heat exchanger, full flow filter; lubricating system capacity: 4 imp qt, 4.8 US qt, 4.5 l; carburation: 2 Solex 44 PHH horizontal carburettors; fuel feed: mechanical pump; cooling system: water; cooling system capacity: 8.8 imp qt, 10.6 US qt, 10 l.

TRANSMISSION: driving wheels: rear; clutch: single dry plate; gear box: mechanical; gears: 4 + reverse; synchromesh gears: I, II, III, IV; gear box ratios: (I) 3.52, (II) 2.32, (III) 1.52, (IV) 1, (Rev) 3.29; gear lever: central; final drive: hypoid; ratio: 3.9 : 1.

CHASSIS: integral; front suspension: independent, wishbones, anti-roll bar, coil spring, rubber elements, telescopic dampers; rear suspension: independent, swinging half-axles, single joint low pivot, trailing radius arms, coil springs, rubber bellows, horizontal compensating coil spring, telescopic dampers.

STEERING: recirculating ball, damper; turns of steering wheel lock to lock: 3.5.

BRAKES: drum, 2 leading shoes; braking surface: total 164.92 sq in, 1064 sq cm.

ELECTRICAL EQUIPMENT: voltage: 12 V; battery: 56 Ah; dynamo: 160/240 W; ignition distributor: Bosch; headlights: 2 front and reversing.

DIMENSIONS AND WEIGHT: wheel base: 94.49 in, 2400 mm; front track: 56.69 in, 1440 mm; rear track: 58.46 in, 1485 mm; overall length: 166.14 in, 4220 mm; overall width: 69.29 in, 1760 mm; overall height: 50.39 in, 1280 mm; ground clearance: 6.10 in, 155 mm; dry weight: 2414 lb, 1095 kg; distribution of weight: 48 % front axle, 52 % rear axle; turning radius (between walls): 17.2 ft, 5.25 m; width of rims: 5.1''; tyres: 6.40 - 13; fuel tank capacity: 14.29 imp gal, 17.17 US gal, 65 l.

BODY: convertible; doors: 2; seats: 2.

PERFORMANCE: max speed in 1st gear: 31.1 mph, 50 km/h; max speed in 2 gear: 47.2 mph, 76 km/h; max speed in 3rd gear: 74.6 mph, 120 km/h; m speed in 4th gear: 108.7 mph, 175 km/h; power-weight ratio: 20.1 lb/h 9.1 kg/hp; useful load: 761 lb, 345 kg; max gradient in 1st gear: 50 %; spe in direct drive at 1000 rpm: 18.3 mph, 29.5 km/h.

PRACTICAL INSTRUCTIONS: fuel: petrol, 96 oct; engine sump oil: 3.52 imp 4.25 US qt, 4 l, SAE 10 (winter) 20 (summer), change every 3700 miles, 6000 k gearbox oil: 3.87 imp qt, 4.65 US qt, 4.4 l, change every 11200 miles, 18000 k final drive oil: 1.98 imp qt, 2.38 US qt, 2.2 l, SAE 90, change every 11200 mile 18000 km; steering box oil: 0.26 imp qt, 0.32 US qt, 0.3 l, SAE 90, chan every 11200 miles, 18000 km; greasing: every 11200 miles, 18000 km; sparki plug type: 200°; tyre pressure (medium load): front 26 psi, 1.8 atm; re 27 psi, 1.9 atm.

VARIATIONS AND OPTIONAL ACCESSORIES: hardtop; 190 SL Coupé.

PRACTICAL CLASSICS BUYING FEATURE

Buying a Mercedes 190SL for restoration

Chris Graham points out the problems, and the costs.

"**B**uying for restoration" is a phrase that is happily bandied about these days amongst enthusiasts but few, I fear, completely appreciate the full implications of the remark. As *Practical Classics* has repeatedly discovered with our own in-house restorations, this process frequently overshoots the limits initially set for both time and finances. This of course is equally likely (if not a little more so) to occur with the home restorer, and in his (or her) case it can prove nothing short of disastrous. Some cars will demand many thousands of pounds for their complete restoration, only to repay their tireless 're-creators' with a fraction of this cost if they reach the classifieds. On the other hand however, there are cars which, although costing a great deal to restore properly, are actually capable of registering a profit at the end of the day should this be desired, and the Mercedes 190SL can be one such car.

(Above) The stately lines of Roy Brown's 1961 Mercedes 190SL help a great deal in compensating for the large amounts of time and money spent on the car's superb restoration.

(Below) The large steering wheel is positioned close to the driver and the comfortable but upright seats (which are adjustable to three positions by three levers) give an engaging period feel. I found headroom slightly limited.

The ravages of the Second World War took a severe toll on the Daimler-Benz motor company (an alliance which had been set up in the early 1920s between the two rival German companies, in an effort to produce a united front against the terrible economic conditions existing in Germany at that time – prices were going up several times a day!..). With nearly three-quarters of their factories having been destroyed by bomb damage, the early post war years were most definitely a time for recovery of a most basic nature. It was not until 1948, as the result of a currency reform, that the company could begin the production of cars once again. Initially some of the tried and trusted pre-war favourites were continued, but as the years rolled by advances were made and new models rose from the drawing boards.

This continued in a predictable fashion up until 1953, when a totally new bodyshell design was introduced. Up to this point all post war Mercedes-Benz cars had been built with separate tubular chassis which was in itself advanced by many standards, but this new design saw the development of a pressed

Buying a Mercedes 190SL for restoration/continued

steel unit construction bodyshell that provided its own strength. It made the new car lighter and quieter, easier to produce on a moving production line, and much simpler to maintain. The first car to feature such a construction was a model called the 180, and it was a step on, and a little development from this, that produced the 190SL.

The first prototype was revealed in 1954, and in its Roadster form featured a plexiglass aero-screen and cut-down lightweight doors without windows. However, after the initial launch, things went a little quiet and nothing was heard of the new model. This unnatural silence lasted until 1955 when, in March, the car was in effect re-born. It was immediately noticeable that the bodywork had been altered quite considerably; in an effort, it is presumed, to liken it more to the successful 300SL (its high performance relative). The engine chosen was a straight four cylinder, single overhead camshaft unit, of 1897cc capacity. It was coupled to twin Solex dual carburettors, but these were rather complicated and so were rarely used in other Mercedes engines.

The welded body-chassis development was continued on from the 180, to the 190SL. The new car featured a central tunnel to provide the main support and accommodate the driveshaft, and box sections that were welded to the floor pan and to the body panels down each side. It was available in two basic forms, the Coupe (with detachable hardtop), and the Roadster (with soft top, but provision for a hardtop).

Apart from the obvious differences between the open and closed models another recognisable feature was the bucket seats with the tipping backs finished in a material called MB-Texleder, in the Roadster (leather upholstery was an optional extra).

The road to restoration

Assuming that you manage to locate a 190SL at the right price, one which will provide a suitable basis on which to begin a restoration, the first thing that you should check is that the car is complete. In recent years the spares scene with regard to body and trim items has become very limited. Therefore, if you can start with a complete car, so much the better. Pay particular attention to the smaller items of trim like chrome finishing strips, door fitments and the like, as these are just the sort of items that may escape your notice in the initial excitement of seeing the car, but will prove costly to replace later on. Check under the bonnet too, and in particular in the region of the carburettors. Being such a large and heavy unit, the twin carburettor assembly was given a metal supporting bracket by the designers, but it has been known for this member to 'go missing'. This can lead to the carburettor flanges becoming cracked – not a welcomed condition.

On the protype 190SL there was a ventilation slot cut in the front of the bonnet. However, before production got under way, this was filled in to produce a 'power bulge' from front to back. In reality this car can be prone to overheating, so perhaps they had got it right the first time after all! Another development that occured between the prototype and the production models concerned the bumpers. Originally they ran straight across the car, irrespective of the body curvatures. But as an afterthought, they were tailored more closely to the natural contours, a feature perhaps taken from the 300SL.

Technical Data

Produced between May 1955 – February 1963 (25,881 built)
Engine capacity 1897cc (four stroke, four cylinder)

Bore x stroke	85 x 83.5mm
Compression	8.5:1 then 8.8:1 from 9/59
Max. power	105 bhp at 5700 rpm
Max speed	105mph
0-60mph	13.3 seconds
Fuel consumption	22mpg

During the 190SL's production term (May 1955 to February 1963) the company did not incorporate any form of rust prevention treatment, which has unfortunately taken its sad toll on the elegant bodywork of many examples. The damage was somewhat limited by the fact that this model was fitted with aluminium doors, boot lid and bonnet. However, all four wings, the floor (including the boot) and certain areas of the chassis assembly do suffer badly.

A lot depends on how the car has been treated throughout its life. Unfortunately though it is likely that in the majority of cases the cars have led a relatively hard life. Being positioned at the lower end of the Mercedes range, but still retaining a certain sporting image, made the 190SL an attractive proposition as it represented fine quality but at a price. It was far more expensive than its British counterparts however this was somewhat justified by its significantly more advanced specifications. Many examples today are suffering the consequences of what could be described as a 'mis-spent motoring youth', and of course this simply adds to the severity of the rebuild.

For this article we decided to adopt a slightly different approach from the usual, and focus our attention on one car which has (conveniently) just been fully rebuilt. As it now stands this gleaming red 190SL provides a superb example of how the car should look,

Initially Mr Brown thought that if the restoration did not work out, at least he would get some money for the number plate! From the rear the 190SL appears reasonably wide and flat which adds to its sporting ambition. Originally the cars were fitted with crossply tyres, but radials are the sensible option these days.

Boot space in this car is adequate although perhaps a little shallow – specially shaped luggage was available to fit. There is reasonable luggage space behind the seats. The bumpers are constructed from three sections and the hardtop features an ingenious ventilation system. The front edge above the windscreen is louvred so that air is ducted through to the back window to keep the outside clear.

and it must be added that it is used as an everyday car in London throughout the year. Its owner Mr Roy Brown is truly devoted to the shapely charms of the car, but as I found out, in the early days before the restoration, the car was certainly not a wonder to behold.

Starting at the rear of the car, the boot floor was rusted around its edges. The floor contains two spare wheel wells and these, if the drain holes become blocked, can be prone to rusting. The lip of the boot, onto which the lid shuts, is covered with a rubber and this can be a nuisance. The overall curvature of the boot section causes any water that becomes trapped under this rubber, to run to

The areas under the rubber sealing strips around the boot lip are a prime target for rust, as the water settles here.

The state of the front nearside wing virtually as found.

With the offside front wing, the grille and the front panel removed, the corrosion caused by the double skinning is clearly evident.

This chrome finishing plate can also hide a good deal of trouble. Note on the left of the plate, a small circular cover for the jacking point. There should be one of these at the front too, but the earliest cars were supplied without.

A view of the old rear nearside wing illustrates well the problem. The brakes were developed from Mercedes' race experience and the wide alloy drums feature a turbo cooling system as the picture shows.

On Mr Brown's car the chassis in the region of the rear spring top was badly corroded. The area that is cut away here had to be replaced with sound metal cut to shape, as replacements are no longer available. This area is a particular weakness of the car.

the corners where it lies and promotes corrosion. The inner rear wheel arches are also a prime target, and once they have rusted, attention is turned to the outer arches. Both the front and rear wings on the 190SL feature fluted splash guards that are finished with a chrome strip. This decoration sometimes retains water between it and the wing and rust results, or in cases where the corrosion is particularly bad on the inside, the flute moulding itself acts as a mud trap, and it rots from the inside out. A chrome trim piece is also the cause of trouble at the front corner of the rear wheel arches. Water gets trapped behind here with the same outcome.

The top mountings for the rear springs are definitely a very suspect area on this car, and so should be checked thoroughly. On either side of the car at the rear there are two chassis members that run up over the rear axle and then taper away on either side of the boot. The rise up over the axle incorporates the top mounting for the rear springs, and appears to be particularly likely to corrode. The unenviable result is that the rear of the car suddenly drops as the springs surge up through the body in wonderful unison. Moving a little further forward, the floor of the passenger compartment should be the next area to inspect. In places it is double skinned and as the car has a removable roof, water is the deadly enemy again here. It can gather between the two skins with expensive results. Running down both sides of this section of the car, underneath the doors, there are box sectioned chassis members. These have been proved somewhat susceptable to the passing years, and the jacking points in particular (one at the front and one at the rear) which are housed within these members, do rust badly.

The front wings corrode in a similar fashion to the rears, but there is an extra problem area at the front created by a strangely designed front 'nose' panel. This panel, which forms the divide between the front of the bonnet and the radiator grille, forms a double skinned section. This on the face of it seems to be of little consequence. However,

The dashboard is interestingly laid out, and certainly very well equipped. There are dials for fuel, oil pressure and water temperature as well as a rev counter and speedometer. The car boasts several fairly advanced (for its time) features in the instrument line including; a foot operated wash/wipe button, a switchable (from side to side) parking light arrangement, a built-in headlight flasher and a hot start button, on the minus side the umbrella handle brake lever under the dashboard was never popular, and the indicators which are operated from the horn ring on the steering wheel, can be a handful.

The interior of Mr Brown's car was completely re-trimmed in leather. The cost of the materials alone was around £600, but friends in the trade helped to keep labour charges to a minimum. Trim items are now next to impossible to obtain, so check methodically over any proposed purchase.

Buying a Mercedes 190SL for restoration/continued

on Mr Brown's example, the space between the two panels opened out into the wheel arch with no protection at all. As there was apparently no splash panel fitted, all the corrosive elements from the wheels were able to pass straight into this compartment, which lead to the inevitable corrosion. Presumably it had originally been sealed with some form of compound which had long since shaken itself free.

The engine and its compartment seem to provide the least of the worries from the restoration point of view, although sizeable expense is always on the cards should major work be needed here. Points to look out for when running the engine include the speed of the tick-over, and the oil pressure. Worn engines needing attention will tend to tick-over faster than they should. They can get as high as 1400 rpm, but the correct reading should be 800 rpm. An engine in good condition should register an oil pressure of 90 psi under normal driving conditions, and 50 psi on the tick-over. Lower readings might indicate the pressure of bottom end problems, and with the cost of a well engineered engine rebuild possibly nudging the £2,500 barrier, mistakes at this stage can be expensive. As far as corrosion is concerned in this area, there are only two points to watch out for. The inner front wings double as the sides to the engine bay, so rust is a possibility here, and also check the battery and brake booster housings. Both of these items (one on each side of the engine), are situated in recesses that are provided with drain holes. But, as with all drain holes, they do sometimes become blocked providing a rust promoting situation. The engine itself is by all accounts a most reliable and well made unit that has a lengthy life expectancy – in other words, it is built to the usual Mercedes standards. A point to be noted is that the head is cast from

Mechanically speaking this particular Mercedes engine is a basically reliable and strong unit. Rust can be a problem in the two recesses created for the battery and the brake servo booster (marked A and B respectively). The brake servo booster was an optional extra until 1956, when it became standard equipment. The twin Solex carburettor assembly is complex, and it is considered wise to leave them alone if they are performing well.

The price of spares
Front wings – Remanufactured **£250** each. Short block **£750**. Head **£350**. Starter motor **£85** new, **£45** reconditioned. Crankshaft **£150-175**. Carburettors **£980** a pair. Seats **£100** to re-finish. Bumper **£350** front or rear. Hood and frame **£1000**. Wheels **£45** new, **£15** secondhand.
It should be noted that these are representative British prices, from Germany they are on average about a third cheaper.

a light metal whereas the block is cast in iron, and that the joint between the two can suffer from corrosion.

Working on the engine is not made easy by the fact that some of the serviceable ancillaries such as the starter motor, the dynamo and the steering box are positioned low down on the unit, and are obscured by the complex carburettor arrangement.

The only criterion which seems to govern work of a mechanical nature on this car is expense. All the main engine parts are still available from Mercedes (or if you are lucky, from enthusiasts on the secondhand market), but at a price. There exists a considerable variation in the prices charged by Mercedes for such components, with some items seeming very expensive, but others being reasonably priced. For example, a pair of carburettors will cost in the region of £980, but on the other hand, a water pump can be bought for £100!

One interesting point to bear in mind concerns the type of oil required by the gearbox – it needs automatic transmission fluid. One suggested reason for this is that the syncromesh is particularly fine on this car, and that anything thicker than automatic oil simply clogs it up.

All things considered...

As I said at the beginning, the Mercedes 190SL can provide a financially viable restoration project (if completed correctly). Roy Brown stresses that his example in effect cost him one year of his life, in terms of his own time. It was a task that required complete dedication. Money of course played an essential role, but what has resulted is most definitely a fine car. Although in no way matching the performance capabilities of its more expensive stablemate the 300SL the 190SL provides a well equipped and comfortable touring machine. Should prolonged motorway journeys be required, the car will respond with ease. The differing roof options make for a car for all seasons, and help to provide interesting variation from the driver's point of view. Although strictly a two-seater, provision was made for the 190SL to be fitted with a third, transverse seat in the back. This was situated behind the driver's seat with its associated footwell being on the passenger's side. Having just discovered about this optional extra, I was then told by Mr Brown that he has had three people in the front with ease, and has even slept in it quite comfortably himself – truly a practical classic!

190SLs appear only rarely on the market these days, and in recent years seem to have become even more scarce. Popular opinion suggests that there has been an upsurge in the car's popularity as a result of the enormous amounts of money now being asked for the 300SL model. So to obtain a reasonable car that will be suitable for a complete restoration, you must now expect to pay anything between £3000 and £5000. Then in reality, if you cannot do everything yourself, you must be resigned to perhaps a further £10,000 for the restoration. Unfortunately a high proportion of the work required on the body (probably the major undertaking with one of these cars) is very specialised. The complex curves and structures on the car demand the attention of a skilled and highly experienced craftsman. Such talents, as we all know, are not cheap to hire. Finally, a word of warning. In Mr Brown's experience, it is unwise to deal with spares suppliers in Germany by post, as the distance and language problems involved can lead to mistakes. And the only way to avoid them is to go to Germany yourself – it could be worth it in the long run. □

The Club
The club to join is **The Mercedes-Benz Club Ltd.**, Membership Secretary Mrs T. Bellamy, 75 Theydon Grove, Epping, Essex CM16 4PX.

The writer would like to thank Mr Roy Brown and Nigel Cooper (Nigel Cooper Cars), 16-17 The Arches, Kingsdown Close, London W10 6SG, telephone: 01-229 1180), for their help with this feature.

The white walled tyres suit this gleaming red example well. This picture illustrates the wrap around rear window incorporated in the hard top. This was a modification that came with time, as the early models featured a smaller and more oval window.

Multi-national 300SL Gullwing line-up pictured at the Nurbürgring in 1956. Can anyone remember the occasion?

The Gullwing

In 1952 Mercedes-Benz introduced one of their most famous models, the 300SL. It was a car destined for great success on the track, and the road. Story by Mike McCarthy

No one can say that the Mercedes-Benz win at Le Mans in 1952 was particularly popular with the partisan French crowds. The war had been over for seven years, and Franco-German scars still hadn't fully healed. But that was only a minor point. The real hero of the race was a Frenchman, Pierre Levegh, who was to make tragic history three years later on the same circuit.

Levegh had driven his Lago-Talbot steadily up the field, aided by the failure of the Jaguars and Ferraris and Gordinis, until at dawn on Sunday morning he was leading. But he was an obstinate man, and intended to drive – and win – the race single handed: his co-driver never got a look in. The inevitable happened: exhaustion set in, and just over an hour before the end he missed a change, and the engine over-revved and blew. Under the directions of the legendary Alfred Neubauer the surviving two Mercs swept into first and second places, driven by Lang/Riess and Helfrich/Niedermeyer respectively. The car they drove was a lightweight silver coupé, the 300SL.

The 300SL story really starts a year earlier, when Mercedes-Benz introduced their first post-war big car, a limousine powered by a 3-litre, single ohc engine. This developed 115bhp (DIN) at 4600rpm, but a couple of months later a more powerful coupé, equipped with triple Solex carburetters to give 150bhp (DIN) at 5000rpm was introduced.

By 1951 Mercedes-Benz as a company was well on the road to recovery, and the management had not forgotten the publicity lessons to be learnt from racing. They tried to resurrect the pre-war M163 single-seaters, but their only outing – to Argentina – ended in failure. The cars were no longer competitive. But the Neubauers and Uhlenhauts of this world are not easily put off. Money was short, too, so the Chief Engineer, Fritz Nalinger, suggested a sports car, using the new 3-litre engine, and other 300 components. It was not the best that could be done, but it was a reasonable compromise.

High strength to weight ratio

Uhlenhaut and his team set to. The engine was quite a hefty lump, so they 'added lightness' in a way that was to stamp the major characteristic of all 300SLs from then on: they produced a light, multi-tubular triangulated space frame. With this form of construction, if properly designed not only are all stresses in the tubes in the right direction – longitudinally as against in bending – but the resultant overall structure has a very high strength-to-weight ratio.

However, you don't get something for nothing, and in this case the chassis around the cockpit area had to be fairly deep to attain sufficient bending and torsional stiffness. The result was another 300SL characteristic: since the doors couldn't open all the way to the bottom, Mercedes came up with the novel solution of pivoting the doors around the roof centre line so that they opened upwards. Thus, for purely technical reasons, was born 'The Gullwing', a nickname by which the 300SL will forever be known.

So, when the 300SL was introduced on March 13 1952, as a pure sports/racing car, the theme was set. The space frame encompassed the engine at the front

1955 Swedish Grand Prix touring car race: Karl Kling finished first in his 300SL. Only SLs were entered

In the same year, John Fitch's SL came fifth overall in the Mille Miglia

The epic 1952 Le Mans race featured a Mercedes-Benz 1-2 once Pierre Levegh's Lago-Talbot failed after 23 hours. Here the second-placed Helfrich/Niedermeyer car leads a team-mate

and was enclosed in a lightweight, almost ovoid, streamlined bodyshell. The engine, canted over at 45deg and equipped with twin Weber carburettors, was pumping out a respectable 173bhp (DIN) at 5200rpm. Suspension was by twin wishbones, coil springs and hydraulic dampers at the front and, following Mercedes tradition – though perhaps not one of their better ones, as we shall see – a coil sprung swing axle at the rear.

The 300SLs may have been giving away capacity and camshafts to the main competition (Jaguar, Ferrari, Aston Martin and Gordini to name some) in 1952, but with Neubauer's uncanny instinct, by hare-and-tortoise methods they finished second in the Mille Miglia, came first, second and third at the Berne Grand Prix (after losing Caracciola in an accident that was to prevent him racing again), first and second again (as mentioned) at Le Mans, took the first *four* places in a sports car race that preceded the German Grand Prix (using open cars incidentally) and finally, finished first and second in the prestigous (for American sales reasons) Carrera Panamericana.

At the end of the season Mercedes-Benz withdrew (temporarily) from racing, to concentrate their efforts on a much more ambitious project: Formula 1. The fact that Fangio and Kling finished first and second in the 1954 French Grand Prix is history, and another story altogether.

And so to production. Which very nearly didn't happen!

Toe-in-the-water exercise

Mercedes-Benz regarded the 300SL sports/racers as a toe-in-the-water exercise, to regain racing experience. But their New York importer was an astute businessman and a sports car fanatic. He suggested a 'productionised' 300SL, an idea which, though it appealed to the Mercedes-Benz board, looked commercially unviable. Who needed a loss-leader, as the 300SL would be, when the all-conquering W196s and 300SLRs were soon to appear? Importer Hoffman came up with the answer: he simply placed a firm order for 1000!

The production 300SL retained the major characteristics of the sports/racer, but was in fact a totally different machine. The one was for the track, the other for the road and occasionally the track.

For a start, it followed Mercedes' racing practice under the bonnet by equipping the engine, suitably modified of course, with Bosch fuel injection. The system was derived from that used in diesel engines, and required considerable work on the heads – but the result was 215bhp (DIN) at 5800rpm.

The extra power was needed, of course, because in 'civilising' the car it had put on weight. The chassis was still a space-frame, but uprated to carry heavier loads. The suspension, front and rear, was derived from the production 300 saloon but remained essentially that of the sports/racer. The brakes were massive Al-fin drum devices, and the steering by recirculating ball.

But the most dramatic changes were to the body. Gone was the utterly clean simplicity, totally devoid of any excrescenses, of the sports/racer. For a start a rectangular grille, incorporating the three-pointed star, replaced the small oval one. Bumpers protruded fore-and-aft. Headlights were raised and moved forward, with side-lights underneath. The door opening retained the 'Gullwing' arrangement but was enlarged. The final external touch was those other characteristic 300SL features, the sweep-spears (for want of a better term) over the wheel arches. Inside, of course, racing spartan gave way to luxurious leather and 'style', though the folding steering wheel, to aid entry and exit, was retained. The boot was filled with petrol tank and spare wheel, but there was a luggage space behind the seats.

Between 1954 and 1957 Mercedes-Benz produced a mere 1400 coupés, the peak year being 1955 with 867 cars. In 1957 it was replaced by the Roadster, which killed two birds with one stone: a redesign of the chassis allowed a 'proper' door for one, and the rear suspension was redesigned. These were the most significant changes, but there were others, such as redesigned headlights and disc brakes.

Winged flight

The Mercedes Gullwing 300SL is one of Mike McCarthy's dream cars and, thanks to the generosity of Delwyn Mallett, he's recently been able to fulfil his ambition to drive one

You remember Delwyn Mallett, don't you? He was the gentleman in last month's issue who owned two Abarths. And a few Porsches. And the Gullwing which – brave soul – he allowed me to drive.

He's had the car for about eight years now, buying it from someone who had a pair! He vividly recalls picking it up, and first driving it, heart pumping and adrenalin just about coming out of his ears – particularly when he took it through a tunnel and heard the reflection of that lovely exhaust note.

The full history of the car isn't known, but he believes it was first sold in Germany, then went to America where it moved around quite a lot, finishing up in Maryland. It was imported into this country by a Swede who had painted it orange with a black stripe down the middle, and stuck roundels on the side. After passing through two or three more pairs of hands Delwyn finally bought it. The genuine mileage is uncertain, but it has been back to the factory at some time where the engine was rebuilt and brought up to Roadster specification, with a hotter cam and cooling modifications.

It was while the car was orange and black that Delwyn first saw and fell in love with it. When he bought the Gullwing the car had been resprayed traditional silver, and it wasn't until later that he discovered that it was the same car. Talk about dream fulfilment!

As you clamber into the driver's seat (slide your bottom all the way into seat, then bring your legs in) you realise why the Roadster has proper doors. Entry and exit may show off a pretty pair of female legs to advantage, but portly millionaires could look decidedly clumsy – *not* a good thing. The steering wheel does, in fact, fold under to make life easier, but only when the wheels are pointing straight ahead.

The 'choke' is an enrichment device for the fuel injection system, and is only needed when the engine is really cold. At other times it just rumbles into life at the press of a button.

Cockpit light and very airy

A previous owner has had the seat squab raised slightly, so there is a slight feeling of sitting on, rather than in, the car. This I personally like, though Delwyn, more used to Porsches and Abarths, isn't too keen on it.

With all that glass around you the cockpit is incredibly airy and light, with near-enough 360deg visibility. The interior mirror, though, is almost a waste of time it's so small and low, and if there's any luggage in the space behind the seats, it becomes pointless. The other drawback is that all that glass area can act like a hot-house in sunny weather. In fact Delwyn has been known to drive with the doors (roof?) open, which can cause some embarrassing attention. As if the car didn't get enough anyway . . .

The seating position and cockpit layout is ideal as far as I'm concerned. There's a large, wood-rimmed wheel replacing the standard white plastic device,

and that frankly, gaudy facia – all chrome knobs and buttons and very American instrumentation, though the large speedometer and tachometer are clearly marked and easy to read. The pedals are well spaced and the gear lever 'falls nicely to hand', as they say.

On the move, at low (town) speeds, everything about the car is heavy . . . the steering, for example, and in particular the clutch (a cross-London drive can be quite tiring according to Delwyn). The brakes too require a hefty shove, but with those massive drums all round they are effective. At higher speeds the whole car seems to lighten up (except for the clutch) and the steering comes into its own, being direct and full of feel, though it never really loses all its weighting. The gearchange is pleasant, being light and direct, though it can be criticised in that it has a very positive gate, so you cannot slur second to third changes. It's best not to try racing changes, though, for they merely result in a loud (and possibly expensive) clonk. Firmness and precision is the order of the day.

The performance, for a car coming up to its 30th birthday, is something else again. At the moment the engine tends to hunt and surge below about 2000rpm, and with the very high gearing – 25mph/1000rpm – fitted to Delwyn's car, you seldom use top in traffic. But once above that, and using a lot of throttle, it pulls like a proverbial steam engine, with a seeming never-ending surge of torque. In deference to the car's age I only used 5000 of the 6000rpm available before the red line, and Delwyn only uses 5500rpm himself. But between 2000rpm and 5000rpm the actual revs seems almost academic, so smooth and flowing is the engine's urge. And with it goes some of the most beautiful noises any true enthusiast could wish for, a cross between a growl and a bark. XK owners with well-tuned cars will know something of what I mean, but the Merc's notes are truly distinctive. It's pure magic.

In a straight line the car sits rock steady, just minor corrections of the steering wheel keeping the car on a dead straight path. But then we come to the roadholding and handling . . .

Dreaded rear swing axles

Before I drove it, Delwyn took me out for a quick spin to show me the ropes. Part of the route involved a roundabout with a tricky, S-bend, exit. Shortly before, we'd been hammering around this section in one of his Abarths without any problems – in fact that little car clung on like a leech, and was great fun. The Merc was a different story.

The car is powerful, with a relatively light rear end – and the dreaded swing axles. I say dreaded because, even at moderate speeds compared to the Abarth, lifting off caused swift and rather dramatic tail-end breakaway, which, if you could predict it, was catchable. *If* you could predict it . . . The technique for a Gullwing seems to be slowly into, then power progressively out of, a corner. Under those conditions the tail squats under weight transfer, the negative camber on the rear wheels increases, and the car will drive through the corner or bend smoothly and neutrally. I must confess, again in deference to the car's age (and Delwyn's nerves!) I didn't try any really hard cornering, just enough to give me the feel of the car – but I would love to get it on, say, a circuit, airfield, or other open area where I could play around with it and find its true limit myself. I'd also need to spend quite a long time with it before I would feel truly comfortable with it.

I asked Delwyn if this was typical of 300SLs, and from his experience his car is no better or worse than others. While realising that the car is on skinny tyres, and it isn't new, I must confess I was a little disappointed with its road manners. Other cars of that period I've driven seem to behave better. They say racing and press-on drivers prefer oversteer: that is definitely the Gullwing's characteristic, but I cannot believe they'd like it at the relatively low cornering speeds at which the Gullwing displays it. Perhaps I'm being too harsh on the car, and I'd love to know what owners who drove the cars when they were new thought about them: would they really see everything else off the road?

So to me the Gullwing, one of my own dream cars, only partially lives up to its reputation. In a straight line, and on known corners, it's everything I always thought it was – but we don't lift off in the wrong conditions . . .

PHOTO BY KURT WÖRNER

MERCEDES-BENZ 300SL

One of the most exciting cars of any era

BY THOS L. BRYANT
PHOTOS BY JOE RUSZ

Is THERE A car enthusiast anywhere in the world who hasn't lusted after the Mercedes-Benz 300SL Gullwing coupe? I've never known anyone who didn't fall in love with this spectacular sports coupe at first glance. Even the experts, like the staff members of *Road & Track* in 1968 in a Classic Test of the 300SL, characterized it as a car in a class by itself: "If only one car built since World War II could be called a classic, it would have to be the Gullwing 300SL."

The S is for Super and the L is for Light, while the 300 refers to the 3.0-liter displacement of the inline 6-cylinder engine. This magnificent car first appeared as a competition car only in 1952, and proceeded to take the racing world by storm. First and 2nd in the 1952 Carrera Panamericana, the 24 Hours of Le Mans and the 1000 Kilometers at Nürburgring. After that year of conquest, the Mercedes factory turned its attention to Grand Prix racing and the 300SL slipped from the limelight.

But there were people who wanted this racing machine converted to street use—and one man in particular, Max Hoffman, importer of a wide variety of European cars to the U.S., put his money behind his words. Hoffman guaranteed the factory that he would purchase 1000 300SLs if the works would build street versions.

Road & Track published its first road test of the 300SL in the April 1955 issue, and confessed that the staff was afraid the car would be a mediocre performer. However, the long wait and the skepticism gave way to unbridled enthusiasm: "In fact, we can state unequivocally that in our opinion the 300SL coupe is the ultimate in an all-round sports car. It combines more desirable features in one streamlined package than we ever imagined or hoped would be possible."

This exciting thoroughbred was based on a rigid tubular frame made up of a great number of steel tubes that surround the passenger compartment and the engine bay as well. The earlier competition cars boasted aluminum body panels, but the production versions were fitted with steel bodies with aluminum used for the engine hood and rear deck lid. The styling, to my eye, is absolutely gorgeous—a long sweeping hood, short rear deck, interesting character lines above the front and rear wheel wells, and, of course, those doors. Because the tubular space frame came up quite high on the sides, Mercedes decided to make the doors open upward rather than out, and hinged them very nearly at the center of the roof. Who could resist the look of those gullwings rising upward to give the 300SL a truly unique aspect?

The powerplant for the 300SL was a single-overhead-camshaft six with Bosch fuel injection putting gasoline directly into the cylinders. The bore and stroke was 85.0 x 88.0 mm for a total displacement of 2996 cc. Compression ratio was 8.5:1 and the engine pumped out an impressive 240 bhp at 5800 rpm and 202 lb-ft of torque at 4000. The 300SL's performance was nothing short of fantastic for its day: 0–60 mph in 7.4 seconds and the standing quarter mile in 15.2 sec at 95.0 mph. In the words of the 1955 R&T test: "Tramping on the accelerator pedal produces instantaneous acceleration in any gear at any speed. Two aspects of this warrant comment. With first or second gear engaged, full throttle at, say, 1000 rpm literally forces you back in the seat. As the tach needle sweeps toward 4000 rpm, you think— 'man, what acceleration!' Then all hell breaks loose, for at 4000 rpm things really begin to happen."

Mercedes-Benz offered three final-drive ratio choices for the 300SL, and the R&T test car was fitted with the 3.64:1 ratio. Optional were a 3.42:1 and 3.25:1. Even with the low (numerically high) 3.64 ratio, the 300SL was capable of more than 140 mph, while the 3.25:1 final drive gave the Mercedes a top speed near 160 mph.

Writing in the January 7, 1955 issue of *Autosport*, the

1955 Mercedes-Benz 300SL, courtesy of Nürburgring Rennsportmuseum.

legendary British journalist John Bolster found the 300SL exciting to drive: "Fuel injection pays dividends in giving instant response to the throttle, and, at the other end of the scale, it allows the car to accelerate in top gear from little more than walking pace. No luxury limousine has a more flexible power unit. The engine is quiet and smooth when cruising, but takes on the 'hard' feel of a racing unit when really extended. The exhaust is at all times virtually inaudible, which is astonishing to say the least."

Driving the 300SL was not a tricky exercise, as the clutch was quite positive and the gearshift light in action. Synchromesh on all four forward speeds made the Mercedes gearbox a delight to use, and virtually the only criticism leveled at the 300SL's transmission was the obtrusive noise level of gear whine. The gear ratios were ideally matched to the engine's performance capability, particularly to the flat torque curve between 3500 and 5500 rpm. And this meant the 240 horses could be transmitted into super performance.

Mercedes engineers designed a suspension system to take advantage of the 300SL's high speed ability. Up front were unequal-length A-arms, coil springs, rubber auxiliary springs and an anti-roll bar. At the rear, conventional swing axles, trailing arms, coil springs and auxiliary rubber springs kept the live axle in place. While the suspension design produced a comfortable ride over nearly any road surface, handling at high cornering speeds could be a challenge to the less-than-expert driver. The recirculating-ball steering was quite quick, with only 2.0 turns lock to lock, and rather on the heavy side. Initial response was neutral, but you had to be wary of the quick transition to swing-axle oversteer. Because of this trait and the narrow wheels and tires (Dunlop Extra Super Sport 6.50-15s mounted on 15 x 5K steel hub/aluminum rim wheels with a knockoff nut), the 300SL's cornering power was not great. But at the hands of a truly skilled driver, the Mercedes coupe could be made to corner at relatively high speeds, and the car was quite competitive in sports car racing in America in the Fifties.

Out on the open road, the 300SL was a treat, as R&T pointed out in the 1968 Classic Test: "Straight-line stability, though, is commendable in the 300SL, and for everyday brisk driving the car is still great fun to drive. The brakes, monstrous finned steel-aluminum drums (10.25 x 3.5-in. with vacuum assist)—with copper-impregnated lining on the leading shoes, conventional organic lining on the trailing ones—also reveal that engineers weren't able to achieve as nice a balance of high- and low-speed brake performance in 1955 as they can now." That judgment is based on hindsight, of course, and the road tests of the Gullwing in 1955 evaluated the braking performance quite differently: "Applied repeatedly, there is absolutely no sign of brake-fade, or loss of control. In our opinion these are the best brakes ever employed on a production automobile," reported the April 1955 R&T road test.

The comfort level within the 300SL Gullwing was one of its most endearing characteristics. Getting in and out over the wide sills was not the most graceful of exercises, but once in place, driver and passenger were seated in a pleasant though not overly luxurious environment. The seats were bucket-style, amply wide for comfort but with lateral bolstering. And the high doorsills also served to hold driver and passenger in place during hard cornering. The large, 2-spoke steering wheel was hinged at the hub so that it could pivot downward to aid the driver in getting into and out of the cockpit.

The instrument panel was excellently designed, with large dials for speedometer and tachometer. There were smaller gauges for fuel level, oil pressure and water and oil temperature. A small clock sat in the middle of the dash, while the optional radio nestled below the dash over the transmission tunnel.

Although the side windows within the Gullwing doors could not be raised or lowered, they could be removed to aid ventilation on warm days; and there were those owners who took great joy in driving around town with the doors in the raised position! Mercedes had done a good job in providing an effective fresh air ventilation system through dash-mounted vents, and the heater also worked well.

Behind the front seats, there was a large flat luggage space that could carry a considerable amount of baggage for touring. Mercedes offered a set of matched, fitted leather luggage as an option. Beneath the rear deck lid, there was a good-size trunk, but it was mostly filled with the spare tire, although there was room for carrying small parcels. Beneath the floor of the trunk was the 34.5-gal. fuel tank—fortunately, gasoline sold at about 30¢/gal. in those days in the U.S., so it wouldn't break you to fill the 300SL's tank with the required premium fuel. And oil was equally inexpensive, which was good news to the 300SL owner when he discovered that it took 16 quarts to fill the engine!

The Mercedes-Benz 300SL Gullwing was one of the most exciting sports cars to ever put tire to road. Some 30 years later, it is still a car that turns heads when it passes, and it still performs at a level that puts much more modern cars to shame. In 1955, the list price was a moderately expensive $7463. Today, excellent examples of the Gullwing can fetch as much as $100,000 from collectors who have come to appreciate this wonderful coupe with the unusual doors.

The Mercedes-Benz 300SL Gullwing showing its spirit in the rain-plagued 1956 Mille Miglia.